FINDING
FAITH

Also by Brian McLaren

The Church on the Other Side
(formerly titled *Reinventing Your Church*)

FINDING
FAITH

A SELF-DISCOVERY GUIDE
FOR YOUR SPIRITUAL QUEST

BRIAN D. McLAREN

ZONDERVAN™

GRAND RAPIDS, MICHIGAN 49530

ZONDERVAN™

Finding Faith
Copyright © 1999 by Brian D. McLaren

Requests for information should be addressed to:

Zondervan, *Grand Rapids, Michigan 49530*

Library of Congress Cataloging-in-Publication Data

McLaren, Brian D., 1956–
    Finding faith : a self-discovery guide for your spiritual quest / Brian D. McLaren.
      p.   cm.
    ISBN 0-310-23838-2 (softcover)
    1. Apologetics. I. Title.
  BT1102.M44 1999   98-48165

Interior design by Sherri L. Hoffman

Printed in the United States of America

05 06 /❖ DC/ 10 9

There is a dramatic story in the New Testament
commonly referred to as "The Conversion of Cornelius"
(in Acts 10), about how the apostle Peter helps a
Roman officer find a deeper faith. When you read it,
you realize that the story could just as easily be
called "The Conversion of Peter," because Peter seems
to be as profoundly changed through their encounter as
his new Roman friend. That's how I feel about my
many friends who are seeking faith. In my attempts to
teach or help or encourage them, I keep receiving
more than I give. To those friends, present and
future, I gratefully dedicate *Finding Faith*.

CONTENTS

Part 5: Milestones in My Spiritual Journey

PREFACE

Several months ago, I took a day off to walk along a favorite stretch of the Potomac River, where it winds through the Appalachian Mountains before entering the coastal plain of Maryland where I live. It was a day to think, to sort through some of my questions and doubts, to struggle with some new understandings that were forcing my faith to adapt and stretch to new dimensions. It was a day to think about what would go into this book as well.

I remember reaching a certain point along the old towpath just below one of the locks of the old C & O Canal. A very simple thought dawned on me there: I need faith. Here I am, someone who is writing a book on faith, and I am realizing as never before how I need faith not only to live my daily life to the full, but to grow and nurture and sustain my faith itself and also to write the book that you are now holding.

I suspect that the very act of reading this book will be an act of faith for you, just as writing it has been for me. Realizing this, I can imagine that you are now walking with me alongside the river, and that we are now, as of this moment, on a journey of faith together. This book can become our extended conversation.

I realize that for some readers, it is easy to relate to the experience of walking along a beautiful bend in a river, shaded by tulip poplars, sycamores, and black, white, and red oaks. It is also easy to relate to the experience of internal struggle, of thinking about life, of straining within one's mental maps or paradigms, of grappling with those deep questions that murmur in the back of our minds like the river beside the path.

But as soon as I talk about faith, I know many readers find it hard to relate. Make-believe, self-hypnosis, manipulation, group hysteria, anti-intellectualism, obscurantism, closed-mindedness, backward-ness—for many, the images or associations related to faith are the very opposite of what I was thinking about that day along the river. For you, faith is perhaps like death, a subject you know you shouldn't deny or avoid, but one that is profoundly uncomfortable. You wish, and I wish for you, that faith could be a subject of joy, vitality, hope, and healing.

It is for people like you that I have written this book. If it can help you who struggle the most, I know it can help many others too, others whose struggles with faith are not perhaps as radical or extreme, but who struggle nonetheless. (The people for whom faith comes easily and whose faith is never called into question probably would never pick up a book like this anyway, although I wonder if it might do them some good if they did.)

I am grateful for the people of Cedar Ridge Community Church in Spencerville, Maryland, who have helped me learn faith in so many ways. There is a biblical story (in Acts, chapter 10) about the apostle Peter who went to participate in the conversion of a man named Cornelius. What followed was not only a conversion for Cornelius, but also for Peter as well. Similarly, I have been converted in many new ways through my contacts with the people who have come through the doors of Cedar Ridge, with their questions, needs, hopes, and thirst for truth. A community of faith where love and hope abound is a too-rare thing these days, and I am privileged to enjoy such a community.

Both in the church and in my associations outside of it, I have made many friends who would call themselves atheists or agnostics, or who follow religious paths very different from my own. Several of them (Glenn, Gregg, Tony, and others) agreed to read this manuscript and "field test" it for me. I thank them for their insights, questions, and responses, which have made this a better book than it would have been.

As always, I am grateful for my best friend and partner, Grace, and for our four amazing kids, Rachel, Brett, Trevor, and Jodi, who are launching their own journeys of faith. Of course, I could also mention the one to whom I am grateful for all of these wonderful people, and for the beauty of that stretch of the Potomac River, and for all of the rich experiences of life. But that's getting ahead of myself, because that's who this book is ultimately about.

Let's keep walking together.

INTRODUCTION

The Predicament of an Intelligent Person Seeking Faith

So here you find yourself at some point in your journey through life and you're seeking for faith, which is another way of saying you're seeking for spirituality, and for God, since faith is the doorway into spirituality and the primary means of connecting with God.

DIMENSIONS OF THE QUEST

The search you have embarked upon is a quest of staggering proportions. Its dimensions are wide and deep, breathtaking at times, inviting you to the dizzying rim of some awe-inspiring vistas, leaving you wordless in humbled silence. Though a healthy faith is bigger than the intellect, the search for faith cannot bypass the intellect. The sincere spiritual seeker must engage the mind fully, even while transcending cold or calculating rationalism. This is a journey that will require you to think bigger than you ever have before, and then to think bigger still.

But the search for faith also involves noncognitive parts of us—emotions, longings, aspirations, dreams and hopes and fears; drives, desires, intuitions. It often forces us to face some ugliness in ourselves, some hard facts about life, requiring courage, honesty, and determination. Faith involves admitting with humility and boldness that we need to change, to go against the flow, to be different, to face and shine the light on our cherished illusions and prejudices, and to discover new truths that can be liberating even though they may be difficult for the ego, painful to the pride. The search for an authentic faith must be the most life-changing quest anyone can ever launch. It's no Sunday school picnic.

WHOM CAN YOU TRUST?

Another challenge: To whom do you talk about this search? Perhaps you could go to a minister, pastor, rabbi, or priest. But don't they have a vested interest in the outcome of your search? Can you trust them to be unbiased, or might they push you, stack the deck, suppress some evidence and inflate other evidence, subtly making it hard for you to say no?

You might go to a counselor, but then again, the counselor may see your search as a pathology and try to cure you of it.

It's not always easy to consult your spouse, either. "Searching for God? I just wish you'd help with the dishes or clean out the car," you might hear. Or, "You don't have to become more spiritual, dear, just less grouchy." Or, "So now it's spirituality. I wonder how long *this* will last." A friend's response might be similarly discouraging: "Oh, great. Does this mean you won't play cards with us anymore? Are you going to make us hold hands in restaurants and pray before we eat? Will I have to apologize from now on if I say a four-letter word in front of you?"

You might consult a college professor of comparative religion or a historian conversant with the development of world religions, someone for whom the subject is purely abstract and intellectual. But might her very objectivity and professional detachment create another set of problems? Wouldn't you find yourself apologizing for taking this whole thing so seriously—so personally—in the first place? Wouldn't you find it hard to express your personal longings in the company of someone who studies those very personal longings as sociological or psychological or historical phenomena?

The fact is, thankfully, there are many ministers, counselors, friends, and professors who could be of real help to you in your search, who understand your desire for unhurried and unpressured guidance, who will not coerce you to conform your search to their expectations, who will offer guidance while leaving room for you to reach your own conclusions. I hope I can be of help to you in precisely this way. I am a pastor, but before entering ministry, I worked in secular higher education (as an academic counselor and college English instructor). And in each role, I have become more and more sensitive to the predicament of the intelligent adult who begins searching for faith, for spirituality, and for God. I can't pretend that I'm completely neutral, a totally objective third party. Here's my bias: *I sincerely hope you find what you're looking for*. Toward that end I am dedicating myself in these pages.

WHAT YOUR SEARCH IS NOT

If I understand you and your situation correctly, there are two things your search is not. On the one hand, it is not an act of desperation. You are not in such a frenzied emotional state that you're willing to believe anything as long as it brings relief. Sadly, some people are reduced to this condition, and they jump on the assembly lines of cults and extremist groups, ready to conform, ready to make false confessions, ready to sacrifice their personal responsibility for the benefit of belonging to a group that is sure about everything.

No doubt there are things from which you seek relief, and conversely, things you desire: a sense of purpose for your life, perhaps; forgiveness and peace to replace the guilt and fear that nag you; an integrated philosophy or worldview that makes sense of life with all its grandeur and squalor; an explanation for the spiritual experiences that have come unbidden into your life. But these triggers to your search require something more than a desperate emotional placebo for you. You would actually aspire to know some truth. Your search is for a relationship with a God who really exists, and if no such God exists, then you want to know that too, straight up.

The Physics Lecture

On the other hand, neither is your search merely objective, detached, theoretical, academic. One of my favorite novelists (Walker Percy) loved to picture the difference between your search and the more objective, abstract type of search with a story something like this: Imagine a group of physicists and astronomers gathered for a lecture on cosmic background radiation. As the lab-coated lecturer drones on, the group is listening, taking notes, rubbing their chins, crossing and uncrossing their legs, maybe nodding a bit, occasionally mumbling, "Interesting," or something of that sort. Suddenly, a woman walks briskly onto the stage and whispers something in the lecturer's ear. He hands her the microphone and she says, "Ladies and gentlemen, a fire has broken out in the lobby. Please stay calm. Leave quietly and quickly through the exits on your left. Do not use the rear exits, as they are already smoke-filled and unsafe. Please follow me—this way."

At this moment, no one keeps rubbing his chin, crossing and uncrossing her legs, taking notes, or mumbling, "Interesting." The reason? Before, during the lecture, their situation allowed them the luxury of abstracted, disinterested detachment. But now, their real-life situation has been addressed, and the category of communication has changed from knowledge or information (a lecture on astrophysics) to news (of a threat to safety and life and how to escape it). Flooded and numbed by information as we are, it is often hard for any message of news to get through to us. Life often has to send us some pretty strong wake-up calls to make us susceptible to news, open to it, hungry for it. You must have had some of those wake-up calls to bring you to this point.

So, here you are. You are not just an abstracted listener in a lecture series about the psychology of spirituality, the demographics of religion, the history of theology, or theoretical ethics. Rather, you have had your wake-up call. You are a person who knows you are alive, who feels the immediacy of "something more" in life that has never been adequately accounted for . . . a person who knows you will one day die, and who feels the urgency of finding your place in the universe before you vacate it . . . a person who wishes to be honest and feels dishonest denying the existence of a spiritual dimension to life (as some secular people may pressure you to do), and yet who feels dishonest repeating without question the creeds (as the religious folk may pressure you to do).

Three Needs

Many of us were brought up with some sort of faith as children. Our parents, our extended family, our ethnic group, our society likely reinforced their religious views in us. But as we grew older, we questioned many of the beliefs that were passed on to us. Perhaps we saw hypocrisy all too evident in the lives of the religious, or we asked questions our tradition didn't answer. Perhaps we met good people of other faiths and felt that their goodness somehow made our faith superfluous. Or perhaps we learned things from science, history, or philosophy that contradicted the tenets of our faith, so we rejected our faith or sidelined it for so long we forgot it was there. Perhaps our initial coming into faith was part of our adolescent identity crisis, tied in with youthful idealism ("Let's change the world through God and love and belief!"), alienation ("At last, a group that accepts me!"), insecurity ("Maybe God can help me take a shortcut around the difficulties of growing up."), or even rebellion ("I'll show my parents—I'll change religions!"). Or perhaps we found ourselves "faithfully" going through the motions, but never really feeling or experiencing anything ourselves. Eventually, we couldn't sustain the charade, or we just lost interest.

One way or another, we outgrew the faith of our childhood or youth. Now we're seeking for a faith that we can hold with adult integrity, clear intelligence, and honest feeling. So, many of us need in this way *to renew or replace the faith we lost*—to fill the old vacancy in a new way, to see faith with fresh eyes, or better—to let a mature, refreshed faith become the new eyes through which we see life.

Others of us have faith, but it is weak or damaged. We feel that we're walking on a sprained ankle or trying to enjoy a delicious meal with a bad tooth. Perhaps we've been spiritually undernourished, malnourished, or mistreated and injured by a church or religious family member. We don't have confidence in our faith, and it brings us more pain than comfort. Or we have a faith that is little more than a set of concepts to us. This kind of faith is often called nominal, meaning "in name only." It doesn't affect our behavior, at least, not positively. Perhaps for some of us, faith is like a vaccination—we have just enough in our system to keep us from getting "infected" with a full-blown "case" of vibrant faith. There's faith there, but it needs to be "set on fire"; it needs to come alive; we need to really "catch" it. In these ways some of us need *to invigorate the faith we already have.*

Still others of us were brought up in a secular context. Faith to us seems strange, an oddity, an embarrassment, superstitious, primitive, the customs of "some other family's culture"—natural to them but foreign to us. Yet we find our secular worldview unfulfilling, able to tell us much about the world, but unable to account for much of our own experience as men and women. We need *to find the faith we never had before.*

That's why this book was written: *to help you replace the faith you lost, invigorate the faith you have, and develop the faith you desire but never had before.*

More "How" Than "What" or "Why"

Like you, I am a spiritual seeker, and I have many friends who are spiritual seekers at varying stages in their journeys. Obviously, my work as a pastor keeps me in a community of such people every day, so the struggles of spiritual seeking are always on my mind. This is the book that I wish had been there to help me and my friends in our own spiritual searching. I hope it will help you. I hope it will encourage relationships and conversations among spiritual seekers wherever it is read—relationships and dialogue that will be mutually beneficial and encouraging in many ways.

Instead of trying to tell you "the answers" via dogmatic pronouncements (as many well-meaning people have already tried to do for you, no doubt), I would like to try to help you find the answers yourself. Instead of trying to tell you *what* to believe or focusing on *why* you should believe, my goal is to help you discover *how* to believe—how to search for and find a faith that is real, honest, good, enriching, and yours.

GOOD QUESTIONS AND TRUE STORIES

This goal will require an approach that focuses more on questions than answers. My job will be to lead you to and through important questions, in a sensible order, since good questions are among the most important tools for a good quest. While some questions tend to lead to dead ends or vicious circles of controversy, other questions, approached in a sensible order, can help a person progress in his or her search at a good pace, not rushing, but not wasting time either. Rather than presenting one answer only—what I might feel is the "right" answer—I'll try to guide you through each of the more plausible answers and encourage you to make your own choices. Again, I won't pretend to have no beliefs myself, which would be dishonest. Instead, I'll try to be open about my own conclusions without imposing them on you. You may agree with me; you may not. I'll feel I have been of some service to you either way simply by stimulating your thinking.

Along with questions, I have found that stories can be of great help in the search, so you will find many true stories—my own and others'—included in each chapter. (As you'd expect, I've changed some names and details to avoid invading anyone's privacy.) The last few chapters, comprising part 5, focus more directly on my own experiences, struggles, and breakthroughs. One of my main credentials as a pastor is that I myself have had most of the doubts or spiritual problems anyone else has ever come to me with, so I hope the accounts of my struggles will offer you something to identify with and learn from too.

READER-FRIENDLY?

There is no one right protocol by which to search for God. There is no simple formula or easy recipe that you can follow to arrive at faith. The way that is most natural for me to express my understanding may not be the way that is most natural for you to progress in your understanding. The physicist and the artist, the social worker and the engineer, the salesperson and the programmer will approach the spiritual search differently and will find different parts of this book more and less helpful. So, although I've tried to organize this book in a reader-friendly way, I encourage you—in fact, I urge you—to skip around and use this book in the way that's most useful for you.

In fact, here's a quick self-assessment that can help you determine where to start, what to skip, and so forth.

Which of these statements best describes you?

- My problems with faith are primarily philosophical and intellectual. *(If so, you'll probably want to read the whole book in the order it's presented.)*
- I already have a basic faith in God, but I am eager for more spiritual experience. I already have a conceptual kind of faith; I want a faith I can *feel*. *(If so, you may want to skip parts 1 and 2.)*
- Before I consider what you want to say, I want to know a bit more about who you are and what you believe. *(If so, feel free to read part 5 first of all.)*

The Chapter Previews should further help you tailor this book to your own needs. At the end of each chapter, you'll find a section called Your Response, which can be used in two ways. First, if you write your responses, you will compose a kind of personal creed, which can help you in your spiritual journey. Second, if you use these questions for dialogue with some friends, you can enjoy one of life's greatest pleasures—people talking openly about life's deepest matters. Following the response section, you will find recommended resources (books, tapes, videos, websites, and more) and finally, sample prayers, which can help you express and exercise your faith as it grows.

Speaking of reader-friendliness, I should add that I've tried to write in a way that educated readers (the kind of people who would be picking up a book like this in the first place) will understand and enjoy. I haven't tried to show off my best vocabulary or impress you with quotes from my vast reading (you should know I'm winking here), nor have I imagined seminary or philosophy professors as my audience (they're too tough a crowd for me). Rather, I've simply tried to write conversationally, clearly, and intelligently, as I would want someone to write for me. I do not pretend to be a scholar; I hope rather to fill the role of a helpful friend. (Occasionally, you will probably be able to tell I am a preacher . . . but I hope not too often!)

FOR THE ALREADY-CONVINCED

I should offer one more disclaimer for those who are reading this book but are already committed believers of whatever persuasion. My guess is that many of you will be disappointed in what follows for several reasons:

1. I don't seem to validate some of your most dearly held doctrines and may even question them.
2. I don't go far enough, in your opinion, to push for closure and definition.
3. I don't use terms and arguments that you are already familiar with, that helped you most in your search for faith, and that would identify me as "one of us" for you.

I'm sure you understand that I can't please everyone, and though I believe in trying to be "all things to all people" when possible, that is patently impossible to do all at the same time in the same book. As C. S. Lewis said in his introduction to *Mere Christianity*, ". . . you can not even conclude, from my silence on disputed points, either that I think them important or that I think them unimportant. . . . All this is said simply in order to make clear what kind of book I was trying to write." I hope you'll also understand that my real focus here is not to earn the nod of the already-convinced reading over my shoulder, but rather to help the unconvinced person across the page from me. To be of the most help to him or her, I may have to disappoint you. I'm sorry about that.

Also, please understand that we live in a very dynamic time, at the hinge between modern and postmodern worlds. Many of the answers that were most helpful to you and me twenty-five years ago land with a thud today, and other questions that you and I never thought of twenty-five years ago are electric and unavoidable today.

If you are one of the already-convinced, I hope this book will help you learn ways to be more understanding of and therefore more helpful to your spiritually seeking friends. I hope so, because books take people only so far, and then friends are indispensable. In fact, if you are a credible believer, your life itself offers more important data for your spiritually seeking friends than anything I could write. The best use of this book will likely be as an extended foreword or footnote to the message of faith that is told through the life you are living. In that way, I am honored to be your colleague.

Together, through your life lived well at close range, and through my words in this book, I hope we can help more and more people find faith. Then more and more lives will begin to reflect the benefits of a healthy spirituality, which will positively affect still more people. The ripples can spread far, so let's get started.

YOUR RESPONSE

1. Here's a brief description of my religious background:

2. Here are the more positive features of my religious background:

3. Here are the more negative features of my religious background:

4. My primary goal in reading this book is to. . .
   replace the faith I lost.
   invigorate the faith I have.
   develop the faith I desire but never had before.
   other

5. Questions I hope to explore in reading this book:

6. Chapters I plan to read:

7. Chapters I plan to skip:

8. People with whom I might like to discuss this book:

PART 1

FAITH, KNOWLEDGE,
AND DOUBT

CHAPTER 1 PREVIEW

Does It Really Matter What I Believe?

This chapter attempts to define faith by distinguishing "good faith" from "bad faith." These important terms will be used throughout the book. It also explores the problem of "circularity" (that arguments about faith often seem to be circular arguments) and the idea of a "leap of faith."

WHO SHOULD READ THIS CHAPTER?

If you have heard or made the statement, "It doesn't really matter what you believe, as long as you're sincere," this chapter is a must-read for you. This chapter is also for you if you are bothered by the fact that for many people, faith seems to make them into worse people, not better people.

WHAT QUESTIONS DOES IT ADDRESS?

What is faith? What is bad faith? What is good faith? How can I "get into" faith if I feel like an outsider?

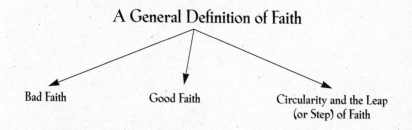

A General Definition of Faith

Bad Faith   Good Faith   Circularity and the Leap
                                        (or Step) of Faith

The most beautiful and profound emotion we can experience is the sensation of the mystical. It is the source of all true science. . . . To know that what is impenetrable to us really exists . . . this knowledge, this feeling, is the center of true religion.

ALBERT EINSTEIN

CHAPTER 1

Does It Really Matter What I Believe?

"It doesn't matter what you believe, as long as you're sincere."
That must be one of the most common statements I hear when
people first start talking about faith. What do you think about that
statement? Personally, I don't think these people really mean what
they're saying, at least not literally.

- They couldn't mean that it's okay for a crazed cult leader to
  sincerely believe his sincere followers should join him in sincerely drinking poisoned Kool-Aid so they can end up in
  heaven together sooner rather than later.
- They couldn't mean it's okay for white supremacists or anti-
  Semites to believe and practice their beliefs, as long as they're
  sincere—which, I say with sadness and disgust, they often
  seem to be.
- They couldn't mean it's okay for totalitarian dictators to suppress religious freedom, since they're sincere in believing religion is an opiate of the masses or a menace to their regime.
- They couldn't mean that it would be okay for sincere religious fundamentalists to control the lives of millions through
  sincere intimidation, censorship, legislation, or threats of violence.
- They couldn't mean that it would be fine with them for parents who believe that life is meaningless to raise their children
  with a nihilistic philosophy of life, freely offering their children drugs, for example, or allowing them to experiment with
  vandalism and violence, not caring about their education or

motivation, abandoning any pretense of teaching moral guidelines, since they sincerely believe that nothing really matters.

The kinds of people who I have heard talk this way about sincerity would never agree with these implications of their statement taken literally.

THIN ICE

Nor would these people want to be associated with the abandonment of truth their statement seems to imply. They would never mean to invite people to the disaster of sincerely believing dangerous illusions. An analogy to walking on ice can help here. If you're walking on a lake that's covered with one inch of ice, no matter how sincere you are in believing you can do it, you're in for a cold soaking at best, drowning at worst. If someone encourages you to try, "as long as you're sincere," they're no friend!

(Conversely, if you're walking on a lake that's covered with twelve inches of solid ice, even if you are plagued by doubt at every step, you'll still be upheld. And of course, if your doubts are so great that you never get out on the lake at all, you'll never know either way.)

So, the issue is less the sincerity or intensity of your faith than it is the trustworthiness of the object of your faith: Is it solid enough, deep enough, trustworthy enough, to be capable of holding your weight? From this vantage point, the "as long as you're sincere" statement seems hard to justify, I think you'll agree.

AN IMPORTANT DISTINCTION

But in a more positive light, when people say, "It doesn't really matter what you believe, as long as you're sincere," I think they are trying to make an important distinction we will explore (and endorse, I hope) in this chapter: the distinction between "good faith" and "bad faith." The Latin term bona fide means, literally, "good faith"—and I think we all sense that some examples of faith ring with an authenticity, a sincerity, and a quality that qualify them as "bona fide" faith, good faith. Conversely, some examples of faith strike us as inauthentic, unwise, unsubstantial, "bad faith."

In this context, here's what I think people really mean by their statement, "It doesn't really matter what you believe....": "Before we argue about whether *what* you believe is right, let's discuss *how* you believe. Before you try to persuade me about the *content* of your faith, let me see the *quality* of your faith." If that's the case, I think these people realize something quite profound: "Right faith that isn't good faith isn't really right faith." (Faith that believes true things, but does so in an ugly or inappropriate way, isn't justified just because it is conceptually correct.) They might even be going further: "I would rather have a wrong faith that is good than a right faith that is bad." (I would rather hold some inaccurate beliefs with a good heart, so to speak, than be accurate in all the details and yet have the wrong approach, the wrong attitude.)

What do you think about those statements? Since people with good faith will by definition want to keep learning, constantly admitting previously held beliefs were imbalanced or inaccurate or incomplete, regularly fine-tuning and adjusting their beliefs to be more in line with what they are learning, wouldn't people with good faith come, over time, to have an increasingly accurate faith? In other words, isn't the goal of a right faith best served by concentrating hard on a good faith? If that's the case, how should we define *good faith*? Even more basic, how would we define *faith*?

A PROVISIONAL DEFINITION OF FAITH

Maybe you heard about the little boy in Sunday school who defined faith as "believing what you know ain't true." We've got to do better than that in our definition of faith. Let's start like this: *Faith is a state of relative certainty about matters of ultimate concern sufficient to promote action.*

Let me forewarn you: We're going to come back later and quarrel with this definition a bit. We'll challenge it, expand it, and improve it. But for now, let's use it as a springboard and break it down as follows:

1. *A state.* Faith is a condition we find ourselves more or less "in"—like being in good health, or in love, or in depression, or in ecstasy, or in confusion, or in doubt. I suppose that psychologists could study it as a psychological phenomenon, perhaps finding certain electrochemical patterns in the brain associated with faith. But faith is also more than a condition or feeling. It is more than just *something we experience.* Faith is the context in which we feel and experience and think about everything in life. It includes data—propositions, ideas, specific beliefs—that form an intellectual framework, a paradigm, in which all other psychological phenomena take place and by which they are evaluated.

A crude analogy to a computer might be helpful. The operating system of the computer is the "state" in which the computer operates. It provides the foundation and framework upon and within which all the operations of the computer occur. Faith is, in this analogy, the operating system of the computer. It is the state or condition or system a person operates in. (That is not to say it is "static," though. As we'll see, good faith continually self-modifies, like an operating system that continually upgrades.)

2. *Relative certainty.* As we will see in the next chapter, we humans don't seem to have the luxury of absolute, unquestioned certainty in many (if any) areas of life—and especially in matters of the spiritual life. So we acknowledge our predicament—that we have to function in relative certainty, which always includes relative uncertainty.

3. *Matters of ultimate concern.* We aren't talking about abstract mathematical equations or the middle name of the vice president or the cost of green beans at the grocery store. We're talking about how we conduct our lives, make our decisions, solve our moral dilemmas, face death and the possibility of afterlife for ourselves and other people, cope with suffering and loss, answer the big questions about our origin and destiny and ultimate value, decide whether life is worth living, establish values, and so on.

Matters of ultimate concern are matters of truth. In this light, faith can be distinguished from pretending, self-hypnosis, self-delusion, or lying by its intention to reach for truth, reality. In other words, faith is an attempt to orient oneself to and concern oneself with what is real and true "in here" (subjectively) and "out there" (objectively). Some thinkers have used this expression: True faith is held "with universal intent." Believing is thus distinguished from make-believe in that the person "in" faith believes she is onto what is actually universally true, not just what is "nice" for her to fantasize about to make herself feel better. She hopes that she is not departing from reality, but rather closing in on it, through her exercise of faith. To proceed otherwise would be to act in "bad faith."

4. *Sufficient to promote action.* How much certainty is sufficient to qualify as faith? If a professed belief is *not* sufficient to promote action, then it would be better called an opinion or an idea or concept. We may hold it as data in our memory banks, but it does not constitute part of our operating system. If an idea (say, that God exists) doesn't promote action (say, to search for God or pray or monitor one's own moral behavior or love one's neighbor), it isn't really faith at all . . . it's just an idea. But if there is sufficient certainty to prompt us to action—action such as reading this book, attending a church service, admitting a fault, reaching out to an estranged associate, or reaching across a barrier of fear or prejudice—there is real faith at work.

WHY REJECT FAITH?

Given this definition, faith seems like a needed thing, a good thing. Why then would anyone want to reject faith? Again, when people say they are rejecting faith, I don't think we should take them literally. Rather, I think what they really mean is that they are rejecting "bad" faith. They have decided that the operating system they inherited or installed is "no good." It doesn't work for them. Maybe it can't account for the data presented by real life. Maybe it doesn't make its adherents into better people. Maybe it is too complicated to be useful. Maybe long-term it is too boring or depressing to be livable. For these and other reasons, people often "lose faith," meaning they discard their *version* of faith. Perhaps this describes your situation, but now you find yourself wondering if you have, to use two clichés in rapid succession, thrown out the baby with the bathwater and jumped from the frying pan into the fire. You wonder if there are more than two alternatives—bad faith or no faith.

BAD FAITH DESCRIPTORS

What do we mean by "bad faith"? If six or eight of us were sitting in a seminar setting, this would be a great question to kick around, maybe filling some poster paper or whiteboard space with possible answers and insights. But given the limitations of our situation here—me writing and you reading—may I offer some of my own observations and opinions? (Perhaps you can get a few friends together and kick these ideas around, and add your own too.)

1. *Bad faith is based solely on unquestioned authority.* In other words, in bad faith, I believe, simply because an authority figure or structure tells me to. I don't think for myself. I don't question. I comply, thoughtlessly believing what I am told to believe. Maybe I am lucky—maybe I happen to follow the one right authority structure; but what of all those poor folk who blindly follow authority structures that direct them to believe differently? Should they be condemned and I praised simply because I was lucky enough to have blindly followed the right guru, or been born into the right family who happened to belong to the right religious denomination? Clearly, tested and trusted authority figures, structures, and organizations can be of great help in developing a good faith (in fact, later we'll talk about the value of participating in a faith community)—but one can't blindly, mindlessly follow the group if one wants good faith. Good faith doesn't appear to be a herd behavior. (The dynamic relationship between authority structures and an individual's questioning and commitment is complex and has important implications for parents trying to pass on a good faith to

their children. Too much pressure and they threaten to ruin what they're trying to strengthen; too little guidance and they inadvertently imply that the subject just isn't that important.)

2. *Bad faith is based on pressure or coercion.* At a party I attended a few years back, I asked a woman—a visiting scholar from another continent—about her religious beliefs. Then, perhaps to be polite, or perhaps from genuine curiosity, she asked about mine. We seemed to be having a pleasant, animated conversation about "matters of ultimate concern." After a while though, she became increasingly uncomfortable. "In my country, it is not permitted for me to question my beliefs, and listening to you talk about your beliefs is raising doubts about my own. It would not be permitted for me to convert to another religion or even to become lax in performing the duties of my religion. I would be shunned by my community and disowned by my family. So, I must not continue this conversation."

With that, she walked away. I was stunned. These thoughts came to mind: This coercive approach may make for national solidarity in her country. It may keep attendance high at religious services. But it doesn't make for an authentic faith sincerely held.

Of course, this characteristic of bad faith is found not just in other countries. Here in America, I've run into many cultic groups with a similar coercive edge. But even beyond cults, we are all largely unaware of the ways the groups and cultures in which we participate pressure us to conform and chastise us when we rattle the cage—of consumerism, rationalism, scientism, and so forth. We're so used to the subtle "tyranny of the majority" that we seldom buck it. How much of what we believe right now is the result of our buckling to the pressures of the culture we are part of? We may not be so different from the visiting scholar I met at that party after all.

3. *Bad faith is often the result of a psychological need for belonging.* Maybe no one is coercing me to believe, but if I am so desperate to belong that I will claim to believe anything the desired in-group requires of me, how can my faith be authentic?

4. *Bad faith appeals to self-interest and base motives.* I recently heard about missionaries of a certain religion in a certain country who actually pay people to attend their services. I've also heard about religious groups that use sexy young women to allure male members. Less extreme, but no less inauthentic, are those groups that promise health or wealth, revenge or power, pain avoidance or easy solutions to all life's problems. This approach violates the "matters of ultimate concern" element of our definition. I doubt God would be very impressed with those who believe in order to become rich, popular, comfortable, lazy, and so forth, with no real desire for the true, the good, or the beautiful.

5. *Bad faith is arrogant and unteachable.* When a person takes pride in feeling "right" and rewards himself with a sense of superiority, when his faith puts him in a high and mighty posture to look down in judgment on others, it's hard to feel that we're dealing with good faith. When the religious indulge in spiritual status-seeking (Look at how much I give! Notice how much I suffer! Aren't you impressed with my knowledge, my piety, my zeal?!), their desire for attention seems even more disgusting than those who parade their material wealth in a quest for social status. That know-it-all spiritual attitude, that pretended certainty that makes one talk, talk, talk but never listen, that obnoxious "you can't teach me anything I don't already know" spirit—these traits are ugly in the irreligious, pathetic in the religious.

6. *Bad faith is dishonest.* If I boldly proclaim, for example, that the earth is six thousand years old, when I have convincing evidence that it is much older, I may outwardly appear faithful, but don't I lack integrity? If my religion tells me to believe that members of another race are inferior, when I know many of these people personally as wonderful people, don't I become a worse person by continuing to recite the "party line"? When I have witnessed corruption in a religious organization firsthand, but continue to publicly uphold it as pure, can I be showing good faith? How could a God of truth be pleased by my saying things I do not mean?

7. *Bad faith is apathetic.* Since real faith inspires action, if my faith produces no action, it cannot be good faith. If I cannot honestly say that my faith makes a difference—if I would behave just as I do without my faith—then my faith is bad faith, if it is faith at all.

Sometimes this lack of action is covered by a surplus of talk. Sometimes the jargon flows thick, like lots of strawberry jelly on moldy bread. Sometimes people substitute the active life of faith with the fascinating lore of faith, terminology, facts, opinions on religious esoterica, and so forth. This immersion in words no doubt positions them well to win at religious "Trivial Pursuit," but that's about it. Who is fooled by the barrage of words, besides the talker himself?

8. *Bad faith is a step backward.* Perhaps I am a young adult, growing up, just graduating from college. I become frightened by career choices. I seem to be striking out in the "dating game." I am paralyzed by the challenges of adulthood. If in this context, I join a high-control religious cult so that they will make my decisions for me, my faith is really an excuse for immaturity. If I am overwhelmed by advances in science, by complexities in ethics, by gray areas in my own personal life, and I throw myself into a religion that tells me easy answers so I don't have to think for myself, my religiosity is an excuse for laziness and fear, not a motivation to growth and courage. Good faith ought to produce good fruit; I ought to become a better person for holding it. A faith that makes me less loving, mature, wise, alive, or responsible sounds to me like bad faith.

In writing this book, I asked several of my friends (agnostics and atheists) to read the manuscript and give me their feedback, all of which was helpful and some of which was downright profound. As I dialogued with one of my friends, something became clear to me in a whole new way: *Healthy people don't step backward or down; they only step forward or up.* This insight explains both why some people leave faith and others accept it; in either case, their move into or out of faith is perceived by them as a step *up.* For this friend, brought up in a rigid, anti-intellectual religious system, science (in this case, science as a package deal with atheism)—honest, accurate, curious, open-eyed—felt like a huge step up from the superstitious version of religion he had been presented with. I'd have to agree with him; it *was* a step up. As we continue our dialogue, I'm hoping he can see that the best alternative to "bad faith" in God is not necessarily no faith (or faith in the science-atheism package). Granted, to step back into the version of religion he grew up in would be a step down, but perhaps there is a step that will present itself to him that will be a step up into good faith.

These descriptors of bad faith are my opinions, and you may disagree. But perhaps they will ring true. At the very least, I hope they'll stimulate you to develop your own working descriptions. As I'll say again later, *I don't think the greatest enemy of monotheism is atheism, agnosticism, polytheism, dualism, or pantheism: It is bad monotheism, monotheism carried out in bad faith.* Show me a person who has rejected faith, and nine times in ten I'll show you a person or group nearby who turned them sour with their example of bad faith. The great spiritual need of our world, as well as of so many individuals in it, then (in my opinion), is good faith. But how would that good faith be described? Again, I can offer my opinions.

GOOD FAITH DESCRIPTORS

1. *Good faith is humble, teachable, and inquisitive.* If I am aware of how contingent and limited my knowledge is, how can I be proud about how much I know? How can I look down on someone else for knowing less? Isn't pride—the sense of certainty that I am right and superior and don't need to learn or listen—the greatest possible barrier to faith? In this way, isn't religious pride the most hideous sin imaginable—because it is incredibly dangerous—and ridiculous? If there is a God, wouldn't good faith begin by humbling oneself before God, acknowledging one's ignorance and asking for guidance and enlightenment?

If I am appropriately humble, isn't it possible that anyone can become my teacher, from a little child to a mental patient, from a sage of old to a comedian of today? Isn't an open mind, eager to learn, the essence of good faith (as it is of good science)? Aren't yesterday's certainties sometimes the enemies of tomorrow's faith, since we'll be tempted to say, "The old wine is good enough; I don't need any new wine"? Shouldn't humble, childlike inquisitiveness be characteristic of good faith, since I'm young, new here, with an awful lot to learn? Wouldn't it make sense to ask God my questions and see if any answers are forthcoming?

2. *Good faith is grateful.* If I reach some conclusions as I humbly and teachably continue on my quest, some working hypotheses to base future experiments upon, shouldn't I be grateful for them? Even if they are only a few very basic things, such as "God exists and loves me and wants me to imitate God by loving everything God loves," aren't these few basic things very precious and worth celebrating? Even if I can't claim to comprehend (or grasp completely) everything, can't I acknowledge that I have at least apprehended some things (having at least touched them, come into contact with them, begun to experience them)? And rather than being puffed up by this "knowledge," shouldn't I be grateful to God and others for helping me learn what I've learned, being sure not to close myself off to further learning?

3. *Good faith is honest.* Shouldn't I feel free to be as accurate as I can about what I am relatively sure about and relatively unsure about? Shouldn't good faith feel free to express both doubt and confidence, neither overstating nor understating its level of certainty? Shouldn't I abhor dishonesty, since it clouds the already difficult search for truth? Shouldn't I seek to honestly acknowledge and remove my own blind spots before critiquing others about theirs? Shouldn't I be as honest about the weaknesses of myself, my faith, and my community of faith as I would want others to be about theirs?

4. *Good faith is communal.* Since my individual understanding is so limited, don't I need connection with a group of trusted companions, so we can help and encourage one another in our common

search for faith, God, and truth? Don't I especially need friends—a faith community—who will gently confront me when they see me losing these qualities of good faith? And just as I value highly my cohorts in my faith community, don't I also need honest, humble dialogue with people of other groups (religions, ideologies, parties, denominations, and so forth), since they may see things I and we are missing, and vice versa? And shouldn't humility and teachability prompt me to include in my faith community people from the past, so I can learn from the writings and art of the great sages through history? Granted, we don't want coercion and pressure, but don't we need mutual encouragement and support from other seekers, past and present, in our spiritual search?

5. *Good faith is active.* If I apprehend what I believe to be truth, am I not obligated to live by it? Shouldn't I abhor apathy (not acting on my beliefs), hypocrisy (covertly acting contrary to my beliefs), inconsistency (overtly acting contrary to my beliefs) just as I abhor dishonesty? Shouldn't my pursuit of truth be "hot" rather than "lukewarm"—suggesting a hunger and thirst for more truth, rather than complacency about what I believe I have already found? And if I believe the search for truth and faith and God are indeed important, shouldn't I sensitively try to influence others (who are open to my influence because I have earned their respect) to take steps forward in their own search—always without coercion?

6. *Good faith is tough.* How much is an easy, untested faith worth? If faith brings all benefits and no costs, how can we be sure our belief is an honest pursuit of truth and goodness, as opposed to a pursuit of benefits? If my faith always gains me respect and compliments, and never rejection or misunderstanding, might I not just be a believer out of social convenience? My faith may feel strong today, but how will it fare under tomorrow's tragedy, depression, disappointment, or delay? When money is tight or when money is flowing freely, when friends are few, when temptations are enticing, when patience is thin, when I'm in the middle of a project and the end seems to elude me, will I abandon my faith? Is a faith that

doesn't cost me anything worth anything? Is a faith any good that doesn't challenge me to do good and become better, even when I don't feel like it?

7. *Good faith is relational.* If I believe there is a personal God behind (and with) the universe, shouldn't my search for truth in God's universe begin with an acknowledgment of my relationship with God? In other words, given my personal limitations and the limitations of human knowledge, wouldn't it make sense to live in dependence on God to help me learn and search fruitfully—and more, to live with expectancy and hope that God will in some way be my teacher and guide? Wouldn't my relationship with God thus become the basis or context for my search for truth? And shouldn't I consider what loyalties and responsibilities are incumbent upon me as a party in this relationship with God?

You might ask at this point, "But how can I have a relationship with God if I am not sure God even exists?" You might even say, "This is very frustrating. You say I need faith to find a relationship with God, and then you say that having a loyal, trusting relationship with God is a necessary component of good faith. This is very circular and frustrating!"

CIRCULARITY?

You raise a good point. Your frustration now will serve to push us beyond the limits of our original working definition of faith (which we said from the start would need some improvement). You may have noticed that our original working definition never even mentioned God; it presented faith as if it were simply an internal reality ("a state of relative certainty," we called it) with no vital connection to anything (or anyone) beyond oneself. In that provisional definition I was trying to avoid this circularity that we must now come to terms with.

Some concepts or theories can be entered into via linear argument, from A to B to C, and so on. But some conceptual frameworks—we could call them worldviews or paradigms—are systems unto themselves, and in that way, they do seem circular from the outside. One can make an approach from the outside, but the only way in is to jump in (hence the phrase, "leap of faith") and test them out from the inside.

I think of a bright young graduate student who came to see me last year. He had been raised in a churchgoing family, but in college had lost whatever faith he had. He heard that I was someone who understood the kinds of questions and doubts he struggled with, and he drove for two hours just to talk with me. At the end of our session, he expressed a desire to come back again, and I encouraged him to bring a list of specific questions so that we could be sure to address them directly.

In our second meeting, he pulled out his list and we began to deal with his questions, one at a time: How can evil exist if there is a good and powerful God? Why are there so many religions? Who is to say that some things are morally wrong? Midway through a question about sexuality and morality, he interrupted me: "Just a minute. This isn't what I need at all. Our time is so limited, and I am quite certain that you will have a logical answer for every question I have on this paper." After a pause, he continued. "I don't want to talk about faith from the outside anymore. I want to move to the inside and see the answers from the inside. The answers will come in time. The important thing right now is for me to move from the outside looking in to the inside." Can you identify with this young man? There is a point where enough questions have been asked and answered, and you are ready to take the step, or make the leap, to proceed in your search *from within* the circle of a faith-relationship to God.

LONG LEAPS OR SHORT STEPS

Be assured, I have no desire to push or rush you in that direction. I'm going to do my best to present all the linear, step-by-step logic I can, so that if you choose to make a move from your current circle to a new one, it will be a manageable leap, or maybe even a single short step. That's all that's required, really. In fact, I think you can imagine that first step of good faith as a kind of simple "Hello! Is anyone there?" shouted into the darkness.

The act is absurd, in a way. If no one is there, I'm shouting to no one and making a fool of myself. Yet if someone is there, how can I know it if I don't take this risk . . . this risk of faith? In order to find if someone is there, I have to act as if I already know that someone is there. The call into the dark is, in that sense, circular, presupposing that someone is there, and more, someone who speaks my language, is predisposed to respond, is friendly, and whose acquaintance and response would be welcome. Significant presuppositions to be sure! But that is our situation with faith. There is a risk involved (the risk of being wrong) and a certain circularity (of needing to believe, however tentatively, certain things about God—such as God's existence and desirability—in order to begin searching for God). I think that this risk and circularity are inescapable. I can't see any way around them. Can you? If I sincerely want to know if someone is "out there," then sincerity will move me to take the risk and make the call out into the darkness.

STILL WORKING ON THE DEFINITION

I said earlier that our working definition was a start, but not the last word in defining faith. We have since taken a step forward by adding the adjective "good," and we tried to define what we would mean by "good faith." We've acknowledged that logic alone will not get us "into" faith, but we have expressed a desire to make the leap into faith a sane, manageable, reasonable one. But I still think we should admit there is more to faith than we've said so far. Our understanding of faith will have to grow as we proceed, but one thing is, I hope, becoming clear: It really does matter *what* you believe, and even more, it matters *how* you believe.

A QUIZ

Let's finish this chapter with a two-question quiz:

Multiple-Choice Question

If I take my four children on a walk by the river, and we sit together on some rocks and watch the river run by, and in that quiet moment I say to them, "Rachel, Brett, Trevor, Jodi . . . I love each of you. I really do. I hope you will believe that"—which three of the following six responses would I prefer to hear from them?

A. "Sometimes I doubt that. But I'm open to being persuaded that it's true."

B. "Can you give me a genetic analysis of your DNA and mine so I can have greater certainty that you are indeed my biological father?"

C. "Could you repeat that? I was so engrossed in watching the river that I didn't hear what you said."

D. "In that case, I would like a new car, unlimited use of your credit card, a phone line of my own, and a complete overhaul of our typical diet."

E. "Why then did you give my brother a birthday gift which cost $8.75 more than mine last year? I've been keeping track, you know."

F. "Thanks, Dad. I believe you do. And I love you too."

True-False Question

T or F: The fact that you are reading this book indicates some degree of good faith, as does the fact that you are about to turn the page and continue reading.

YOUR RESPONSE

1. I affirm the following descriptors of bad faith:
2. I affirm the following descriptors of good faith:

RESOURCES

The film *The Mission* explores the effects of faith on two men, and the agonizing issues they face as they try to apply faith to life. The contrasts between the good faith of these two and the bad faith of the institutional church are staggering and troubling.

Carl Sagan's film *Contact* similarly explores issues of good faith and bad faith—both in religion and science.

PRAYER

I do not want to develop a faith that is sincere but misguided. On the other hand, I don't want to develop a faith that is conceptually accurate but heartless or graceless. I want to learn, and as I learn, I want to be increasingly aware of how much more I have to learn.

CHAPTER 2 PREVIEW

What Is the Relationship Between Faith and Knowledge?

This chapter stimulates thinking about the words "know" and "believe," and argues against the common myth that we human beings have a clear-cut choice between certainty, science, and knowledge on the one hand and faith on the other. It considers, and rejects, the religious claim that the Bible or some other document can provide certainty. It suggests that even science, which we normally think of as being purely rational, has important nonrational elements, and has more in common with faith than most people realize.

WHO SHOULD READ THIS CHAPTER?

This is one of the more philosophical chapters in the book, and so is especially for folk of a more analytical, reflective bent.

WHAT QUESTIONS DOES IT ADDRESS?

How much can we really be certain of? Is some degree of faith inescapable, or is it possible to live without any faith at all? Are religious people justified when they say the Bible gives them certainty?

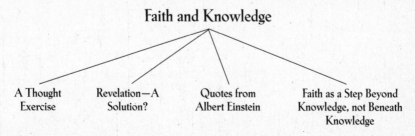

Faith and Knowledge

A Thought Exercise   Revelation—A Solution?   Quotes from Albert Einstein   Faith as a Step Beyond Knowledge, not Beneath Knowledge

We have but faith; we cannot know,

for knowledge is of things we see;

And yet we trust it comes from thee,

A beam in darkness; let it grow.

Let knowledge grow from more to more,

But more of reverence in us dwell;

That mind and soul, according well,

May make one music as before,

But vaster.

ALFRED, LORD TENNYSON, "IN MEMORIUM"

. . . my not being able to give a sufficient reason is not a matter of a defectiveness in my ability to think, but of a real peculiarity in my relationship to the one whom I trust or to that which I acknowledge to be true. It is a relationship which by its nature does not rest upon "reasons". . . . Reasons of course can be urged for it, but they are never sufficient to account for my faith. . . . My rationality, my rational power of thought, is merely a part, a particular function of my nature; when however I "believe" . . . my entire being is engaged, the totality of my nature enters into the process, indeed this becomes possible only because the relationship of faith is a relationship of my entire being. But personal totality in this sense can only be involved if the whole function of thought, without being impaired, enters into it. . . .

MARTIN BUBER, *TWO TYPES OF FAITH*

CHAPTER 2

What Is the Relationship Between Faith and Knowledge?

We stated rather nonchalantly in the preceding chapter that good faith was about the pursuit of truth. But in postmodern times, it's dangerous to use the word "truth" naively. As never before, we are sensitive to how hard it is (some would say impossible) to know truth. We are increasingly aware of the ways our presuppositions and subjectivity color our perception, interpretation, understanding, and communication of "the truth"—and as a result, we aren't at all sure if what we have at the end of the day is even worth calling "truth."

In my opinion, the problem we face is less with the word "truth" than it is with the word "knowledge." Few if any of us doubt there really is something "out there" called truth, even though many of us are suspicious of humans' ability to perceive, interpret, understand, and communicate what's out there with a degree of certainty worthy of the word "knowledge."

A THOUGHT EXERCISE

So let's think about the word "know" for a few minutes. Consider these sentences:

1. I know the capital city of Uzbekistan.
2. I know I exist.
3. I know that 4 x 13 = 52.
4. I know that water is two parts hydrogen and one part oxygen.

5. I know Tim Ayers.
6. I know the town of Hancock, Maryland, like the back of my hand.
7. I know a bargain when I see one.
8. I know that black holes exist.
9. I know that Abraham Lincoln was an American president.
10. I know that Abraham Lincoln was a great American president.
11. I know the meaning of the word "flagma."
12. I know God exists.
13. I know God.

What do you make of the various uses of "know" in these statements? In which cases does the word "know" mean complete, unassailable certainty? How many different meanings does the word "know" have in these statements? How do you know? Now consider the word "believe" in these situations.

1. I believe it's going to rain.
2. I believe in extraterrestrials.
3. I believe in liberal democracy.
4. I believe the square root of 9801 is 99.
5. I believe Abraham Lincoln made a mistake in launching the Civil War.
6. I believe I can be a success.
7. I believe that music is a universal language.
8. I believe it because I saw it with my own two eyes.
9. I believe it is safe to swim in that lake.
10. I believe that all mammals bear live young.
11. I believe that God exists.
12. I believe in God.
13. I believe God.

How do these two words, "know" and "believe," relate? How might knowledge and faith relate? It appears that anyone can *believe* just about anything, but how much can people really *know*?

KNOWING ABOUT KNOWING

The study of certainty is called epistemology. Epistemology gets
you thinking about ~~questions~~ ... knowing and

... ~~a~~intment, an
... ~~l~~eft your wal-
... ~~m~~ent that was
... ~~o~~f your mind
... responsible
... trust it?
... that every-
... ~~jus~~t humoring
... ~~o~~ut of touch
... a character
... seems real,
... it's all real.

... for snow.
... more than
... ~~occur~~ring." The
... The speci-
... ~~ficity of their language ...~~ ... among types
~~of fr~~ozen crystalline precipitation that the rest of us don't even
notice. Is it possible that my language similarly blinds me to many
important spiritual distinctions or realities that others who speak
different languages may grasp? And is it possible that human language in general guides our thoughts into ruts that keep us from
knowing reality in other—perhaps truer or fuller—ways? Is it possible to train our minds to go beyond the normal limits of our languages?

4. In ancient times, everyone "knew" the earth was flat. Before
Galileo's day, everyone "knew" the sun rotated around the earth.
Before Darwin's day, everyone "knew" the earth was created in six
literal days about 4004 B.C. Before the Civil War, many people

"knew" that slavery was completely justified. How do we know that many of the things we think we know today won't be shown to be false in the future?

5. After a highly publicized murder trial in the United States in the mid 1990s, most people of the same race as the accused "knew" he was innocent, while most people of other races "knew" he was guilty. They heard the same objective evidence, but their subjective interpretation of it was, in some cases at least, skewed by their background. How do we know our backgrounds haven't impaired our ability to be objective?

6. Most people brought up in the context of a particular religion believe that religion is true. If you're born in India, you're probably going to "know" Hinduism is the true religion; if in America or Guatemala, it will probably be Christianity; if in an intellectual family in France, agnosticism or atheism; if in Iran, Islam; if in Israel, Judaism. There are exceptions, but it appears clear that the majority of people choose their beliefs based on social acceptance, peer pressure, and other factors rather than on a sober investigation of the objective evidence. Might many of the things we "know" simply reflect the norms of the groups we belong to?

7. Scientific knowledge is based on repeatable experimentation. As data increases, as hypotheses "work" under repeated testing, one makes an inductive leap from specific results to generalizations— which are accepted as "knowledge." Is something true because it works consistently?

UNCERTAINTY PRINCIPLES

Clearly, those words "believe" and "know" signal a lot of complexity, a lot to think about. It doesn't seem possible to assign some arbitrary "certainty factor"—so that if your certainty is less than, say, ninety-four percent, you "believe," and if it is ninety-five percent or greater, you "know." How would one apply such a number—based on a "gut feeling"? How do you "know" your "gut feeling" is accurate? Someone might suggest that the word "know" be reserved for only 100 percent certainty, but again, one has to question whether 100 percent certainty is possible. Ironically, an unreflective person is 100 percent certain of a lot more often than a highly reflective one, because a highly reflective person eventually recognizes a number of "uncertainty principles," including these:

1. That the "laws of logic"—the software that thought runs on—must be accepted on faith, being unprovable (since you have to assume them in order to prove them, which tends to not prove anything!): Thus all thought is ultimately based on faith!

2. That language has powerful effects on our experience of perceiving, thinking, and "knowing."

3. That the groups from which we derive our social identity (sociologists call them "plausibility structures") and our historical setting also have far-reaching effects on what we think we know.

4. That even our personality types—some of which seem by nature to be more questioning and others less so—affect how easily we are persuaded that we know the truth.

5. That at some point, practicality steps in: We are forced to answer a test question, or we have to decide whether to marry Lee or Terry, or we have to fund a project, or we have to get on with life—and doing so requires us to make some assumptions . . . to decide that in spite of our lack of absolute certainty, we have to turn some things into "knowledge," which we call assumptions.

6. That sometimes, even those assumptions have to be questioned.

TWO DISCLAIMERS

Let me interject with two disclaimers. First, I'm not suggesting our elementary schools accept a divergence of opinion on multiplication tables, since some children who multiply thirteen by four and get fifty-seven may simply be working with different logic software! Rather, I am suggesting that we reflect more on how small (nonexistent?) is the sphere within which we actually "know" with complete, unassailable certainty. Second, I am not recommending the absurdities of "absolute relativism" or radical postmodernism—where we say that everything is relative and nobody can know anything with certainty, conveniently ignoring the fact that we seem to believe we know with complete certainty that everything is relative! To argue such a point is itself illogical: Why try to persuade you that my assertion is true if the point of the assertion is that there is no knowable truth? (We'll return to this issue in chapter 8.)

No, rather than promoting relativism or a postmodern despair about being able to know or communicate truth, I am trying to push our thinking about our thinking beyond its normal limits because I believe that doing so can lead us to important insights about faith.

REVELATION—A SOLUTION?

Some of my believing friends feel they have solved the problem. The Bible (or the Gita or the Koran, or whatever), they say, provides direct revelation from God. Therefore, it is absolutely true and trustworthy, providing a sure foundation upon which all knowledge can be built. The Bible thus yields more than faith: It yields certainty, knowledge. Now you should know that I have great faith in the Bible, and have found it to have an importance and value for me above all other books, and I in fact used to be among those who thought the Bible solved the whole epistemological problem simply and cleanly, as many of my friends now feel. But I can't follow that logic anymore. A number of questions come to mind:

1. How do you know with absolute certainty that the Bible is the direct revelation of God? (And again, if you answer that, how do you know your ability to know is absolute and unflawed?) If you accept the authority of the Bible on any

degree of faith, then the point has been made: We all live by faith, not certainty.

2. Even if you had complete certainty that the Bible was originally the direct revelation of God, how do you know with complete certainty that in all its copying, translations, and so forth, it has not been corrupted in some small ways? Even if the scope of the corruptions or uncertainties of translation is small, haven't you still lost absolute certainty?

3. Even if you had complete certainty that your translated copy of the fully inspired Bible were completely uncorrupted, how do you know with complete certainty that your understanding of the document is absolutely complete and accurate? As soon as you acknowledge the potential for imperfections or misconceptions in your reading and interpretation (not to mention imperfections in its exposition and application by preachers like me), haven't you again lost absolute certainty?

4. Even if we were to concede all the previous questions (which, of course, we cannot), we are left with another even deeper question. Even if God—who as creator must know everything about everything—gave us a statement as simple as this: "I exist and I love you," could we fully grasp what the statement means, with unassailable certainty that our understanding was accurate? Do we fully comprehend what God means when using the word "I"? Do we know what God would mean by the word "exist"—surely implying levels of existence far beyond what most of us have ever tried to imagine? What about the word "love"? Can I safely assume that a loving God will meet all my expectations, fulfill all my wishes, since I am loved? If not, what can I safely assume, and why?

Now again, as we'll see in chapter 13, I believe that the Bible has unique and immense value in our search for good faith and our search for God, and I don't want to be seen as someone who tries to discredit the Bible in any way. Rather, as someone who deeply respects the Bible, I think we do it a disservice by implying that it can do something that no book can. In spiritual matters as in used car sales, exaggerated claims may make a fast sale, but customers are soon dissatisfied, and eventually buyer's remorse sets in, along with a lasting distrust of the salesperson who overpromised and underdelivered. Promising absolute, unassailable certainty, even with the benefit of the Bible or any holy book, seems to be an exaggerated claim.

Do you begin to feel the magnitude of our question, "What is the relationship between faith and knowledge?"

A LEVEL PLAYING FIELD

So where are we? As I have said before, we're left, the more reflective we become, with this realization: We're on a level playing field; none of us lives with absolute, unassailable certainty about anything; we all live by faith. What we might call practical certainty—the kind of certainty that allows us to ignore many of these rather abstract and far-fetched questions so we can get along with our lives—is really relative certainty, shot through with faith on many levels. Even the skeptic can only doubt one set of propositions because he believes another. Without some structure of faith, some plausibility structure, we can't get anywhere. We're like weightless, tractionless runners or boxers. We have no leverage. So, some degree of faith is downright inescapable, and faith runs through all we claim to know. (I realize that for some of us, this is such an immense realization that it seems trivial to say it so glibly. It might be best for some readers to put this book aside for a few days to let the dust settle, and see if you can really live with this conclusion.)

ACCORDING TO ALBERT

If it's any comfort, Albert Einstein reached a similar conclusion: In the words of Lesslie Newbigin (*The Gospel in a Pluralist Society*, Grand Rapids: Eerdmans, 1989, p. 33), "There is no knowing without believing, and believing is the way to knowing." Consider these quotes from Einstein:

> As far as the propositions of mathematics refer to reality, they are not certain; and as far as they are certain, they do not refer to reality.

> *IDEAS AND OPINIONS*

> The supreme task of the physicist is the search for those highly universal laws from which a picture of the world can be obtained by pure deduction. There is no logical path leading to these laws. They are only to be reached by intuition, based upon something like an intellectual love.

> *THE WORLD AS I SEE IT*

> The mechanics of discovery are neither logical nor intellectual. It's a sudden illumination, almost a rapture. Later, to be sure, intelligence and analysis and experiment confirm (or invalidate) the intuition. But initially there is a great leap of the imagination.

> *CROSSAN, THE DARK INTERVAL*

"A sudden illumination, rapture, intuition, intellectual love, a great leap of the imagination" ... they sound like the words of a poet or prophet, not a scientist. But those readers who are involved in science will likely agree: Science is a creative process involving many faculties in addition to cold, hard reason. (See chapter 5 for more on the super-rational dimensions to science.) The popular myths of objectivity and certainty notwithstanding, knowledge and belief need not be enemies, but can rather be partners in the search for truth.

WHAT IF?

What then is the relationship between faith and knowledge? What if faith, instead of being a step back from the limits of our ability to know and understand, could actually be a flight beyond the rim? What if the word "knowledge," used to denote certainty gained by rationalistic and empirical means, is actually only appropriate for mundane facts, pedestrian inquiries, common commodities? What if there is another category of reality in the universe, no less real just because it doesn't shrink itself to our instruments and portals of "knowledge"? What if that category of reality—let's call it mystery or spirituality—dwarfs all of our knowledge, as space dwarfs our little earth? Are we humble enough to look up from the little things we are so proud of comprehending and controlling, to face massive realities—humbling mysteries—greater than ourselves, and therefore greater than our ability to squeeze into our little boxes of "certainty" or "knowledge"? Are we willing to step off the narrow ledge of knowledge to soar into broad spaces of faith?

After all, as novelist Flannery O'Connor said, "Whatever you do anyway, remember that these things are mysteries and that if they were such that we could understand them, they wouldn't be worth understanding. A God you understood would be less than yourself."

Is this kind of talk uncomfortable for some of us? Yes, like inviting a data-bound scientist or a numbers-bound accountant to read literature for the first time or experiment with sculpture, exercising an atrophied capacity called imagination. Getting us into water over our heads? Yes—but believe those who have tried it: Swimming and surfing and sailing are not so bad!

FAITH BEYOND KNOWLEDGE

I said earlier that in our postmodern times, we are increasingly aware of the limitations of human knowledge. We are aware perhaps as never before of the gap between what we subjectively "know" and what is objectively true. For people like us, boxed in little bodies with narrow portals of physical senses which are interpreted by fallible, limited (yet amazing!) little brains, absolute certainty is a luxury we have not been given. We can only aspire to relative certainty, which involves relative uncertainty . . . which leaves room for—no, more, which actually *requires*—faith.

We could content ourselves with petty pursuits and leave off any search for truth. But to do so feels cheap, for moral reasons if not for intellectual ones. So, into this profound human dilemma we go, needing to let go of certainty in order to reach for truth. We venture into this very real gap between our understanding "in here" and reality as it is "out there." We move into this territory where the limitations of knowledge are admitted and the value of seeking truth is also held high. Here, without faith we cannot go. It's the only vehicle we have.

We are faced again with the predicament we spoke of in the introduction, the predicament of being not just abstract note-takers gaining "knowledge" or information, but of people in a smoky building needing news of escape routes. We are faced again with the predicament we spoke of in chapter 1, of people needing to know if there is someone out there in the dark, beyond our ability to see. To call out, "Hello! Is anybody out there?" we have to act as if someone is there, even though we aren't sure. That's our human predicament, and that is the domain of faith.

I'M SORRY

I'm sorry. Beyond these musings, I can't map out for you a precise relationship between faith and knowledge. But I can tell you that I have looked at the question from many angles, and after all my considerations, I am more convinced than ever that faith is necessary, faith is inescapable, and faith is a thing of great value—to find, to hold, to treasure, and to grow—if we aspire to seek the truth. How faith grows will be the topic of the next chapter.

YOUR RESPONSE

Which statement best describes you?
I accept that everyone lives by faith to one degree or another.
I cannot yet accept this idea.
I am able to see faith as a step up from where I am now.
I am not yet able to see faith as a step up from where I am now.

RESOURCES

Books that explore this topic from a vantage point of faith are, to date, rare. I expect this to change. By far the best religious thinker I have found in this regard to date is Lesslie Newbigin. See his *The Gospel in a Pluralist Society* (Grand Rapids: Eerdmans, 1989) or *The Open Secret* (Grand Rapids: Eerdmans, rev. 1995). Of course, Walker Percy's essay "The Message in the Bottle" is worth finding and reading too (*The Message in the Bottle*, New York: Farrar, Straus, and Giroux, 1954).

Fiction can perhaps explore this issue better than nonfiction. I recommend Orson Scott Card's Alvin Maker series, beginning with *Seventh Son* (New York: Tor Books, 1993), and his Homecoming series beginning with *The Memory of Earth* (New York: Tor Books, 1994). Card has the ability to show you the same reality from several vantage points, in a way that leads you to question the sole authority of your own vantage point in the real world.

PRAYER

It is very humbling to face the limitations of my own certainty, my own knowledge. I do not want to rest on my own solitary powers of perception and reasoning, but neither do I want to discard them. Rather, I present all of my faculties of thinking and knowing, and hope to be guided through them . . . and beyond them. My faith seeks understanding, and my understanding seeks faith. I see that humility is essential to pursuing faith, and that arrogance will sabotage my spiritual search. I aspire to have a truly intelligent faith, that is reason-plus, not reason-minus.

CHAPTER 3 PREVIEW

How Does Faith Grow?

This chapter explores a four-stage model for the growth of faith and attempts to describe the four stages. It suggests that as faith grows, one outgrows one stage and embraces a new stage, perhaps like growing out of and into new sizes of clothes or shoes. It suggests that this process is often painful, and summarizes my experience of progressing through the stages.

WHO SHOULD READ THIS CHAPTER?

This chapter is relevant to both the spiritual seeker who is still unsure of faith and the already-convinced person who has believed for many years.

WHAT QUESTIONS DOES IT ADDRESS?

Why is the spiritual journey so often difficult? What are the characteristics of each of the four stages of faith development? How does doubt fit in to the development of faith?

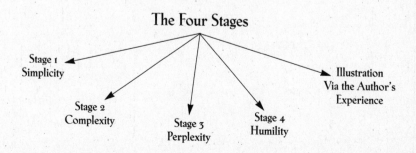

The Four Stages

Stage 1 Simplicity

Stage 2 Complexity

Stage 3 Perplexity

Stage 4 Humility

Illustration Via the Author's Experience

CHAPTER 3

How Does Faith Grow?

I don't want to give you the impression that I live in this constant bliss of relative certainty about these matters of ultimate concern. Much of my spiritual life has been tortured by doubt. Not everyone seems to experience the curse of doubt to the same degree, but those of us who are by nature reflective and who find doubt inescapable gradually must learn to see the curse as a mixed blessing. For example, if I am able to help some readers work through their doubts and not be overcome by them, it is only because I have been there myself. Being of some help to you is a meaningful consolation for me.

But even if there were no such consolations, there isn't any alternative to learning to deal with doubt. It's not as though I could simply give up my current faith and revert to another viewpoint that would never itself become doubtworthy! Even the convinced atheist—if he is the slightest bit reflective—has his doubts about atheism—whether they occur in a foxhole, hospice lobby, concert hall, delivery room, board meeting, or wilderness hike. Doubt is part of the human condition. Nobody gets a guaranteed anti-doubt vaccination, short of a lobotomy.

My experiences with doubt have, ironically, helped me see more clearly how faith grows. In fact, doubt has helped me see a four-stage process of faith development, a process where faith is found and lost and found again, at deeper and deeper levels.

A SCHEMA

In this schema, one gradually outgrows one version of faith, discards it for a more fitting version, outgrows that, and so on. I call this schema "The Four Stages." It was inspired by specialists in cognitive development such as William Fowler and William Perry, psychologists such as Robert Coles and Scott Peck, writers such as Søren Kierkegaard and Walker Percy, and poets such as William Wordsworth and William Blake. It goes like this:

Stage 1: Simplicity

Focus: Right or wrong? Being right, belonging to the right group.

Motive: Pleasing authority figures, being an "insider."

Beliefs: All truth is known or knowable. There are easy answers to every question. The right authority figures know the right answers.

Perception: Dualistic, in terms of right versus wrong, good versus bad.

Mottoes: You're either for us or against us; it's all or nothing.

Authorities: Godlike. God's representatives, with divine right. They help you know.

Like/Dislike: We like bold, clear, assertive, confident people who know the answers. We dislike tentative, qualifying, timid, or unsure people who say, "I don't know."

Life is: A war.

Strategy: Learn the answers. Learn what to think. Learn to identify and avoid "the enemy."

Strengths: Highly committed, willing to sacrifice and suffer for the cause.

Weaknesses: Also willing to kill or inflict suffering for the cause. Arrogant. Simplistic. Combative. Judgmental. Intolerant. Incapable of distinguishing major from minor issues, since every issue is part of the system that has embraced all (as universal, absolute, and inerrant) or nothing (as false, wrong, discredited).

Identity: I find my identity in my leader or group.

Relationships: Dependent or codependent.

God is: The Ultimate Authority Figure and/or Ultimate Friend.

Transition: As Stage 1 people encounter diversity in their ranks, or are disillusioned because of fallen leaders or internal squabbles in the group from which they derive their identity, or are unsettled by the multiplicity of viewpoints, they tend to swing from a desire for internal knowledge and certainty to a desire for external accomplishment and success, thus moving on to Stage 2. The world isn't simple anymore, so the task changes—to make life work in this complex environment.

Stage 2: Complexity

Focus: Effective or ineffective? Accomplishing, learning technique, winning.

Motive: Reach goals; be effective.

Beliefs: Almost anything is doable. Different people have different methods, beliefs, approaches—the key is finding the best ones.

Perception: Pragmatic—looking for the useful, practical.

Mottoes: There's more than one way to do things—find whatever works best for you.

Authorities: Coaches. They help you grow.

Like/Dislike: We like people who give clear instructions and let us know what they expect of us. We like people who motivate us and make us feel like doing things. We dislike people who are too dogmatic (Stage 1) or mystical (Stage 3).

Life is: A complex game. You have to learn the rules.

Strategy: Learn the technique. Play the game. Find what people want and give it to them.

Strengths: Enthusiasm, idealism, action.

Weaknesses: Superficial, naive.

Identity: I find my identity in a cause or achievement.

Relationships: Increasingly independent.

God is: The Ultimate Guide or Coach.

Transition: Three problems push people out of Stage 2 (usually against their will). First, the prevalence of Stage 1 people always claiming to have all the answers prohibits Stage 2 people from escaping questions about truth. Second, the failure of "foolproof" techniques and projects leaves them disillusioned and perplexed— prime characteristics of Stage 3. Third, Stage 2 people survive by fragmenting complex and apparently contradictory truth into categories (scientific truth, religious truth, social or relational truth, political truth). Eventually, a desire for unity and integration causes them to be dissatisfied with their fragmented approach.

Stage 3: Perplexity

Focus: Honest or dishonest? Authentic or inauthentic? Understanding, seeing through appearances and illusions to reality.

Motive: Being honest, authentic.

Beliefs: All is questionable. Nothing is really certain, except uncertainty. Everything is relative.

Perception: Relativistic.

Mottoes: Everyone's opinion is equally valid and equally questionable. Who knows who really is right?

Authorities: Demonic. They're dishonest controllers, trying to impose easy answers on complex realities.

Like/Dislike: We like other questioners, free spirits, and nonconformists. We dislike people in Stages 1 and 2.

Life is: A joke or a mystery or a search.

Strategy: Ask hard questions. Be ruthlessly honest.

Strengths: Depth, honesty, often humor or artistic sensitivity.

Weaknesses: Cynical, uncommitted, withdrawn, depressed, or elitist.

Identity: I find my identity in solitude or a small circle of similarly alienated friends.

Relationships: Counterdependent.

God is: Either a mythic authority figure I've outgrown, an opiate of the masses, or a mystery I'm seeking.

Transition: One of the key struggles in Perplexity is the battle between arrogance ("Those simpletons in Stages 1 and 2 don't see how shallow and primitive they are! Ha! They've never even asked the questions we ask, much less found answers for them! Ha!") and humility. And there is much in this stage to humble a person. Notably, one has to get on with life, and life requires one to make commitments, and commitments grow out of values and beliefs, so one is not left with the option of staying in limbo. One has to make choices. One can't blindly accept a group's or authority figure's agenda anymore, but one has to take responsibility for living life and proceed—chastened and more realistic, often disillusioned and less idealistic—in short, humbled.

Stage 4: Humility

Focus: Wise or unwise? Fulfilling potential. Making the most of life.

Motive: Make the best of opportunities. Serve, contribute, make a difference.

Beliefs: There are a few basic absolute or universal truths, many relative matters, and much mystery. There are enough basics to live by.

Perception: Integrated, synthesizing the dualism, pragmatism, and relativism of earlier stages.

Mottoes: I'll focus on a few grand essentials. In essentials, unity; in nonessentials, diversity; in all things, charity.

Authorities: They're people like you and me—imperfect, doing their best, sometimes admirable and dependable, sometimes untrustworthy and despicable, sometimes sincerely misguided.

Like/Dislike: We like people who combine thoughtfulness with accomplishment.

Life is: A mixture; what you make it; what it is.

Strategy: Learn all the answers and techniques you can (Stages 1 and 2), ask all the questions you can (stage 3), and try to fulfill your potential, admitting how little you really know.

Strengths: May exhibit strengths of earlier stages, plus stability, endurance, wisdom, and humility.

Weaknesses: May display weaknesses of earlier stages.

Identity: I find my identity in my relationship to the whole, or to God.

Relationships: Interdependent.

God is: Knowable in part, yet mysterious; present, yet transcendent; just, yet merciful (able to hold dynamic tensions about God).

Transition: That this is the last stage in our schema doesn't suggest that one lives happily ever after! At this stage of integration, one now faces all the weaknesses of the previous stages. Whenever one enters a new context (a new career, a new religion, a new social network), he or she may well recapitulate the stages repeatedly. After all, humility, like maturity, is obviously not a destination, but rather a journey in itself.

A QUALIFIER, A FEW BRIEF TANGENTS NOT QUITE TAKEN, AND A SUMMARY

Clearly, people don't generally move out of or into a stage in one giant step. There are many hesitant explorations, retreats, renewed explorations. The transitions from infancy to childhood, childhood through puberty, adolescence through adulthood, and young adulthood to middle age certainly don't happen suddenly; a twelve-year-old is a child one minute, a young adult the next, it seems, then a child again, and so on. The same is true of these stages.

By the way, we could describe a Stage 0, where a person simply believes what he or she has been told and taught, without questioning, without even recognizing the possibility of questioning, without realizing there are any alternative beliefs or differing groups out there. Or we could explore cultic behavior as a regressive step in this process, where, say, a young adult becomes intimidated by the complexities or perplexities of growing up and throws himself into a Stage 1 group, against his better judgment, as a "bad faith" act of emotional desperation.

Or we could consider how different religions, churches, denominations, or religious organizations often enfranchise and serve people at one stage, but not others. That could open up some fascinating considerations of how organizations can better serve people through the whole process. Or we could consider how the Bible or other sacred writings appear to people at various stages . . . as the Book of Easy Answers and Absolutes for Stage 1, as the Spiritual How-To Manual for Stage 2, either as an outmoded tool of oppression by Stage 1 authority figures or as a refreshingly diverse and honest artifact for Stage 3 folk, or as a library for lifelong learning for those in Stage 4. But these tangents would take us too far afield. Our focus here is on the finding of faith and the growing of faith— which generally feels like losing faith.

Here's how it works: When a person begins to outgrow Stage 1 faith, it feels like doubt. Then, appropriating a Stage 2 faith feels like finding faith again—and that feeling of satisfaction and renewal lasts until Stage 3 is knocking at the door. Most people don't know there is a more advanced stage waiting outside the door, so to them, this knocking feels dreadful, disloyal, dangerous. Most of us fight it and try to avoid answering the door as long as possible. It feels like the end of faith, not the beginning of a new stage, when the knocking of doubt begins. Even when Stage 4 knocks, Stage 3 usually only lets go after a fight.

MY BACKGROUND

I've seen this pattern play out in my own life. I was brought up in a very conservative Christian group. For most people in this group, the world was created in six twenty-four-hour periods, less than ten thousand years ago. Species did not evolve, but were formed from clay by the literal hands of God. Adam and Eve literally ate a literal forbidden fruit, and that one act explains literally everything that's wrong with the world today. Noah's flood covered every square inch of planet earth. All other religions—including most "Christian" denominations—were simply wrong, from the devil, many hell-bound. Women must never speak in church (although they may sing and teach children) and should let their husbands rule the home. Philosophy and science were evil; studying them was a waste of time (or worse) compared to studying the Bible. For that reason, higher education was often suspect. Why get all that godless learning when the world is going to end any day anyway?

Now before you react too strongly, let me say that there were many wonderful people (my parents among them) in the church of my childhood—exactly the kind of people you'd want for your boss, employee, neighbor, fishing buddy, or golf partner. The sincerity of devotion and genuine neighborliness of many of the "saints" there was among the most beautiful and poignant I have ever seen. Let me also say that the dogmatism of many "secular" families, in opposite ways, of course, can be just as "fundamentalist" as the devotion of religious families. But let me also say that this kind of environment was impossible for a boy of my reflective temperament—there wasn't room there for a person like me.

Stage 1 Doubt

I am by nature a questioner. I can't help it. I have a built-in urge to ask questions, and to me, experts earn their credibility by their willingness to be tested or doubted. In addition, from before first grade, when my dad would sit next to me on the sofa reading books about nature, I have been an incurable book-lover. By the time I was in seventh grade, I had memorized the Latin genus and species name of nearly every North American reptile, not because I was trying to, but simply because I was by that time reading college-level textbooks on herpetology ... my great boyhood passion (until I discovered girls and the fact that girls weren't interested in that sort of thing generally).

In all of that reading, it was inevitable that I would start questioning the dogma of my church. At first, this questioning had to do with the specifics of my denomination: "Why do we think we're so right, and all other Christians are so wrong?" But by the time I was fourteen or so, I was wondering if the whole God-thing was a hoax. Perhaps my secular scientific education had it right after all.

This is a classic Stage 1 dichotomy: There are good guys and bad guys, and maybe the guys I thought were good (church people) were really the bad guys, and the bad guys (scientists, intellectuals) were really the good guys. I was questioning who really wore the white hats, but I wasn't questioning my view of the world in which everyone fit into one of two categories.

Enter Stages 2 and 3

I had some very powerful spiritual experiences and influences in my teenage years which convinced me that I couldn't simply reject God (more on this in chapter 17). I also came across some intelligent Christian writers and thinkers by my senior year of high school (C. S. Lewis, Francis Schaeffer, R. C. Sproul) who gave me some hope that a person didn't have to check his or her brains at the door when entering church. So, having been confirmed in my Christian commitment, I turned my focus from which tribe I was going to join and which authorities I was going to follow to how to make this thing called the Christian life work. This was my entry into Stage 2 faith—preoccupied with hows, techniques, practicalities: How do I learn more of the Bible? How do I pray more? How do I get along with my parents better? How do I relate to people better? How do I find God's will for my life—in my career choice and college choice and dating choices? How do I deal with my sexuality? How do I find more happiness? How do I find more success?

That preoccupation lasted into my college years. But during college, Stage 2 faith began to falter. Stage 3 was knocking at the door, and it was knocking hard. I was an English major, and deconstruction, postmodernism, relativism, pluralism, and all their cousins made my Stage 2 version of Christianity seem more and more like a tacky infomercial on late-night cable TV. Sure, some people have bought it, and it works for some people, but is it really true and right for everybody? Aren't the claims hyped up, exaggerated, falsified by group dynamics? Isn't my "brand" of faith just one of many on the market, in no way superior to anyone else's?

Granted, those making the assault on my faith (professors, fellow students, writers) didn't have it together themselves. It wasn't that they had a better lifestyle or better answers, but their cynicism and skeptical tone were enough to make me lose Stage 2 faith by my senior year.

Stage 3 Struggles

I was fortunate at this time to have good friends who weren't put off by my spiritual malaise, people who gave me room to question and doubt. I remember unloading with one of them, Tom Willett, about the erosion of my faith and my mountain of questions, and then Tom saying something like this: "Brian, I can tell your faith is shaky right now, but my faith is strong, and I just want you to know that reality doesn't look so gloomy for me. God doesn't seem very real to you, but God is very real to this person you know and trust sitting across the room from you." For him to keep faith in God and our friendship meant a lot to me. I also remember him offering me some hope: "As your worldview expands to grapple with all the things you're thinking about, you'll have a perspective much broader than that of most people. You'll be able to help a lot of other people in some pretty deep ways because of what you're going through now." That didn't solve the problem, but it gave me hope that a solution would be worthwhile, if it ever came.

Stage 3 was hard on me and lasted a long time. I wrote a song in those days that conveys Stage 3 pretty clearly. In the song, God is still present, but only as a glimmer on the periphery of sight, like Moses' burning bush, but barely visible. Paradoxically, there's a sense of drifting, disillusionment, and alienation, along with a sense of clarity, liberation from "false security," and revelation. Stage 3 doesn't look like faith from "the inner circle" of Stage 1 and 2 perspectives, but there can be real faith there nonetheless. Here's the song, called "Sunken Corner":

> It's a rainy night. The streets are shining like a carnival with colored lights:

flashing red and blinking yellow, neon blue and mellow
sodium white.

I cannot see the lines they've painted. I'm trying to find the
lane where I belong.

So if you see me drifting, mister, it's just the weather. I ain't
done nothing wrong.

So meet me at the sunken corner. I know a diner there that's
light and cool and clean.

While we taste our toast and coffee, we can relate illusions
that we've seen.

I feel the blaze of revelation, I feel the stir of inspiration rumbling.

It's a process of elimination, an interruption to our conversation. It's coming. . . .

I have some friends snug in the inner circle. You couldn't pay
them to exchange their place with you or me.

But at least we have this consolation: There's not much here
in the way of false security.

You find God in the strangest places, places you would never
choose to be.

I feel like Moses on the mountain: It's burning there—what
can I do but see?

What can I do but see?

Stage 3 was for me a time of simply trying to keep my eyes
open—to see evidences for God and to see questions and issues my
faith couldn't explain or handle (most significantly, the apparent pig-
headedness and bad taste of so many Christians who were supposed
to be better than the average person, but weren't). I sometimes wondered if my faith would survive. But it did. Chastened, seasoned,
pruned, tested, humbled. That's what Stage 4 faith is all about.

Stage 4 Frontiers

I remained more or less in Stage 3 through graduate school. If
there was one catalyst that helped me get beyond Stage 3, it was

my graduate work on novelist Walker Percy. Percy was an adult convert to Roman Catholicism. He had his dark side, his doubts and depressions, but he exemplified in his novels and essays an approach to Christianity that was more stable, more humble, more honest, more thoughtful, full of more intellectual integrity, than anything I had seen in my Protestant evangelical circles. It was a Christianity unlike the fundamentalism of my childhood (too often defined, I felt, largely by its reaction against and retreat from modernity) and unlike the liberal Christianity of the mainline churches (too often defined, I felt, largely by its capitulation to and endorsement of modernity). Instead, it was a Christianity engaged with modernity (and postmodernity)—grappling with its issues, sensitive to its questions and concerns, aware of its spiritual vacuum, in vital dialogue with its artistic and intellectual leaders. It was a "third-way" faith seeking to steer a course which would avoid defensive retreat and isolation on the one hand and capitulation and sellout on the other.

The faith that I've been learning and growing and seeking to live out during the twenty years since then has been of this Stage 4 type. I never would have gotten there without the first three stages, but the first three stages alone never would have brought me to where I am today.

Rough Riding

But again, I don't want to give you the impression that Stage 4 has been a gentle ride, free of hairpin curves, potholes, and roadside breakdowns. Far from it. In fact, I've seen myself repeat the cycle, repeatedly going through all four stages in more or less dramatic ways, recapitulating the journey in a kind of widening spiral again and again, through simplicity, complexity, and perplexity to new levels of humility. That's what mature faith requires—not pride over how much one sees and understands, but humility, the feeling that one is still a child, certain of so little, still so dependent on God and others, with so much still to learn—including so much more to learn about humility. A friend of mine talks about two simplicities, a bold, naive one on this side of complexity and a humbled, seasoned one on the other side. That describes the process pretty well, I think.

Even in Stage 4 faith, there are occasional mornings I wake up and look in the mirror and think, "Have I been a fool to live for things I can't see, instead of going after money and comfort and pleasure like many other people?" Once, when I was the speaker for a large youth retreat, I spent all the time between my messages wondering, "Do I myself believe in God anymore?"

At those times, my faith seeks deeper understanding. My faith looks for evidence, for good reasons to keep on believing. I know that logic and reason won't force me to believe, but I also have learned that clear thinking can often help me to believe. So, to questions of God's existence and character we will turn in the next several chapters, looking for good reasons to believe.

For those of you at a transition between stages, these chapters might help your faith stretch to the next level. For those of you approaching faith for the first time, this logical approach may remove obstacles, shorten the distance between where you are and where you want to be, and thus make the first step into faith more manageable. (For those who find analytical argument tedious and irritating, this would be a good time to skip ahead to chapter 9.)

YOUR RESPONSE

1. In which of the four stages do you see yourself now?
2. What transitions/challenges should you expect ahead in the road?

PRAYER

I may not be sure if anyone is there to listen to what I'm saying. I may even feel a bit silly saying these words. But if there is a good, kind, compassionate God able to hear me, I have to believe that these words will be interpreted as a sincere attempt at prayer and as an expression of whatever small amount of faith I have. I hope that if I am being heard, I will be helped and guided and that the thinking stimulated by this book will be of value to me.

PART 2

GOD, FOR LOGICAL THINKERS

CHAPTER 4 PREVIEW

Can I Believe in Atheism?

This chapter addresses the question, "Is there a God?" and considers the first possible answer: *No,* the answer of atheism. It suggests that many atheists have good reasons for their belief and explores those reasons. It also suggests a number of reasons for moving beyond atheism to consider the other possible answers. It argues that atheism is a belief just as theism is.

WHO SHOULD READ THIS CHAPTER?

If you are a committed atheist, this chapter will probably not convince you to become a believer in God overnight. It will, I hope, nudge you to reopen the question of God's existence and continue your search. If you are not a committed atheist, but have frequent or occasional doubts about the existence of God, this chapter will help you solidify your belief.

WHAT QUESTIONS DOES IT ADDRESS?

Why do some people choose atheism? Why is atheism a matter of faith just as much as theism? Why should people move beyond atheism?

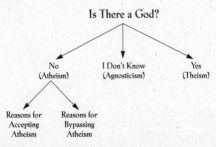

CHAPTER 4

Can I Believe in Atheism?

Our quest for faith now brings us to this blunt, stark question: *Is there a God?* Why waste our time searching for something/someone that does not really exist? Let's abandon from the start the quest for a faith that is comforting but delusional. I agree with C. S. Lewis: "...comfort is one thing you cannot get by looking for it. If you look for truth, you may find comfort in the end: If you look for comfort you will not get either comfort or truth—only soft soap and wishful thinking to begin with and, in the end, despair."

So, is there a God? Three answers present themselves when we raise this question: *No, I don't know,* and *yes.* We'll consider the first answer in this chapter.

NO

The "no" answer is the atheist position. Now it must be granted that this answer is a position of faith, because no one can prove conclusively that God doesn't exist. Consider this diagram:

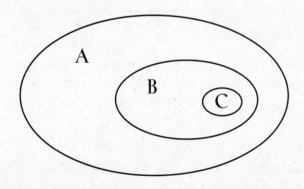

Let Figure A represent all truth everywhere. (Obviously, these figures aren't drawn to any scale!) Let Figure B represent the sum of all truth known by all human beings. And let Figure C represent the knowledge of the person answering no to our question.

Granted, this person can honestly say, "No, in my experience, I recognize the existence of no God." But for this person to deny the huge quantity of experience of the vast majority of other humans through all of history—nearly all of whom say they have experienced God in some way—and to extend his certainty even beyond the realm of all human experience to Figure A, saying that no God exists anywhere out there, even beyond human experience . . . I think you'll agree that this is a statement beyond knowledge, beyond certainty, beyond science, and beyond logic. It is a statement of faith.

NINE REASONS FOR ATHEISM

That doesn't mean the atheist is wrong. It does mean, again, that the playing field is level. The atheist does not have the high ground of logic, reason, science, knowledge, and certainty, as some people seem to feel, leaving the unenlightened masses to muddle along in faith. No, as we've already seen, theists and atheists alike live by faith of one sort or another.

The fact is, there are strong reasons for making a faith commitment to the atheist position. If we could peel back the surface layers, beneath the "No" answer of many atheists we would find some strong reasons like these:

1. All or nearly all religious people I've met are kooks. I find them repulsive, ill-mannered, naive, or unintelligent. I don't want to be associated with them, and I can distance myself by self-identifying as an atheist.
2. I feel that religion is a primitive feature of immature civilization that must be outgrown. I wish to align myself with

the progressive edge of human evolution—hence my atheism.

3. I have chosen a scientific worldview, which prohibits me from believing in anything that can't be verified either by my senses or a mathematical proof.

4. I have certain sexual, moral, or relational practices which would be inconsistent with any belief in God and its attendant morality. I prefer to avoid internal tension and qualms of conscience by excluding God rather than by reevaluating my behavior. I wouldn't want to be a hypocrite by professing a belief that is denied by my actions.

5. I am busy having fun, making money, meeting women (or men), drinking or using drugs, or being otherwise amused, and I frankly don't have the time or energy to consider believing in God, so I reject the possibility as a convenience.

6. I have thoroughly examined the evidence, and I found it less than compelling, so I've made my choice on the "innocent until proven guilty" premise: Without compelling proof to the contrary, I will believe the universe exists innocent of any deity.

7. I used to be very religious, but I had such horrible experiences with belief that I rejected it as an act of self-preservation.

8. I believed in God, but experiences of suffering, injustice, and evil have prompted me to conclude that God must not exist.

9. I watched God evaporate or become obsolete. God was frequently called in to explain mysterious phenomena in life— disease, "acts of God" like floods, tornadoes, or earthquakes. But in each case, other explanations became known (bacteria, genetics, El Niño, cold fronts, plate tectonics), and so the "God of the gaps" had no gaps left to fill.

At least some of these reasons, I'm sure you'll agree, seem like valid reasons. True, they may not be logically watertight, but they sound like the kinds of reasons people give to make other life decisions—like choosing or leaving a career, marrying or divorcing a spouse, and so forth. Many pastors have learned to make this request when people tell us they don't believe in God: "Tell me about the God you don't believe in." Usually, when people describe the God they have rejected, we can say, "I agree with you! I couldn't believe in that sort of God either." Then we try to help them see that there are ways to believe in God other than the way they have rejected.

Any of these reasons might do for you, however, if you want to choose, by faith, atheism as your life option. If you have already chosen it, of course, you have little reason to continue with this book. Otherwise, I hope you'll consider the other two options (agnosticism and theism) before making a final decision.

Following are six good reasons—better reasons, I think—for bypassing the "no" answer.

1. IF THERE IS NO GOD, "THE BIG QUESTIONS" REMAIN UNANSWERED

Where does everything come from? Why does something exist rather than nothing? Why did the Big Bang bang when it did and how it did? Why did conscious, intelligent life develop? Does life have meaning? Does human history lead anywhere, or is it all in vain? Is death the end? Are good and evil, right and wrong ultimate realities, or mere social constructs, human opinions?

Now you might be saying in answer to these "big questions": "Who needs a reason or explanation? Evolution. Chance. Time. It all just happened. It's here. Who cares why or with what meaning?"

Part of me wants to point out that this kind of response can be as facile as the platitudes of many religious folk who answer every question with an unthinking, "The Lord works in mysterious ways" or "Just have faith" or some such statement. It can be a lazy excuse for not thinking; it can be a casual brushing off of a matter of ultimate concern.

Part of me wants to say that, but part of me wants to say nothing. After all, if you're completely content in an atheistic worldview, and the big questions don't seem important to you, or if they seem easily answerable with your current God-free data, then there's not much I can say. I might ask, "What circumstances would serve to make you open to other answers?" But I certainly can't push you in a direction you don't want to go. You are free to stop right here if you prefer, and I will be one of the first to stand to defend your right and freedom to do just that.

Possible Explorations

But if you are open to moving farther in this search, there are a number of directions we could explore to assure you that God is still a credible hypothesis when facing life's big questions. For example, many people find themselves reconsidering God's existence through the study of cosmology (the origin of everything). They ask: If the Second Law of Thermodynamics is true, if everything tends to run down, to cool, to decompose (i.e., to experience entropy), and if the universe has always existed, why wouldn't it have run down already, reaching a steady state of maximum entropy? Clearly, we find ourselves in the middle of a story with a real beginning. Recent discoveries in cosmic background radiation and star formation and decay confirm that conclusion, pointing to a genesis point for the universe some fifteen billion years ago. Again, people ask: Why did everything that is pop into existence? And even more: Why did it pop into existence so amazingly calibrated to make stars possible, and planets possible, and organic compounds possible, and life possible on at least one planet—an amazing series of feats that, the more we learn, become more and more astounding? The old ideas of a Prime Mover and Intelligent Designer begin to seem plausible again.

The classic "argument from design" is not only alive and well; more, some would say—it is making a strong comeback after being temporarily discredited by the now-discredited steady state and oscillating universe theories. "If the universe is like a clock, there must be someone like a clockmaker," the argument from design asserts, or "If the universe is like a symphony, there must be someone like a composer," or "If the universe is like a thought, there must be something like a mind."

Why I'm Nervous

Please don't misunderstand me: I have no desire to stir up creation-evolution debates again. I am all for letting those sleeping dogs rest in peace! True, many intelligent people have found the evolutionary model incapable of explaining the appearance of complex systems: the eye, reproductive organs, blood capabilities, brains, and other "black boxes," to use Michael Behe's term (*Darwin's Black Box: The Biochemical Challenge to Evolution*, New York: The Free Press, 1996). These and other problems in traditional Darwinism (such as the reality of "punctuated equilibrium" reflected in the fossil record) have led some to propose an "anthropic principle"—that the universe somehow conspires to produce intelligent life, that life itself is a fundamental reality like matter and energy, that natural selection may indeed have an intelligent supernatural Selector working behind the scenes to help it along. Nancy Pearcy, a philosopher of science, puts it like this:

> Darwin's purpose was to show that the design in living things was only apparent and could be explained by something other than intelligent design. Darwin's argument sounded plausible, it was worth investigating, but it hasn't worked. There's an irreducible complexity in living things that's not explainable by any mechanistic view. ("I Believe," ed. by Howard Means, *The Washingtonian*, December 1997, p. 101)

But I am still nervous about trumpeting unanswered questions about Big Bang cosmology and problems with Darwinism as evidence for the existence of God. I have seen people of faith make the same mistake too often: appealing to "the gaps" in scientific knowledge as evidence for God's existence, only to find those gaps erased or shrunk as scientific knowledge increases. The "God of the Gaps" project seems like a risky, already-been-tried endeavor to me. For example, Stephen Hawking's Wave Function theory already offers an alternative answer to the "who set off the Big Bang?" question, and some, at least, find the theory satisfying. Regarding Darwinism, I wouldn't be surprised if other "nonmiraculous" mechanisms are discovered that handle the current difficulties in biological evolution. Whether or not life evolves, science does, and its track record for finding natural causes or explanations for supposed supernatural events is impressive indeed.

That's why I am more interested in the evidence for God seen in *what we know* than I am in the supposed evidence to be found in *what we don't know*. To me, finding a "natural explanation" for something seems irrelevant to whether there is a God or not. But maybe that's just me?

Two Evolutions

I know that many religious people have set up creation and evolution as enemies, basically forcing you to choose either their antievolutionary version of theism, or evolution-and-atheism as a package deal. I don't see it that way at all. As I explained in an earlier book (*Reinventing Your Church*, Grand Rapids: Zondervan, 1998), if by the term *evolution* we mean a purely natural, unplanned, undesigned, accidental, mindless mechanism that explains the development of everything (including life and consciousness) within an airtight system of physics and chemistry (without God or Spirit or transcendent meaning) by impersonal randomness plus time plus nothing—then of course, we are looking at an irreconcilable enemy to theism. In this view, evolution is an uncreated, self-existent, and universal principle or force that "selects" and "leads" toward complexity and even intelligence. It starts to look like a god itself, leaving the position filled

and leaving any other aspiring deities standing in the unem-
ployment line outside of reality.

But if by the term *evolution* we mean simply an observation of
adaptive development from simple to complex, a pattern of change
suggested by the data of the fossil record, an elegant process involving adaptation through inherent flexibility and survival of the fittest,
then we have something potentially very different from an enemy
to theism. We have one of the possible means by which God created. As such, the evolutionary process can be seen not as an enemy
of theism, but rather as a creation of God, and a grand one at that.
In this view, it would be a creation intended to produce other creations, a "natural" tool designed and used by a supernatural God,
a creative process or tool (such as erosion or plate tectonics) for producing planet earth as we know it, another great reason to admire
and even worship God rather than doubt or disbelieve.

There are others more qualified than I to guide you deeper into
these subjects, but I simply mention them here to support my rec-
ommendation that you keep your mind open on the existence of
God, rather than close it prematurely. (See the appendix for some
recommended reading on these fascinating subjects.) For now, I
hope you'll agree that it's no sin to have an open mind to at least
consider the big questions, and to keep open the option that God
might be part of the answer.

2. IF WE REJECT THE EXISTENCE OF GOD, WE ARE LEFT WITH A CRISIS OF MEANING

Perhaps you've heard of Jean-Paul Sartre and his fellow thinkers
of the existentialist school in the early twentieth century. Although
I don't share their choice of atheism, I applaud their honesty when
dealing with the question of the existence of God. If he were alive,
Sartre might say something like this: "The difference between us
existentialists and other intellectuals is this: They all say that God
doesn't exist and it doesn't matter, while we say that God doesn't
exist and it makes all the difference."

Many of the existentialists explored, with courage and sensitivity, what it means to live in a godless world. Take Sartre's character Antoine Roquentin, for example, in *Nausea*. Roquentin sits on a park bench and sees a root descending from a chestnut tree behind the bench into the ground between his feet. But he thinks (I'm paraphrasing), "What is 'root' but a term I use to distinguish some stuff from other stuff? The word is merely a construct my mind artificially imposes on reality, not a real quality of existence itself." And as he lets the word "root" go, he sees the root-stuff blend in with the surrounding dirt-stuff. But it doesn't stop there. His experience expands into a kind of deconstructing vision where everything— the bench he sits on, the feet below him, the body to which they are attached, all trees, all people, everything—all are stripped of their categories and names and reduced to meaningless stuff. The experience overwhelms him with nausea.

Wanted: Meaning

That is where the most sensitive and thoughtful among us find ourselves when we come to grips with what it means to live in a world without God. The universe is just stuff, thrown out into space and time, going nowhere, meaning nothing, random noise echoing like gibberish, like nonsense words spoken by nobody to nobody with no intent. Maybe on a good day when the stock market is up and our teeth aren't aching, we can avoid such melancholy conclusions. But when war breaks out, or the lab tests come back positive, or the dreaded phone call comes, something in us—or at least, in most of us—cries out that life should have some purpose, meaning, direction, point. Victor Frankl said it like this: "The will to meaning is really a specific need not reducible to other needs, and is in greater or smaller degree present in all human beings" (*The Unheard Cry for Meaning*, New York: Washington Square Press, 1985, p. 33).

Take Franz Kafka's Gregor Samsa in *The Metamorphosis*. The poor chap, a traveling salesman, wakes up one morning to find himself transformed into a cockroach. The story is told with such droll matter-of-factness as to make one laugh. But like Roquentin, Samsa is facing the reality that if there is no God, then there is no transcendence above stuff, above insectness, above meaninglessness.

To move from fiction to autobiography, consider Leo Tolstoy's *A Confession*. The young Tolstoy began asking questions, as many young people do, about the meaning of his life:

> "Well," I said to myself, "I know everything that science so much wants me to know, but this path will not lead me to an answer to the question of the meaning of my life." …[T]he answer given by this branch of knowledge to my question about the meaning of my life was only this: …You are a little lump of something randomly stuck together.… The lump decomposes. The decomposition of this lump is known as your life. The lump falls apart, and thus the decomposition ends, as do all your questions. Thus the clear side of knowledge replies, and if it strictly follows its own principles, there is no more to be said.… To say that [my life] is a particle of infinity not only fails to give it any meaning but destroys all possible meaning. (New York: Norton, 1983, pp. 41–42)

Perhaps you can live with that kind of answer. But don't let yourself off too easily. What happens if millions of people share this nihilism (the belief that everything is ultimately meaningless)? Consider: What if it's really true that we're just stuff, just lumps of protoplasm, products of blind, mechanical accidents with no design or destiny, pathetic organisms cursed with consciousness, with silly illusions of meaning and values and morality and beauty and art and all the rest, when really we're no different from insects, just blind urges destined to burn out, just fermenting lumps, just stuff swirling in stuff? What would the effects of that belief be, not only on you, but on the world, if millions of people actually believed it? That leads to our third reason for considering the nonatheistic options.

3. IF PEOPLE DON'T BELIEVE IN GOD, THE HISTORICAL RESULTS ARE HORRIFIC

John Lennon encouraged us, in his classic song "Imagine," to envision a world where happy people live free of the tyranny of belief in God. He invited us to imagine "there's no heaven ... no hell below us, above us only sky," to picture "all the happy people living for today ... living life in peace," to envision a world with "nothing to kill or die for and no religion too." Such a world would "be as one," he promised.

The song is beautiful, and it is aptly titled, because you do have to imagine such a world: Reality (so far) offers no actual examples to examine. Quite the reverse. The bitter regimes of the twentieth-century's Hitlers, Stalins, Pol Pots, and their colleagues held as their core ideology atheistic assumptions. Religion was the problem, they felt; eradicate it, and we can get on with helping the world "be as one." Imagine if they had succeeded! David Putnam's *The Killing Fields,* Steven Speilberg's *Schindler's List,* William Golding's *Lord of the Flies,* or Quentin Tarrantino's *Pulp Fiction* offer imaginative looks at human culture uncoupled from substantial faith, views more in line with reality than John Lennon's hauntingly beautiful song.

Please Don't Misunderstand

Please don't misunderstand me. I am not arguing for "putting God back in the schools," breaking down the "wall of separation" between church and state, the creation of fundamentalist nations, making America or any other country "a Christian nation," or anything like that. I think Philip Yancey is right: When religion and politics mix, religion is the loser (*What's So Amazing About Grace?* Grand Rapids: Zondervan, 1997, p. 239ff.). Rather, I'm suggesting that when a society doesn't believe in God, things seem pretty consistently to go south for it; without faith in God, people can't seem to sustain the will to be good, at least, not in sufficient numbers to keep themselves from slipping into nightmarish moral and social decay.

Again, please don't misunderstand me: I am not saying you should choose your belief based on its outcome. (The fact is that theism has had some pretty messy outcomes in many places, too. The additional fact is that the previous fact is grossly understated.) In other words, I am not recommending that you say, "Theism must be true because the practical effects of atheism are so unsavory." That's a logical leap I wouldn't encourage anyone to take. Rather, I'm saying that you should at least give theism a chance in light of the practical implications of atheism. And you might go one step further with me: Although something is not necessarily true because it "works," if something doesn't work, if it has consistently disastrous personal, social, and historical consequences, its impracticality may signal a philosophical "design failure" of some sort.

4. IF THERE IS NO GOD, THE PROBLEMS OF EVIL AND SUFFERING ARE IN NO WAY SOLVED

True, if you do believe in God, you are left with "the problem of evil": How can an all-good, all-powerful God allow evil and suffering to exist in a universe he/she creates and controls? In the face of this profound question, some feel they can "solve the problem" by removing God. Such desperation is understandable when victims of rape, torture, oppression, natural catastrophe, random accident, or devastating disease raise their fists to heaven crying, "Why? Why?" One can't help but sympathize with the grief and rage that lead to this rejection of God.

But what is one left with, having removed the God-factor from the equation? Now, the suffering is no less tragic. There is no hope of it being rendered meaningful or transcendent, redemptive or redeemable, since no interventions in this life or reparations in an afterlife are possible. True, there is no God to blame, but is that so great a consolation? Neither is there a God to reach out to for strength and comfort and a higher perspective. There is no God to make meaning of the madness; there is only madness. Not a good trade, in my opinion.

I don't say this glibly. As a pastor, I'm often the person people come to see when tragedy strikes. I hear their stories, feel their rage, empathize with their doubts. And I've been there, too. It's common and natural to want to blame God in suffering, at the very least to echo Jesus' own words, "My God, my God, why have you forsaken me?" But removing God via atheism solves little and costs much.

5. IF THERE IS NO GOD, WE LOSE THE VERY STANDARD BY WHICH WE CRITIQUE RELIGIONS AND RELIGIOUS PEOPLE

C. S. Lewis argued this point powerfully in *Mere Christianity* and elsewhere. Do away with God, and you've done away with transcendent meaning and power behind words like right, wrong, good, evil, justice, or injustice. Without God, all you're left with are human tastes and opinions which, in the long run and big picture, have no more weight than we give them, and who are we anyway?

Do you see this? Who's to say that lying, adultery, and child molestation are wrong—really *wrong*? Sure, society might make it illegal or call it socially unacceptable—but human cultures have at various times legally or socially disapproved of everything from believing in God to believing the world revolves around the sun, from having more than one wife to refusing to take a second wife under some circumstances. Human taste, opinion, law, and culture are hardly dependable arbiters of Truth! Democracy is a fine form of government, but it makes a frightening basis for morality. Dare we think that holocausts are moral because fifty-one percent of the public votes yes? Is right determined by vote, or force, or who can shout the loudest?

Many people have arrived at a similar conclusion: If there is no God, everything is permissible. Atheism leaves no standard beyond ourselves or outside ourselves to look to, to appeal to, to help us discern what is really and ultimately right and permissible, or wrong and impermissible—a powerful reason to consider alternatives.

6. IF THERE IS NO GOD, WE DON'T MAKE SENSE

C. S. Lewis asked us in *Mere Christianity* (New York: Macmillan, 1943, p. 46) to imagine a world where eyes had never evolved:

> If the whole universe has no meaning, we should never have found out that it has no meaning: Just as, if there were no light in the universe and therefore no creatures with eyes, we should never know it was dark. *Dark* would be without meaning. Similarly, the fact that eyes exist suggests that light must exist. And the fact that we have spiritual longings . . . the fact that we even have a meaningful category of thought and speech called "spirituality . . . suggests that there is some corresponding reality out there which we have the capacity to "sense." That capacity would be called faith, and that reality, God.

"Just a minute," you should be saying right about now. "I don't buy that. Maybe these so-called spiritual longings are illusory. Maybe they're misguided. Maybe they're an evolutionary bug that hasn't been naturally selected out of the programming yet. Give us time, and we'll evolve beyond this fluke of spirituality." And I would say, yes, maybe you're right. But I must ask you to consider how you would eliminate this spiritual longing from humanity without also eliminating the things that mean most to us when we say the word "humanity."

Francis Schaeffer, a theologian and philosopher whose writings have helped me a great deal over the years, understood this well. He told the story of a young man who had written him a letter after hearing one of his lectures. The young man said something like this: *Why am I so empty? Why am I so unfulfilled? Why do I have these spiritual longings? Moss grows on the rocks in my backyard. Squirrels jump from branch to branch in the trees. The moss doesn't seem unfulfilled; the squirrels aren't plagued with questions of purpose and meaning. They're happy in their ignorance. Why do I have an insatiable thirst for a drink of something that doesn't seem to exist?* Schaeffer, of course, answered him by affirming that there is indeed a reality corresponding to his thirst. His longings are not an evolutionary fluke or cruel cosmic prank, but rather evidence of an aptitude for connecting with and relating to God—who really is "there." Please don't reduce this line of thinking to a facile argument along the lines of "if I think something could exist, it must exist," which is obviously misguided. We aren't proving anything here with mathematical certainty; we're simply suggesting that if human beings have a seemingly incurable, innate, core hunger and thirst for spiritual meaning, then that is at least evidence—though certainly not proof—that there may be a reality corresponding to the desire.

Even among many who do not yet believe, there is an undeniable longing for faith, expressed by rock groups like U2 ("I still haven't found what I'm looking for") and novelists like Richard Selzer (*Wittenburg Door*, summer 1989, p. 27):

> My entire life has been one long search for faith. I haven't found it. I do not believe in God. Having said that, . . . I want you to know that I love the idea of God. I love piety. Without it, you lead your life unmoored, in a state of isolation. You are a tiny speck in a vast universe. I'm jealous, frankly. I feel as though I've missed out on the greatest thing that can happen to a person—faith in God. It must be wonderful.

There's more we could say, but the point is already clear enough: Atheism is a faith option open to you, but there are reasons to at least consider other options. This brings us to the second option. Instead of "no," some people answer the question, "Is there a God?" with this answer: *I don't know*. That's the topic of the next chapter.

YOUR RESPONSE

Choose one:

I am an atheist because:

I am not an atheist because:

RESOURCES

Michael Behe's *Darwin's Black Box* (New York: Free Press, 1996) details some of the reasons scientists are reconsidering the argument from design. The writings of Hugh Ross (such as *Creation and Time*, Colorado Springs: Navpress, 1994) and Fred Heeren (*Show Me God*, Wheeling, Ill.: Searchlight, 1995) further explore the relation of science and faith from an already-convinced perspective. Patrick Glynn's *God: The Evidence* (Centerport, N.Y.: Forum, 1997) summarizes the decline of the secular-atheistic paradigm on several fronts. I especially appreciate John Polkinghorne in this regard (*The Faith of a Physicist*, Minneapolis: Fortress Press, 1996)—Polkinghorne is both a trained scientist and an ordained Anglican priest.

C. S. Lewis's *Miracles* (Touchstone, 1996) is one of the best explorations of atheism and theism I am aware of.

As for fiction, you might try Walker Percy's novels *Lancelot* (Ivy, 1989), *The Last Gentleman*, and *The Second Coming* (the last being a sequel to the former) which explore the question of God's existence in an entertaining, often hilarious, yet ultimately intelligent and human way.

Bruce Cockburn and David Wilcox explore faith in some extraordinarily moving and sensitive ways in their music. Cockburn's songs "Rumours of Glory," "All the Diamonds in the World," and "Broken Wheel" have been released on various albums under Columbia and Gold Castle labels. David Wilcox's "Someday Soon," "That's What the Lonely Is For," "Show the Way," "Big Mistake," and "Hold It Up to the Light" are all found on *Big Horizon*, A & M Records, 1994.

PRAYER

I may still not be able to say I believe there is a God capable of hearing and responding to my prayers. But intellectual honesty and curiosity— and perhaps spiritual need—require me to keep the question open. If anyone is there to hear me, I want to say that I am reaching out to you; I would like to come in contact with you; I would like to explore a relationship with you. I am becoming, if not yet a believer in God, a spiritual seeker for God and for truth. Please help me.

CHAPTER 5 PREVIEW

Which Form of Agnosticism Is Best?

This chapter explores the "I don't know" answer of agnosticism, and defines three types of agnosticism: *closed agnosticism* (which says, "It is impossible for anyone to know, so I reject faith of any sort."), *ignosticism* (which really means, "I don't care, and I choose to remain ignorant on the matter of God's existence."), and *open agnosticism* (which says, "I don't know" as an honest but open-minded statement expressing a lack, to date, of conclusive evidence). The chapter advocates open agnosticism over the other two.

WHO SHOULD READ THIS CHAPTER?

If you refer to yourself as an agnostic, this chapter should help you sharpen your self-understanding.

WHAT QUESTIONS DOES IT ADDRESS?

What are the three types of agnosticism? Why are they all, to a degree, faith positions? What are the reasons for and against each type?

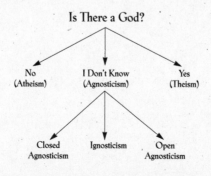

CHAPTER 5

Which Form of Agnosticism Is Best?

"I want to believe." So reads the poster hanging prominently on the wall of Fox Mulder, of the popular TV show *The X Files*. Whether the poster refers to faith in extraterrestrials, faith in God, or just faith in general, I'm not sure. But it expresses the way a lot of people feel. Just the other night, a good friend of mine expressed it like this: "I don't believe in God, but I wish I could. I don't find my lack of belief comforting or helpful in the least, especially when I think about death." I asked him what obstacles kept him from believing, but he couldn't really identify anything specific. He explained, "Maybe it's not just an intellectual thing . . . maybe there's a volitional element to it. Maybe I'm just not willing to believe. But I'm not an atheist; I'm not closed-minded. I guess you'd call me an agnostic."

Ask an agnostic like my friend if there's a God, and his honest answer will be: "I don't know." Agnosticism is a popular option for all those who, for the reasons we considered in the previous chapter, find atheism too great a leap of faith or too extreme a solution to the problems they see in theism. Agnosticism breaks down into three types: (a) Closed Agnosticism, (b) Ignosticism, and (c) Open Agnosticism. In this chapter, we'll try to determine which forms are more and less credible and desirable.

AGNOSTICISM IN GENERAL

The term itself was coined by Thomas Henry Huxley (1825–1895). His definition (from an 1889 essay, "Agnosticism and

Christianity") is fascinating in the context of our discussion here: "Agnosticism is not properly described as a negative creed, nor indeed as a creed of any kind, except insofar as it expressed absolute faith in the validity of a principle, which is as much ethical as intellectual. . .: that it is wrong for a man to say that he is certain of the objective truth of any proposition unless he can produce evidence which logically justifies that certainty." In the same essay, Huxley characterized—and critiqued—a well-known religious leader of his time (Cardinal Newman) with these incisive words: ". . . for him the attainment of faith, not the ascertainment of truth, is the highest aim of mental life." By this definition, I am eager to sign on as an agnostic. As is clear from chapter 2, like Huxley, I am careful in my use of the word *certainty,* and I hope every page in this book affirms an agreement with Huxley that the ascertainment of truth is indeed the highest aim of mental life. Huxley and I would differ, of course, on our assessment of the value of faith in the pursuit of the category of truth called *spiritual* truth; in fact, Huxley might not even agree that such a category is valid. Many agnostics today would be closed to even the possibility that there is a category of truth for which faith would be an appropriate or necessary means of exploration. Those agnostics we could call "closed."

CLOSED AGNOSTICISM

Closed agnosticism says, "It is impossible for anyone to know for certain whether there is a God or not, so I decide not to believe at all, one way or the other." In other words, the agnostic doesn't directly reject God, but he does reject faith.

The closed agnostic focuses on a key issue: the relationship between faith and knowledge (which we considered in chapter 2). Since faith is not knowledge of the type preferred by the agnostic, faith is discardable. Again, I would be quick to agree with the agnostic that many things that pass for faith are not worthy of an intelligent person's self-investment. Many things that pass for faith seem to be more make-believe than genuine belief, more self-hypnosis

than perception of a reality beyond the senses, more a case of reason-minus than reason-plus, more a matter of crouching beneath
understanding than soaring beyond understanding. Many things
that pass for faith have more to do with brainwashing than heart-
cleansing, with cultic tyranny than spiritual freedom.

WHAT IF?

But what if, given the nature of the standing of a finite creature
in relation to an infinite creator, the agnostic's preferred type of
knowledge is not the appropriate medium of experience? What if
we are requiring light to be known through a microphone, or sound
to be registered on a photovoltaic cell, or an emotion to be mea-
surable on a bathroom scale? What if all forms of knowledge, which
are appropriate for every single other entity in the universe, are in
this one case inappropriate for "knowing" God—since an uncreated God would, by definition, be in a separate category from every
created thing? What if, simply because God is in a category apart
from every other thing or force or entity in the universe, another
medium of experience is required, and what if this medium of experience involves faith of some sort? And what if this sort of faith is
not an example of "bad faith" (i.e., make-believe, self-hypnosis, and
so forth), and not an unwarranted claim of certainty, but rather an
honest kind of good faith, worthy of the self-investment of intelligent people, an act of integrity and humility, not escape and self-
deception?

SCIENTISTS WHO DON'T DO EXPERIMENTS

In a strange way, the closed agnostic exercises a fascinating kind
of faith: faith in the unprovable hypothesis that religious faith is
bunk, and faith that his preferred form of rationalistic (i.e., arising
from within the mind, with no outside revelation), empirical (i.e.,
knowable by one of the five senses) knowledge is the best, or only,
medium to be used to know anything worth knowing in the universe—another unprovable hypothesis. I find it fascinating to look

again at the words Huxley used to described agnosticism: "*an absolute faith* in the validity of a principle" (italics mine). He was aware that agnosticism itself is a kind of faith, and he was honest to admit it.

In the preceding paragraph, I used the word "hypothesis" to describe the agnostic's faith. The word deserves a closer look. As a key component in the scientific method, the hypothesis involves a hunch, an intuition, an unproven possibility that is not known, but is of sufficient interest to draw out the scientist's curiosity to do an experiment. An experiment is a quest, a journey, an often painstaking, disciplined, protracted search to test a hypothesis. Without the hypothesis, there is no motive or draw to experimentation. To reject working with hypotheses would in one way sound scientific: "I am only going to work with what is already proven by scientists of the past." But it would at the same time prove that the one making this rejection was not himself a scientist, since testing hypotheses is what scientists by definition do. Closed agnostics, then, might be comparable to people who love to read science, and believe science, and respect the findings of scientists, but who don't want to experiment themselves.

Clearly, one can be overhasty in stopping at closed agnosticism without investigating other options. Many people who may claim agnosticism, and who seem at first glance to be intellectually rigorous closed agnostics, really have committed themselves to the second option, known by the newly created term "Ignosticism."

IGNOSTICISM

Ignosticism, beneath its "I don't know" answer, means "I don't care." The ignostic agnostic says, "This subject is trivial to me. It's unimportant, not worth forming an opinion about. You might as well be asking me if I think the birds on an imaginary planet in an imaginary universe have gray or brown feathers. I don't know; I don't care; it doesn't matter. Whatever. I'm happily *ignorant* (hence the term) about the subject."

Like closed agnosticism, ignosticism may be seen as somewhat elitist, saying something like this: "Never mind that most people through most of history, including many of the best and most brilliant in every culture, have found faith a satisfactory means for seeking God; never mind that they have felt faith was very important, worthy of sacrifice and in some cases even martyrdom. Their devotion can be dismissed as a delusion; they wasted their time and lives on something not that important."

Atheists believe that all religions are false. Agnostics (both closed agnostics and ignostics) believe that all religions are superfluous. Theists, although they don't necessarily believe that all religions are equally true (a commonly heard claim we'll address in chapter 8), do believe that there is some truth in all religions. Theism certainly has its share of elitists, but it by no means corners the market: It doesn't dismiss all the religious believers of history as purveyors of bunk.

That's not to say the ignostics are wrong. Obviously, since truth is not determined by democratic processes, and since the minority has frequently been right, they may be in this case. But I think you'll agree that the ignostics themselves are making a huge faith commitment . . . . a commitment to a set of priorities that basically excludes the spiritual side of life. If you choose ignostic agnosticism, please be aware of the magnitude of your decision, and admit that you're determining your priorities at least in part by a leap of faith. As we considered in reference to atheism, no amount of induction or deduction that I am aware of can prove that God does not exist, and given the real possibility of God's existence, deciding that the quest for God is immaterial is, at the very least, a long leap of faith.

GOOD RISK?

You may have heard, in this regard, of "Pascal's Wager." Blaise Pascal, a brilliant mathematician and philosopher of the seventeenth century, put it something like this: If God exists, not seeking God must be the gravest error imaginable. If one decides to sincerely seek for God and doesn't find God, the lost effort is negligible in comparison to what is at risk by not seeking God in the first place. In other words, Pascal concluded that ignosticism is a risk too extreme for a thinking person. If there is a God, you stand to gain everything by searching for God, and you stand to lose everything by not searching. If there is no God, you stand to lose little by searching, except, perhaps, for time that could have been spent in other pursuits.

I tend to agree with Pascal, although his argument can seem flippant and superficial in some presentations. Many people obviously think Pascal was dead wrong; they are very willing to take the risk of not believing. Those people may be making a huge mistake, but if God exists, God seems to make it frighteningly easy for them to make this mistake. Or maybe it's just the ignostics themselves making it look easy.

OPEN AGNOSTICISM

Some of you may feel uncomfortable with either of the two previous options. You consider yourself agnostic, but not of the closed or ignostic variety. You may be an open agnostic, who says, "God may exist, and I'm not closed to the possibility. Neither am I closed to the option of searching for God. But in all honesty, I've never had any spiritual experiences that would suggest to me that there is a God to seek, or believe in, or obey. I'm open, but sufficient evidence has not yet presented itself—or sufficient barriers to belief have not yet been removed."

Open agnostics fall along a continuum, from those who are open but not actively seeking, to those who are actively seeking. We could imagine Christopher Columbus, perhaps as a child, sure, as were many people of his day, that the world was flat. That would be analogous to someone in the atheist, closed agnostic, or ignostic position. At the point where Christopher first imagined that the world may in fact be round, we could say he became an open agnostic—not sure, not committed, but open to the possibility. Imagine the process that must have unfolded, as a possibility became a hunch, and a hunch a belief, and a belief a quest, and a quest an actual adventure. The adventure was filled with uncertainty and error (poor Christopher thought he had reached India)—necessary prices to pay for discovery.

At what point did agnosticism become faith in our analogy? I suppose it's impossible to say, just as it's impossible to answer the question "When did night give way to day this morning?" Open agnosticism is like that; it is often the dawn of faith. If I were not already a committed theist, I hope I would be an open agnostic on the seeking end of the spectrum.

VULNERABLE TO CONVERSION

As you might expect, open agnostics are very vulnerable to conversion—either to atheism, closed agnosticism, or ignosticism on the one hand, or to some embryonic form of theism on the other. If I were having a cup of coffee with an open agnostic (Joe), I would imagine a dialogue unfolding something like this:

Brian: So you're an agnostic, but you're open to the possibility of God existing.

Joe: Yes, exactly.

Brian: If God exists, would it make sense to you to pray?

Joe: Pray? I'm not sure where I'd begin.

Brian: Well, if a God is intelligent enough to create the universe, and personal enough to create conscious life, it might make sense to say, "God, are you out there?"

Joe: Kind of like picking up the phone and saying, "Hello? Is anybody there?"

Brian: Exactly. And to take it a step farther, I could also imagine saying, "If you're there, please help me to know you."

Joe: Yeah, I wouldn't have any problem with that. It makes sense. I might feel kind of silly, like I'm talking to myself,

but there wouldn't be any harm in it, I suppose, as long
as we wouldn't have to take it any further than that.

Brian: My guess is that you'd only take it any further than that
if you wanted to, and you'd only want to if your prayers
were in some way answered.

Joe: It sounds like an experiment.

Brian: Yes. Faith itself is a kind of experimental process, and
open agnostics are well placed to begin experimenting.

Joe: But doesn't it then require faith to gain more faith?

Brian: That's a great question. Do you have enough faith to pursue more faith?

Joe: It sounds like I do.

If that's how you feel, then perhaps you are ready to move from
open agnosticism to a tentative, preliminary, experimental,
exploratory theism. Even if you aren't sure a God exists, if you have
enough faith to wonder, and even more, to ask, and even more, to
seek . . . well, that's a very good start. There's a pilgrimage going on
here, a spiritual quest or journey: One begins, perhaps as an atheist or ignostic, then moves to closed agnosticism, then opens to
open agnosticism, and then has the courage to call herself or himself a spiritual seeker. This is a significant step, a major decision.
This decision faces you at this point in our exploration, because
there's little reason to continue unless you have enough faith to continue searching. It's a yes/no matter to be worked out in your own
mind and heart. "Yes" means we're ready for the next chapter.

YOUR RESPONSE

Choose one:

I am a closed agnostic because:

I am an ignostic because:

I am an open agnostic because:

I am a spiritual seeker because:

RESOURCES

There is a genre of books that we could call "Literature of Testimony," in which people tell their stories of coming to faith. One of the most famous is C. S. Lewis's *Surprised by Joy* (New York: Harcourt, Brace, 1975). Another is Leo Tolstoy's *Confession* (trans. by David Patterson, New York: Norton, 1983). There are hundreds more examples by figures known (Jimmy Carter, William F. Buckley) and less known (Joni Eareckson Tada, Corrie ten Boom), with more being published each year. These books offer the evidence of human experience ... always subjective, but not for that reason ignorable. Lewis's story has also been depicted on film, by the BBC and in the film *Shadowlands*.

There is also a genre of books giving evidences for faith called "apologetics." Hans Kung has written quite a bit in this area from a Roman Catholic perspective, as has Josh MacDowell from a more Protestant perspective. Again, C. S. Lewis is hard to beat, having come to faith through real intellectual struggle himself. See *Mere Christianity* (New York: Macmillan, 1943). Billy Graham's writings shouldn't be forgotten; although very simple, they are also very clear and have helped many people.

Peter Kreeft's *Yes or No: Straight Answers to Tough Questions About Christianity* (San Francisco: Ignatius, 1991) offers a very readable and reasonable exploration of common questions. I highly recommend it.

PRAYER

God, I want to grow in faith. I don't want to remain stagnant or slip backward. I want to develop a faith that enriches my life, overflows to my neighbors, and in some significant way adds something positive to the world. Through this, I want my life to honor you. Help me, when difficulties come, not to give up, let go, or turn back. Help me be like a child, learning and growing, resilient and energetic, all the days of my life.

CHAPTER 6 PREVIEW

If There Is One God, Why Are There So Many Religions?

This chapter considers the third answer—*yes*—to the question, "Is there a God?" It suggests that the welter of religious options can be simplified to four: pantheism, polytheism, dualism, and monotheism. It briefly describes each, and suggests that pantheism and monotheism are the two main alternatives for people today. While acknowledging value in each option, the author recommends monotheism, and then describes "good faith monotheism."

WHO SHOULD READ THIS CHAPTER?

This is one of the more important chapters in the book for people who are not already convinced regarding monotheism.

WHAT QUESTIONS DOES IT ADDRESS?

What are the four main options within theism? What can pantheism and monotheism learn from one another? Why does the author think "bad monotheism" is the worst enemy of "good monotheism," and what does he mean by these terms?

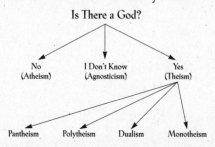

Is There a God?

No (Atheism) I Don't Know (Agnosticism) Yes (Theism)

Pantheism Polytheism Dualism Monotheism

CHAPTER 6

If There Is One God, Why Are There
So Many Religions?

When you're just starting to search for God, it can be bewildering, overwhelming, just trying to figure out where to begin. Which version or model of God do you pursue? There seem to be so many out there!

It can feel like shopping. I speak as one who does not love to shop. (That sentence qualifies as one of the year's greater understatements.) When I need something, my motto is "Get in, select, pay, get out"—as fast as I would if I were venturing through a swarm of thirsty mosquitoes. When I need to buy a car in the next year or so, I want to give my savings to my brother, and say, "Hey, Pete, will you go pick the best car for me?" That makes sense because there are so many makes and models, so many accessories and options. I feel completely unqualified to make a choice, and I'm paralyzed by the range of options. Pete, however, is much more knowledgeable than I, and I trust him. Shopping—especially for a major purchase like a car—is an ordeal I'd rather avoid.

A car can be mine if I pay for it, even if someone else searches for it. Not so, I would think, with a spiritual quest.

FOUR MODELS

The good news is that the situation isn't as complex as you might think. There are four basic "models" of God, and two of them stand out as more worthy of further investigation. Here are the four basic models:

1. God is everything. The universe itself is God. God is the whole, the sum of all the parts. This model is called pantheism.
2. There are many gods. No single one of them is supreme. This option is called polytheism.
3. There are two Gods, one good or creative, one evil or destructive. They are caught in an eternal struggle, perhaps like the positive and negative charges in electricity. This model is called dualism.
4. There is one God. This God is good, supreme, and creative. This option is called monotheism.

Of course, you can imagine some other options too—monotheism with a God who is, for example, evil, powerless, apathetic, or uncaring—or dualism where both Gods are evil, and so forth. But for a variety of reasons, no one has ever decided to believe any of these options, at least not for very long, or with sufficient passion to convince many other people to believe similarly.

In your quest for God, then, you have these four options. Let's begin with the middle options, since they are rarely believed these days, and relatively easy to dismiss.

POLYTHEISM

Polytheism, followed by a wide array of people from the ancient Greeks and Romans to primitive tribespeople to modern-day wiccans and some New Agers, asserts that the universe is peopled (or godded) by numerous deities. Among primitives, perhaps trees and animals were seen to have spirits, or one's ancestors were believed to have entered the realm of the gods—and as such should be revered.

Some practitioners of witchcraft and New Age who speak of many deities shouldn't always be taken literally when they speak this way. What they call gods may actually mean to them concepts, or myths, which they do not believe to have actual reality outside of their own imagination or psyche, or perhaps the collective psyche of a culture. People often speak of having "demons" in this way, not asserting a belief in devilish spirits, but in dark and ugly sides of their own psyche. (Of course, many other people believe in actual demons too.) People who speak in this metaphorical way about gods or deities may in fact be atheists or agnostics incognito, or they could be pantheists, dualists, or monotheists too.

Bona fide polytheists exist, but they are quite rare, especially among educated people. Why? For one thing, polytheism seems to raise more questions than it answers. For example, if there are many gods, might not one of them be supreme, the originator of the others, or might there be an even greater being behind these beings, that "God farther back" being the only real entity worthy of the name God?

DUALISM

Also uncommon are dualists, believing that there are two opposite, eternal, ultimate deities. This should not be confused with the more typical monotheistic belief in God and Satan; clearly, in that scenario God is ultimate and supreme, and Satan a created (and later deformed) being. Neither should it be confused with the somewhat similar "Star Wars" vision of "the Force," which is good and creative, with a "Dark Side" split off from it, which is evil and destructive. Rather, true dualism sees two eternal, parallel forces, neither of which is "higher" than or prior to the other, both of which are equally ultimate.

In history, dualism behaves like an unstable chemical compound. It wants to resolve in one of two directions—either toward pantheism (where the two entities actually comprise one larger, ultimate entity) or monotheism (where one entity is ultimate and the other, contingent).

And thus our quest moves toward this tentative conclusion: There appears to be a God, most likely either of the pan- or monovariety. Both varieties deserve our serious consideration. Perhaps there is truth to be found in both? Yet they differ significantly. . . .

PAN- OR MONO- DIFFERENCES?

On a "macro" level, pantheism says that everything is God. Monotheism says that everything was created by God. Pantheism says that if you subtract the universe—all its matter, all its energy, all its spirit—you have subtracted God. Monotheism says that if you subtract the universe, God has not been diminished one iota. Pantheism suggests that you and I are part of God, that we are, in fact, God. Monotheism suggests that you and I have a distinct existence as creations of God, and as such are capable of relationship with God. Pantheism emphasizes the fundamental unity of all things including God. Monotheism celebrates the unity of God and the diversity of all things.

PANTHEISM'S ATTRACTIONS

Pantheism has much that attracts a thinking person. First, in our divided and polarizing world, we seem to need some centripetal force to counterbalance the centrifugal forces that thrust us apart—hence a certain attraction for pantheism's emphasis on the unity of all things. Second, pantheism not only elevates humanity to the level of divinity; it also elevates all of nature—every bird, every tree, every rock, every drop of water and grain of sand equally sharing the status of being part of God. In our world where neighbor fails to respect neighbor, and where humanity fails to respect the environment, this elevation seems healthy, restorative, therapeutic. Third, pantheism easily explains the experience we all (I hope) have from time to time—when watching a sunset, pondering a flower or tree, touching a whale, observing a baby's birth, making love, grieving a death—the feeling that what we experience is holy, sacred, precious. The pantheist might say, "Of course: All is God. Your experience is simply God awakening to the experience of Itself."

But pantheism has some rather troubling implications. If distinctions are lost in ultimate oneness, and if humanity is part of the deity, then rapist and rape victim, murderer and murdered, child molester and molestee, oppressive dictator and despised minority are equally expressions of the One. The cost of avoiding divisions turns out to be the distinction between good and evil. Both are comprised in the One. Whatever is, is . . . and it is the One; it is God. There is no space "outside" God for evil to be planned and enacted and even celebrated; the whole grim process of evil, then, must take place within God.

If you believe that is the best model to fit the universe and your experience in it, then you may decide to become a pantheist. But please be realistic, and face the full logical implications of pantheism before you sign on. Take it as it is, or don't take it at all.

FIXING PANTHEISM

You might be tempted to try to "fix" pantheism, to domesticate the implications of saying that good and evil are illusory categories, that both are part of God. You might say, for example, that God/the universe itself is evolving toward something better (through, for example, a process where justice is served through life experience, where bad actions bring bad consequences, leading to gradual self-correction within "the system"). You might say that good is triumphing and evil is being purified like dross from gold ore, that truth is overcoming and misperceptions are being exposed and eradicated like darkness by light. But when you say these things, at that same moment, you are acknowledging a higher principle of goodness behind the universe, a preexisting standard of good to which the universe is being conformed, a universal code or conscience by which goodness and evil, truth and error, wisdom and folly are distinguished. And the more important to you that this preexisting standard of goodness behind the universe becomes, the more you start sounding like a monotheist rather than a pantheist. Soon, you start thinking that the standard or conscience or principle behind the universe is greater than the universe itself and is distinct from it and independent of it and prior to it: voilà, a singular supreme entity . . . sounds a lot like monotheism to me.

As you can see, as attractive as pantheism seems to me, and as superior as it appears when compared with atheism, agnosticism, polytheism, or dualism, I find myself drawn beyond pantheism to monotheism. Pantheism certainly has much to offer, and our understanding of monotheism is enriched, I believe, by dialogue with monotheism's primary theological colleague. Incidentally, if Christian monotheism is true, pantheism might not be so much false as it is "not true yet," for Christians believe that history is flowing toward a goal in which God is in everything, and everything is in God (see, for example, Ephesians 1:10, 22–23; 4:6, 10), a vision not unlike that of one version of pantheism (called panentheism, to be precise).

DRIVING ME BEHIND THE MANY

My honest sense in my own search is that logic drives me behind the many, behind the two, behind the all, to one God "over all, through all, and in all."

I see a dynamic tension between pantheism and monotheism. Just as the pantheist can, in my opinion, go astray by coupling good and evil within God, so the monotheist can go astray by completely uncoupling God and the universe, acting as if there is no relationship between the two. Just as I believe the pantheist has much to learn from the monotheist, so I believe the monotheist can benefit from dialogue with the pantheist.

MONOTHEISM'S DOWNSIDES

As the pantheist could readily point out, monotheism has apparent downsides too. For example, as soon as we say there's one God, the natural question arises: Which one? As soon as we ask that question, aren't we inevitably setting ourselves up for Crusades, holy wars, jihads, division, controversy, bigotry, confusion, contradiction, overwhelming complexity? Aren't we right back to where we started—with an impossibly complex "shopping" task? Aren't the very complexity and strife unleashed by monotheism the turnoffs which turn many people on to pantheism—or to atheism or agnosticism? Is there any way to accept monotheism without falling into endless controversy? At the end of our search, will we find ourselves preaching frantic damnation on street corners to passersby, because they don't believe in the same one God we do?

Do you feel our predicament? Logic may drive us toward monotheism, but once we're there, we may not entirely like what we've found. What do we do now? The path ahead, I think, requires us to pursue monotheism—but to do so carefully and to acknowledge that monotheism itself, like faith, can take many forms, good and bad. As I see it, good monotheism's greatest enemy isn't pantheism or even atheism or agnosticism, but rather bad monotheism. What would constitute good monotheism? Here are three of my own opinions on that question.

IDENTIFYING GOOD MONOTHEISM

1. Good Monotheism Makes for Peace

Let's say we monotheists differ with the pantheists by saying that the universe is not identifiable as God; but let's say we agree that the universe in many wonderful ways reflects God, just as a painting reflects the artist, or a song the musician, or a poem the poet, or a novel the writer. (Actually, the ways in which God is seen in the universe must be even more wonderful and immediate than these analogies. More on this in a minute.) In this way, although we can't exactly say that when we see all things we see God, we can say that in or through all things we can see some beautiful reflection of or fascinating clues about God. (In the case of evil things, we see something about God by contrast, or by conspicuous absence.)

If the universe is full of reflections of God in this way, then as monotheists, we would expect every religion to have caught some glimpses of God's glory, being surrounded, as we all are, by the beauty of God reflected in creation. That means that we can begin, instead of with quarrels, with dialogue, listening and sharing with members of each religion, affirming all the common ground we find we share—not, as the pantheist would say, because all things are God, but because all things created by God reflect their creator, and thus the universe is riddled with what songwriter Bruce Cockburn calls "rumours of glory." That means we can look for, and affirm, the points where each religion and individual have caught on to the rumors and recognized the clues. We can be irenic, not combative, and respectful, not insulting.

2. Good Monotheism Affirms God's Connection with the Universe

The very word *religion* offers insight in this regard. The prefix "re-" means "again," and the root "lig" (as in ligament) means "connect." Religion, then, is about the reconnection of the creator with creation; it's about reconnecting people with God, people with one another. The human predicament, monotheists believe, is that disconnect is possible, and not just possible, that it is actual, that it has happened. We intelligent creations have the capacity to at least partially disconnect from God via willful rebellion, defiance, resistance, indifference, or ignorance—and we have used that capacity with tragic results. When we disconnect from God, we find ourselves becoming internally disconnected, "dis-integrated," hence experiencing shame and fear and duplicity and hypocrisy. Our disconnect from God and ourselves leads inevitably to further fragmentation, disconnection from other people, disconnection from our environment.

If our disconnection from God creates our own human predicament, it also creates a dilemma for God, if we can speak in such terms. Put crudely, God has a problem.

A. If, on the one hand, God allows our disconnection in the name of freedom ("They shouldn't be forced to obey; they shouldn't be forced to worship; love cannot by definition be forced. They made their bed; let them lie in it. Let their choices stand."), then we plunge toward destruction. Like branches disconnected from the tree, without God we will wither and die. These questions naturally arise: "Doesn't God care? Would it even be responsible of a creator to make creatures capable of such self-destruction, and then provide no way of escape for them if they chose the bitter path?"

B. If, on the other hand, God interferes excessively with our disconnection in the name of love ("I can't let them destroy themselves and each other. I care too much for them to allow that.") or justice ("No one will defy my just will."), then do we become robots, puppets, rats in a behavioral conditioning experiment? These questions naturally arise: "Doesn't God respect our dignity and freedom? What does it prove if God forces us to comply?"

This divine-human dilemma is resolved easily by two forms of monotheism:

A. *Determinism* resolves it by saying that, yes, people are hopelessly disconnected from God, and that, yes, God cares for some and shows it by forgiving them and reconnecting them. (Natural questions: "Why some and not others? Why not everyone?" To which honest determinists say, "We don't know.")

B. *Universalism* resolves it by saying that, yes, people are hopelessly disconnected from God, and that, yes, God cares for everyone and shows it by reconnecting everyone. (Natural questions: "What difference does it make if a person is good or bad then? Hitler and Mother Teresa receive the same treatment? People are reconciled with God whether they like it or not, even against their will?" To which honest universalists say, "We haven't figured that all out yet.")

Other monotheists don't see an easy resolution here and are content (or maybe not content, but at least resigned) to leave the dilemma to be just that, seeing its resolution as a mystery . . . for now at least. Like the others, they say, "We don't know; we haven't figured that all out yet," although they make this admission earlier along than the others. In spite of these differences, all of these monotheists agree on this: God cares about the universe and doesn't want to let it disconnect, wither, and die, and God is involved in the unfolding of a dramatic story of reconnection, a story we all find ourselves in the middle of. Our "re-connecting" is what "re-ligion" is all about.

3. Good Monotheism Emphasizes the Role of Creation in Revealing God

Good monotheism (unlike the "industrial-strength monotheism" too common in recent centuries) does not allow the distinction between creator and creation to so devalue creation as to make creation little more than a utilitarian resource. Far from it!

Let me illustrate it in this way. I live near Washington, D.C., which has many beautiful art galleries. In the National Gallery hangs a beautiful painting by Rembrandt. It is one of the paintings into which the artist painted his own face. Art lovers feel a reverence for the painting; you can sense it when they enter that room of the gallery. (In fact, it is often their reverence for the painting that leads them to learn more about the artist and develop a reverence for the artist.) There is a hush, a concentration, a thrill, a wonder. Similarly (as we'll see in more detail in a later chapter), healthy monotheists feel a reverence for all that exists. (There are important ecological implications here, aren't there?)

ART GALLERY

We find ourselves living in an art gallery: Every goldfinch and osprey, each trout and barracuda, all Appaloosas and elephants, all mica and magma, each woodland fern and live oak, every red raspberry and green tomato, even all hydrogen and oxygen . . . are unique masterpieces, amazing wonders. And not only can we enjoy the art, but we can also know the Artist, relate to the Artist, tell the Artist about our feelings of gratitude, wonder, and awe. And not only that . . . we can conceive of ourselves as artwork in process, as part of an awesome, unfolding master-creation in progress.

And more: All of creation thus reveals the artist. We are surrounded not only by beauty that inspires, but beauty that teaches. The Christian doctrine of the Holy Spirit and the Jewish concept of the Wisdom of God both support this view, suggesting that God speaks, teaches, and enlightens through all of life. Jesus' use of parables similarly would reinforce this view. For his disciples, there was no classroom but the field, the dirt road, the cottage, the mountainside: All of life was the classroom, full of vehicles for enlightenment. Christian monotheists like me, in fact, have a special reason to see a strong linkage between the creator and the creation; we believe that God actually did paint himself into the picture, thus honoring and ennobling the picture to an astounding degree, showing profound solidarity between creator and creation. Not everyone sees it this way, of course. At any rate, our next step is to deal with some problems with monotheism, as I am describing it, that might have already begun to bother you.

YOUR RESPONSE

> I am pursuing the following model in my spiritual search:
>> Pantheism, because...
>> Polytheism, because...
>> Dualism, because...
>> Monotheism, because...
> I affirm the following characteristics of "good monotheism":
>> Makes for peace
>> Affirms God's connection with the universe
>> Emphasizes the role of creation in revealing God
>> Other

RESOURCES

C. S. Lewis's *Mere Christianity* makes a strong case for monotheism.

For information on world religions and their views of God, one of the best guides is Huston Smith, *The World's Religions* (Harper-SanFrancisco, 1991).

PRAYER

God, I may have sufficient faith to believe you exist (although I may still have doubts at times), but I need increased understanding of which approach to you is best, for me at least. Should you be understood more as the sum total of everything, as pantheism suggests, or as the supreme being who created the sum total of everything, as monotheism suggests? I ask for guidance and enlightenment in this regard. Help my pursuit of you to be a "good faith" pursuit. Although I am thinking hard and searching for you sincerely, I am also aware that without help from beyond myself, my efforts have little or no chance of succeeding. Please help me. The fact that I am praying suggests that, though I can't claim to understand fully or to be free of doubts and questions, I indeed have some degree of faith that you are a personal God who is capable of a relationship with me, one of your creatures. If I didn't believe this to some degree, I wouldn't be talking to you at all.

CHAPTER 7 PREVIEW

Do You Seriously Expect Me to Think of God As an Old Man with a Long White Beard?

This chapter addresses a number of common objections or frustrations that people have with monotheism, regarding God's personality, gender, subtlety, and the like.

WHO SHOULD READ THIS CHAPTER?

If you feel that monotheism as it is usually presented is somewhat beneath you, that it seems backward or outmoded or just doesn't make sense, this chapter may help you. If you are one of the already-convinced, this chapter should help you better understand and help others who have these objections.

WHAT QUESTIONS DOES IT ADDRESS?

In what way can we speak of God being personal and relational without making God sound like a "big old guy in the sky"? What is deism, and why is it attractive? How can we understand and deal with the apparent chauvinism involved in referring to God as "he"? Why isn't God more obvious?

Common Problems with Monotheism

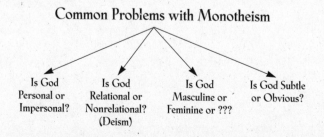

| Is God Personal or Impersonal? | Is God Relational or Nonrelational? (Deism) | Is God Masculine or Feminine or ??? | Is God Subtle or Obvious? |

[S]ome ... think that God is a Wizard-of-Oz or Sistine-Chapel kind of being sitting at a location very remote from us. The universe is then presented as, chiefly, a vast empty space with a humanoid God and a few angels rattling around in it, while several billion human beings crawl through the tiny cosmic interval of human history on an oversized clod of dirt circling an insignificant star. Of such a "god" we can only say, "Good riddance!"

DALLAS WILLARD, *THE DIVINE CONSPIRACY*

CHAPTER 7

Do You Seriously Expect Me to Think of God As an Old Man with a Long White Beard?

In this chapter, we need to clean up some messes that we may have inadvertently created in our dialogue so far.

We began a previous chapter with the question "What is God?"—and we never really answered it. The question has a certain charming naiveté when you think about it. Who do we think we are—we small creatures with three-pound brains, a few limited senses, and life spans barely long enough to get to know our neighborhood, much less the planet, and much less the galaxy, and much less the universe, and much less still its creator! Who do we think we are to be able to define or even describe the creator of DNA, galaxies, dust mites, blue whales, the carbon cycle, light, and a billion other realities we have no notion about whatsoever, no awareness of at all?

A PATERNAL ANALOGY

Yet even given our limitations, perhaps some real degree of knowledge is possible. Consider this analogy to my children. Imagine them when they were younger, say under eight. If you had asked them, "Who is your dad?" how would they have answered? They couldn't have told you about my height, weight, temperature, blood pressure, heart rate, or any other vital statistics. They were incapable of saying anything intelligent about my genetic makeup. They didn't know much about my philosophy of life, what books I had read, what places I had visited, which degrees I had earned, what music I liked, how many languages I spoke. They certainly didn't comprehend my sexuality or my financial position, nor could they identify with many of my adult emotions—including the depth of my love for them. My doctors, teachers, and colleagues knew more about me, in these senses, than they did.

Yet in another sense, they knew me intimately, in a way beyond anyone else. They knew the smell of my skin, the feel of my hair (which I had more of back then), the strength of my hands, the fine nuances of my smile. And more—was I faithful or inconstant, generous or stingy, forgiving or hard, playful or grim, kind or cruel? And even more—who was I *to them*? Who could know these things better than they? True, their limitations as children gave them certain disadvantages in understanding their father, but their relationship as *my* children gave them other incomparable advantages.

THE RELATIONAL ADVANTAGE

And this, I believe, is the key to our approach to the question we'll pose in chapter 9 in our quest: How might God be experienced? The answers have to be in the context of our relationship to God. In other words, we're not a group of fish trying to learn about camels—to which we have no relation and next to nothing in common; we're fish trying to learn about water. We're not birds studying the distances between two stars in a distant galaxy—places inaccessible and irrelevant to us; we're birds exploring wind and air. We're not scholars researching an ancient Chinese emperor—a matter of objectivity and disinterestedness; we're sons and daughters who want to get to know our father—someone with whom we have an essential relationship. We're creations in the universe God created—we're part of God's universe, and God is therefore part of ours: We're related.

But now that we've focused our search broadly within monotheism, and now that we're speaking of God as father, we must address three issues we'll need to deal with sooner or later—and it might as well be sooner. First, aren't we making a huge leap to speak of God as personal (he or she) to begin with—rather than as impersonal (it)? Second, even if God is personal, what reasons do we have to believe that God is relational—that a big, transcendent God would want to be involved in our puny, pedestrian lives? And third, why speak of God as male, as father—why not as female, as mother?

1. Personal or Impersonal?

Many people resist the idea of a personal God, and with good reason. When they think of a person, they think of rather quaint but silly images—such as God as a Santa-esque old man with a long white beard . . . or as an immature tyrant prone to throwing temper tantrums . . . or as a forgetful manager who needs constant reminders (via prayer) lest he forget important details in his universe . . . or as an absentminded professor who naively started this experiment called the universe which since has gone more than slightly out of control.

Our problem in this regard is probably a matter of words—perhaps confusing "personal" with "human." To illustrate, think of the following items: gravity, helium, water, coal, a fern, a frog, a parrot, a golden retriever, a chimpanzee, a human being. The first three bring us from energy to matter, from gas to solid, and from invisible to visible. When we get to the fern, we move from nonliving to living. From fern to frog, we cross the boundary to animate. I don't know any frogs very well, but with my limited exposure, they seem to have a little, but not much, in the way of personality. Parrots have more, and golden retrievers and chimpanzees more still . . . and human beings, more still. Now, with each step up the ladder, we didn't lose the qualities of the previous steps; rather, we added more capabilities, more depth . . . while we subtracted previous limitations, going from energy to matter to form to solidity to plant life to animal life to warm-blooded life to mammalian life to primate life to human life.

Let's imagine we inserted a million rungs in our ladder after human beings, each rung suggesting more developed, less limited beings, with personalities as far beyond our own as ours are beyond a bullfrog's—not less developed with each ascending rung, but more. And we could insert another million, and another, and we'd be getting some idea of the way in which we can speak of God being personal.

So, we're not saying that God is personal to the same small degree and with the same limitations we are. Rather, we're saying that God is personal not in a way less than us, but more. And we're saying that the fact that we share this quality called personality means there is a bridge, a connecting point, a common language, a medium of communication. It means that both we and God come equipped with a telephone or modem so we can interface. Obviously, one party's potentials dwarf the other party's, but nevertheless, connectivity is possible. That's a pretty wonderful thought.

It's illogical to think otherwise, really. A creator can't create beings greater than himself. The fact that personalities (humans, chimps, golden retrievers) exist in the universe demands, it seems to me, that the creator must not be below personality—just as the existence of living creatures suggests that God must be in some way alive, must be, in the truest sense, the Life that all living creations reflect. Now I know many people who don't like to speak this way. They prefer to speak of God as a force or perhaps a principle, and I think they do so to avoid confusing themselves with the kinds of silly human notions we mentioned earlier (Santa Claus, petty tyrant, forgetful manager, and so forth). If by "force" we mean something mysterious, powerful, and beyond our power to fully comprehend, we're speaking accurately. If by "principle" we mean something true in and of itself, requiring no proof or argument, again, I think we're speaking accurately. But if by force or principle, we mean something nonliving and nonpersonal, something on a lower rung than many creations including ourselves and golden retrievers and ferns, then, again, I think we're imagining an absurdity. Don't you agree?

2. Personal But Nonrelational?

Many people will grant that God could not be less than personal, but they argue, "Don't you think the Creator of the Universe has bigger fish to fry than answering the prayers of elementary-school children and old women?" The objection has some merit, but not much, as illustrated by the following counter-objections:

A. What's wrong with elementary-school children and old women?
B. Actually, I can't think of the Creator having any fish to fry at all—i.e., problems to solve. Furthermore, I can't think of anything more important—or interesting, for that matter—than an elementary-school child or old woman. Who do you expect would deserve more of God's attention—lawyers?
C. You don't think that God has limited energy and strength, do you—that God works up such a sweat keeping galaxies spinning and black holes swallowing ("big fish to fry") that God doesn't have the time (time? with God?) or energy or concentration left to pay attention to this little planet or individual people on it?
D. You haven't fallen into the "big is important" fallacy, have you—that physical size somehow corresponds to actual importance?
E. Or you don't think that God lacks mental ability, do you—that God's eyes (so to speak) don't focus down to details such as sparrows, kids, grandmothers?

Of course, in these wisecrack retorts I risk not taking this question seriously enough. And I would be making a mistake to do so, because deism—the belief in a personal but distant, uninvolved creator—is a belief I respect, held by many people (past and present) whom I also respect. Deism, like a lot of movements, makes more sense when you see what it was against, in historical context. To do that, imagine a pair of sensitive, intelligent people in the eighteenth century having a beer in an American pub. . . .

Frank: Did you hear about the latest war?
  Jeff: Where now? Every time you turn around, there's another war.

Frank: Sad but true. This one's in Flogistan.

Jeff: Don't tell me: religion's behind it. Those Flogistanis are a religious lot.

Frank: Of course. What else could it be? One party believes that cleanliness is next to godliness, and they've passed laws requiring everyone to bathe at least annually.

Jeff: Don't tell me—the other party believes that man's natural aroma is God-given, and therefore shouldn't be eradicated by soap or covered by cologne.

Frank: Exactly! How did you know? The Cleanliness Party killed two hundred . . . after torturing them in God's name by making them eat soap. The Natural Aroma Party retaliated by spreading human excrement through the capital city, also in the name of God. Dozens have died because of disease; a plague has broken out. Not only that: full-scale civil war has erupted, each side claiming it is God's army, inflicting his wrath on the other side.

Jeff: A real curse, this religion business, always causing wars, death, division, killing. Wouldn't it be nice if we could conduct our lives free of religion. Imagine there's no heaven. . . .

Frank: Yes, but we need God as the Creator and sustainer of moral law. If there is no God, then everything is permissible.

Jeff: Good point. Let's postulate that the deity exists and should be honored as the giver of life, liberty, moral law, and reason. And let's postulate that the deity wishes us to use our reason to solve our problems, without bringing him into it.

Frank: Brilliant! Such a belief will lead to the elevation of human beings instead of their constant descent into petty and pathetic religious squabbles which, in spite of their triviality, are all turned into God-sized Major Issues. To promote this new concept, the deity should be conceived of in the most high-tech imagery possible . . . how about as a Clockmaker? He designed and created the clock, wound it up, set it in motion, and has no need or desire to interfere or intervene. It is our responsibility to . . . act responsibly, under God.

Jeff: I think we've got something here, my friend. Let me buy you another drink. . . .

I can imagine, if I were drinking nearby and overheard their conversation, being the first one to sign on as a deist. Aren't they right to be outraged at the atrocities and trivialities committed in God's name? I never cease to be amazed at the ridiculous trivialities we believers can focus on and fight about.

Deism made sense in its day as a reaction against religious wrangling and warfare. But reactionary movements often lack lasting stability and staying power, and deism is a case in point. Today, deism tends to be a stopover on the flight, not a final destination. People (or families) moving from faith to agnosticism or atheism, or the reverse, often stop there for a while (or a generation). Deism, as I see it, was against something worth being against, but in the process became for something not worth being for: A distant, uninvolved God whose personal care for individuals is severely limited. This is yet another case of bad monotheism (here, constant religious bickering) being good monotheism's worst enemy. We should be grateful for deism's attempt to remedy the situation, and learn from deism (with its emphasis, for example, on human responsibility, and its sense of proportion—not making God the arbiter of trivialities or the justifier of pettiness), without limiting ourselves to deism's severely limited, uninvolved Deity.

Although few people would call themselves deists today, the term probably fits a good many people, including those who say they believe in God as a Life Force of some sort, but not a personal, relational God. As I've said, I think many people have moved in this direction for understandable and commendable reasons (such as avoiding the cantankerous spirit of bad monotheism). But I must mention one less commendable reason. Deism can be attractive as a low-cost, convenient religious option . . . low cost and convenience being fine qualifications for choosing a bank, perhaps, but questionable for choosing a focus for one's faith. As C. S. Lewis aptly said in *Mere Christianity,* this form of deism

> gives one much of the emotional comfort of believing in God and none of the less pleasant consequences. . . .
>
> When you are feeling fit and the sun is shining and you do not want to believe that the whole universe is a mere mechanical dance of atoms, it is nice to be able to think of this great mysterious Force rolling on through the centuries and carrying you on its crest. If, on the other hand, you want to do something rather shabby, the Life-Force, being only a blind force, with no morals and no mind, will never interfere with you like that troublesome God we learned about when we were children. The Life-Force is a sort of tame God. You can switch it on when you want, but it will not bother you. All the thrills of religion and none of the cost.

There are other ways to deal with the cantankerous spirit of bad monotheism, as we will see. The deists, it seems to me, were right—a Supreme Being wouldn't be about fueling petty party feuds; but neither, I think, would a Supreme Being refuse to come close to us, get involved with us, allow us to come into relationship with him. What do you think?

3. Male or Female?

The fact that I just used the word "him" for God brings us to the problem of gender. This is largely (but not totally) a problem of some languages, such as English. (In many languages, I understand, this problem hardly exists.) Consider these facts about the English language: (1) In English, we can speak of an inanimate genderless thing (stone, table, dirt), but not an inanimate male or female thing (such as a ?—we can't even identify such a thing!). Why? Because to us gender is only a characteristic of living things. (We might as well speak of a solid gas or a poisonous nutrient, since a gendered inanimate object is to us equally an absurdity.) This situation is quite different in the Romance languages, for example, where everything has gender. (2) Of course, in English, we do sometimes ascribe personality (and along with it, gender) to an inanimate thing—like a ship, for instance, calling it "she"—but when we do, we only ascribe gender after we have personified the object. (3) Conversely, in English, when we speak of living things, we have the opposite problem; the more personal they are, the less we speak of them without assigning them a gender. If we don't, we seem to call their personality into question. For example, we have no problem calling a worm (a creature seemingly low on personality, agreed?) an "it"—but we refer to our golden retrievers as "he" or "she." Regarding humans, we feel uncomfortable calling a baby of unknown gender an "it" for very long; we need to know if "it" is *really* a "he" or "she."

So, we seem bound by the rules of our language to ascribe gender to God to express our recognition of God as a personal being. But consider this: If God is not bound by human personality as we know it, then surely God is not bound by gender as we know it either. If that's the case, to call God "he" or "she" would mean "he + she + ." In other words, God is not less than male or female, but neither is God equal to male or female in human terms: Just as God does with our categories of personhood, surely God must include and transcend our gender categories as well.

BEYOND SEMANTICS

But here is where our problem moves beyond the semantic to the practical. Along with our language limitations, we humans have had—and still have—some very restrictive views on the females of our species (please excuse me for stating the obvious). These restrictive views have varied from culture to culture, finding expression in everything from forced female circumcision to excluding women from democratic processes, from considering them as ineducable to counting them as property.

And no doubt, wherever languages like English lead people to refer to God with masculine pronouns, there has been the temptation to assume that God is actually masculine ... thus implying that man is more godlike, and woman less so—and thus justifying and perhaps even encouraging all kinds of oppression and subjugation and mistreatment of women. To remedy this situation, some have tried to balance "he" and "she" references to God (an option I don't prefer for a number of reasons that would take us even further on a tangent to discuss). Others have tried to avoid using pronouns for God altogether (an option I prefer when stylistically appropriate). Still others have hoped that by capitalizing the first letter (e.g., "He" or "Him"), they would be showing that God has a category of His (or God's?) own ... thus transcending the merely human categories of gender; and others still continue to use standard English practice with masculine pronouns, keeping in mind their belief that God is not a male.

As you've probably noticed, I follow the second practice when I can, and revert to the fourth practice otherwise. It isn't a neat solution, but I don't see one ... given the limits of human language, and in our case, the human language called English. Perhaps this challenge goes along with the challenge of faith: Just as faith forces us to deal with realities that exceed our understanding, so it challenges us to deal with realities that stretch our normal language and prove it less than fully adequate. (This is, of course, as we would expect. After all, Whom are we talking about?)

MATERNAL IMAGERY?

Having addressed the language problem, though, this digression is not complete until we go beyond language and deal with the issue of imagery. If God is not limited to he-ness, would not maternal imagery be as effective as paternal? And we can quickly say, "Yes. It's only logical." The Bible itself uses maternal imagery for God on a number of occasions and asserts in its opening chapters that male and female together reflected God's image. In modern times, after viewing a movie like *The Spitfire Grill* or *Lorenzo's Oil,* or throughout history everywhere, after observing the real-life love and dedication and sacrifice of mothers, can anyone doubt that one gets beautiful and brilliant glimpses of God in the quiet heroism of mothers?

Why, then, do paternal images seem to dominate, especially in the teachings of Jesus? Why are maternal images so rare?

Our search for answers could explore any number of possibilities. For example, the Bible was originally written by and for people of patriarchal cultures; in that context, paternal imagery would be the highest and most honoring imagery available for God, whereas maternal imagery could imply an insult or lesser honor. In fact, in those cultures, advanced age (which may have begun at forty or fifty!) was also revered: As a result—imagery of God as an old man with a white beard, which seems quaint or even silly to us, was an attempt to relate God to the most respected, venerated model available to their imagination.

In addition, maternal imagery was common for territorial deities in the ancient world, and the imagery was often highly sexualized, "celebrated" via temple prostitution—more reasons for ancient writers to avoid it. Also, people of the ancient world generally held the "garden model" of femininity: The seed of life was carried by the man, with the woman's womb serving as the garden in which the seed could be planted. It was the man, therefore, who carried the vital function, with the woman being in the passive receiver role— far different from our more egalitarian (and genetically accurate) views of conception and gestation today. In that context, only paternal imagery would do justice to the vitality and vigor of God.

Today, we would feel much freer to use maternal imagery than the ancients. In doing so, of course, we would want to be careful to avoid stereotyping women (inferring, for example, that they only reflect the tenderness and gentleness and emotional side of God, ignoring their strength and bravery and intelligence) and excessively sexualizing God (an underrated danger we may now be somewhat oblivious to, content as we often are to see God in exclusively, perhaps excessively, masculine terms). If some overmasculinize their image of God, we aren't helping ourselves and our children to swing to the opposite extreme by overfeminizing God, and neither are we helping the situation by trying to "neuter" God, I would imagine (a rather horrific thought). God, in whose image male and female were created, must include all authentically masculine and feminine qualities and at the same time transcend them.

WHY ISN'T GOD MORE OBVIOUS?

Returning to the point of these digressions, we're trying to tie up some loose ends, preparing ourselves for the question of how one might experience God, with the starting point of relationship . . . with a natural metaphor for that relationship being a parental (both paternal and maternal) one. But our digression misses a fundamental question: Why do we need metaphors at all? Why isn't God more obvious? We don't need to talk about finding ways to experience, say, sunlight or rain or tiredness or gravity . . . these things are unavoidable. You can't help but experience them because they're so real, so common. Why isn't God as obvious and unavoidable as rain or gravity?

The "problem" could lie with God. This problem could simply be evidence that God doesn't exist, or that if God exists, God simply wants to be left alone and have us get on with our lives and civilization without reference to God. Or there's another option: Perhaps God has reasons for not wanting to be obvious. I can think of an analogy in the church where I serve as pastor. We have an internet discussion group, where people can post messages and raise questions and offer answers. It's a great place for intelligent discourse and educational dialogue. As pastor, though, I try to be a silent participant. If I were to give too many answers in too many postings, others would be tempted to pull back . . . my presence would intimidate them. The discussion group would stop being a community dialogue, and would become a one-way monologue, with people asking questions and "Mr. Know-It-All" answering. Since my goal is for them to develop (not for me to show off how much I know), I must stay in the background, seldom posting a message of my own.

Or to return to a paternal image, as a father I similarly don't want to loom too large in my children's considerations. For example, I don't want them to choose the career or marriage partner that I would choose ... my "will" is that they make those choices themselves. I want them to be their own people, to develop their own personalities, to live their own stories ... not to huddle in my shadow. True, I don't want to be ignored either, but my desire to see them develop into unique people forces me to restrain myself, to not always give my opinion, to not step in and help every time they might ask for help, to not "do their homework for them," but rather to help them develop by *not* helping them sometimes.

Similarly, if God's goal in the universe is for us to develop—for us to make unpressured choices, to become who we will be not because "the Big Guy's looking" but for other more natural, unforced reasons (like courage, love, integrity, or justice) ... then perhaps God is forced to stay "subtle," behind-the-scenes, present but not too obvious, involved but also ignorable, here but hidden. C. S. Lewis said it like this in *The Screwtape Letters*: "He wants them to learn to walk and must therefore take away his hand."

Maybe God's very silence is actually intended to tell us something ... revealing a God who listens more than speaks, a God who wants to make room for us to live our lives without constant intrusion, interference, or domination. It's worth thinking about.

WHY AREN'T WE LESS OBLIVIOUS?

At the same time, God's apparent hiddenness could be a problem of ours. Perhaps many of us aren't looking for God; we're looking instead for our own interests, our next date, our next deal, our next purchase. Further than that, some of us may wish God not to exist . . . since God's existence would likely entail moral limits and social responsibilities that we're interested in avoiding. We may actually be suppressing evidence in order to maintain our illusion that we are not accountable to anyone. Or some of us might be so overcome by our troubles and worries that God could be putting signs of his existence all around us, and we would be oblivious.

Meanwhile, some of us are searching for God, and still God seems resistant to showing up sometimes. I know I have felt this way. The little faith I have has at times been stretched so thin . . . I've waited so long . . . searched for some sign of God's existence and presence and concern, but found nothing for so long . . . God seemed to me to be taking very big risks with my endurance and character: More than once I have been on the verge of giving up on God altogether. God has seemed to me at times like a coach who pushed me so hard during practice that I almost quit the sport entirely.

Even here, though . . . if faith and endurance are virtues, perhaps God has reasons to test us. Perhaps a tested faith is more valuable than an untested one. Perhaps exercising endurance makes faith stronger, just as it does with muscles or concentration or commitments to friends and family. Perhaps the only growing, strengthening muscles are stretched and tired ones.

Having said all this, maybe we're ready to continue with our quest. No, nobody's asking you to think of God as an old man with a white beard. All we're saying in our pursuit of the monotheist path is that there is one God behind the universe, and this God must be amazing to have created all that exists—amazing, and relational—and thus worth "knowing" or experiencing.

YOUR RESPONSE

1. I believe God is impersonal/personal, because. . .
2. I believe God is relational/nonrelational, because. . .

3. Here's how I will deal with issues of gender-inclusive language in reference to God:

4. Here's how I respond to the question, "Why isn't God more obvious?"

PRAYER

I do not wish to limit my thinking of you, but I am aware of my own limitations—constrained as I am by language, human thought patterns, my own experience and education, and the like. I feel that I am looking at an infinite sky through one small window. Yet rather than disparaging this limited viewpoint that I have as a disadvantage, I can be grateful for it: at least I am not staring at a windowless wall with no capacity to relate to you at all. This window—this set of experiences and starting points that are unique to me—is what I have been given, and so I continue in my search for you as you are, simply being myself, as I am. Please meet me where I am, and I will try to remain teachable and humble, open-minded and open-hearted, so that you can reveal more of yourself and your truth to me.

CHAPTER 8 PREVIEW

Don't All Paths Lead to the Same God?

This chapter is one of the more difficult chapters in the book. It addresses the issue of pluralism—how we deal with the multiplicity of religions.

WHO SHOULD READ THIS CHAPTER?

If you are familiar with or curious about the terms pluralism, postmodernism, and relativism, or if you have ever asked the question, "Don't all paths lead to the same God?" you shouldn't miss this chapter.

WHAT QUESTIONS DOES IT ADDRESS?

If all religions are inspired, why do they contradict one another? How can one talk about which religions are right/wrong,

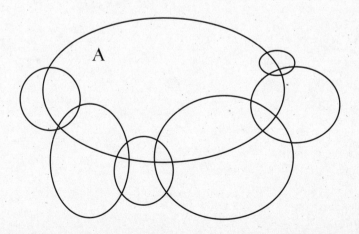

better/worse, more/less helpful, and so on, without sounding elitist or judgmental? Is it possible that all religions possess some value even if they are not all equally true? How can one hold to a religion in a way that does not make him exclusive, elitist, or judgmental?

The preceding diagram will be used to illustrate the relationship between various religions (the smaller circles) and the truth (the big circle, A).

CHAPTER 8

Don't All Paths Lead to the Same God?

This chapter is a test. It's a test of your ability to think clearly and keep your balance in an emotionally charged situation. It's a test of your objectivity. It may even be a test of your faith. If there's any part of this book that many people will not "like," my guess is that it will be this chapter. For that very reason, it's pretty important.

A NEW SITUATION

At the beginning of the twenty-first century, the search for faith is in one way different from the search at any other time in history. Imagine a young Philistine fellow about three thousand years ago. His search for faith was in many ways easier than ours. (Actually, he may not have had to search for it at all.)

For example, he had the "advantage" of one option, not many. Sure, he was aware of many other nations—the Jews, the Hittites, the Amalekites, the Hivites. He was aware that they had other gods. He knew that his religion was not the only religion in the world. But he had this "advantage," if you will: All the other nations were enemy nations, and so their gods were enemy gods—not an appealing option to him and patently wrong. .

He had another "advantage": The assumption in those polytheistic times was that gods were parochial, territorial. One god might be the right god for this geographical region, another for that. Choosing "the right god" was as simple as knowing where you were. When in Philistia . . .

He had still another "advantage": He didn't have as much history behind him. The history of his religion consisted of the stories told by his father, his grandfather. There was little or no record of the scandals of his religious hierarchy centuries ago, or of its negative effects on the socioeconomic order in the previous century, or of its psychological effects on the development of children over the years. His faith could present itself as something pure, perfect even—an impossibility for us these days.

And yet another "advantage": There was little or no science. Claims made by his religion went pretty well undisputed. There was certainly no respected scientific establishment with a built-in skepticism for supernatural claims, constantly posing challenges to the claims of his religion.

And yet another "advantage": All his associates shared his belief. He didn't buy milk from the local convenience store owned by the member of one religion, study chemistry from a professor of another, jog after work with three members of three different religions, and come home to a spouse of yet another. His entire social milieu reinforced his faith . . . that "we" are "right." That "our" truth is the only true version.

And on top of all these advantages, our young Philistine fellow didn't have the "trilemma" faced by nearly every spiritual seeker today:

1. Some forces pull him to a particular commitment to a particular faith.
2. Some forces pull him to an equal tolerance for all faiths.
3. Some forces pull him away from any faith commitment at all.

Can you identify with this trilemma?

THE MIDDLE ELEMENT

If you're like most people these days, it's the middle element of that trilemma that is most troubling. Don't all paths lead to the same God? Why choose one faith over another? Isn't one a fool to narrow his options, when there are so many options to consider? Why not develop a tolerant, "accept-everything" faith, filled with the desired elements from each "aisle" in the religious market, like a grocery cart at the grocery store—a little bit of Hinduism, a few items from Christianity or Islam, some good Buddhist products thrown in, plus several excellent Jewish brand names? Isn't it intolerant to claim that one religion is true, or truer than the others? Doesn't that imply an insult to all others? Doesn't it show unpardonable intolerance?

It almost makes you wish you were an ancient Philistine. From another vantage point, though, the advantages of our imaginary Philistine youth are themselves imaginary. If the goal is to find a faith that is relatively easy to accept and hard to doubt, then he had advantages indeed. But if the goal is to find a faith that is true— tested, considered, chosen, wanted—then you'll probably agree our situation is preferable, in spite of the middle element, which we will call *pluralism*. So let's face pluralism head on.

PROBLEMS WITH PLURALISM

"Pluralism" has several meanings, but for our purposes, pluralism means living with equal tolerance and respect for all belief systems. Sounds good, right? It means mirroring in our private lives the "religious freedom" laws of constitutional democracies—affording no preferences to any one religion. Sounds good, right? It means believing that all religions are equally true; that it doesn't matter which one you follow, as long as you're sincere. Again, this all sounds good to many people. You might be surprised to hear my concerns about applying pluralism to one's personal spiritual search. I can explain my concerns with this "formula": If all religions are equally true....

... Then God Lies or Else Is Confused

If God told Mohammed that everyone must make a pilgrimage to Mecca, and God also told Jesus that it doesn't matter where you worship God, God speaks with forked tongue. If God told the followers of Moses that while it is morally wrong to eat ham, beef and chicken are okay . . . but meanwhile God told the Hindus that eating any meat at all is immoral, what's God's problem—a poor memory? If God tells some people that men should dominate women, not allowing them to vote or drive or be seen in public with any skin exposed, while God tells other people that men and women are equal partners in the gift of life . . . or if God tells some tribes and races they can be slaveholders, while telling others (perhaps the slaves themselves?) that all people have equal dignity . . . I'm sorry, but God just lost me.

. . . Then God Prefers Some Religions Over Others

If God tells one group of people that they should turn the other cheek when they are attacked, and then a few hundred years later tells some other people that they have the right to "convert with the sword" (i.e., "believe my religion or die"), I can't help but feel that God didn't like the first group so much.

. . . Then All Religions Lie

Each religion claims that its approach is not just *an* option . . . it claims to be *the* option, or at least the *best* option, or a better option than some others. But if all religions are in truth equally valid, then each religion that claims superiority (which is, in fact, every religion) is lying.

. . . Then Only One Belief Is Really True: Pluralism

If all belief systems claiming any superiority over their competitors are patent liars, then only one belief system is true: the belief system of pluralism, since it is the only one telling the truth that all belief systems are really equally valid.

. . . Then Pluralism Is True, But Pluralism Is Also False, Which Is Illogical

Follow me here. If all religions are equally true, as pluralism claims, then each religion is false when it claims that some or all other religions are not true . . . which proves that pluralism (which claims that all religions are equally true) is false when it claims that all religions are true. Does that make sense? It shouldn't!

AN OPEN MIND

Now having slammed pluralism (as we have here defined it) in this way, I hope you don't think I am for religious bigotry, holy wars, inquisitions, and the like. The fact is, I love living in a plural society— a society of many races, religions, cultures, languages. How boring a monochrome society would be, after enjoying a full-color one. What's more, I share pluralism's disdain for any form of religious oppression, discrimination, or bigotry. I applaud every attempt for peace done in pluralism's name, since peacemaking is, to me, a truly spiritual work of faith. But in the end, I think pluralism (as we've defined it here) is a miss, a near miss in some ways, but a miss nonetheless, not only for logical reasons (as we've seen) but also for practical reasons.

Practically speaking, different religions do agree on many things and they are allies on many fronts, but they disagree on many things too (as we saw in earlier chapters). They lay out very different paths to very different god-concepts and very different concepts of what life is all about. The world will turn into a very different place, depending on which ones exert themselves in our world. It matters, very practically, which one *you* believe for *your* life and future; you'll live a very different kind of life depending on which path you follow. And it also matters, very practically, which ones your neighbors on this planet believe; it matters for the life and future of planet earth. Remember, bad religion can do some pretty horrific things. Not all religion is benign. You've probably heard the saying that one of the reasons we need good religion so much is that the alternative is not *no* religion, it's *bad* religion. So, how do we proceed in our search?

FOUR GUIDING PRINCIPLES

I have four guiding principles that have helped me face our modern faith trilemma.

1. Honor the Truth Wherever It Is Found

Many years ago, I committed myself to the Christian faith (more on that later). As a Christian, I am taught to seek the truth, wisdom, and humility. That means that if a Buddhist teaches me, I must gratefully honor the truth—because truth is truth, whoever brings it. Not only that, I should gratefully honor the bearer of that truth as well. The Bible is full of people of other faiths being used as messengers or conveyers of important truths. As a young Christian, I was too proud to admit that a Muslim could teach me, or that a Hindu could teach me, or that an atheist could teach me, but I have grown to learn to honor the truth wherever it is found. Doing so, I believe, doesn't make me less mature as a Christian, but rather more.

2. Honor the Glory Wherever It Is Found

Some matters are not matters of truth; they are matters of goodness or beauty, which I'll refer to here together as "glory." When a Muslim mother cares for her children, works long hours, sacrifices, gives her all for their well-being, I see the glory of God in her as much as if she were a Jew, a Christian, my own mother. When an artist paints a beautiful painting, when a dancer moves with grace and wonder, when an architect lifts my spirits with light and space and texture and line, when a musician plays with heart and skill, when a teacher helps my child understand negative numbers, I don't need to ask whether she was an atheist, a Zoroastrian, or a Buddhist nun. The glory deserves to be honored wherever it is found, because it is ultimately a reflection of God's glory. Who else's could it be?

3. Honor People Especially When You Disagree

For me, as a Christian, I am commanded to love everyone— everyone. Everyone. Those with whom I agree are, in a sense, the easiest to love. But even the most faithless people love those who agree with them, so loving my colleagues is hardly an expression of faith: It's just an expression of common decency. My faith is proven by my ability to love with understanding and honor without bias those who are most different from me. I may not honor what they say or do. If they are spreading hatred, if they are stirring up fear or racism or greed, naturally, I'll oppose their words and deeds. But I will try to honor them as people.

This bears a bit of elaboration. Have you noticed that relatively few people really aim to be evil, and that those who are evil often show up in surprising places—including "our" churches . . . and our shoes? Sometimes, those with whom we disagree prove themselves more honorable than we are. I remember one night I was leading a discussion group. We were talking about a passage of the Bible, and this one fellow, a visitor, was very talkative. By his third or fourth comment, I realized from his terminology that he was a member of a certain cult group notorious for mind control and other unsavory practices. I felt alarmed. He obviously was trying to infiltrate our group and cause division and attract converts to his group.

After the meeting, I cornered him. I was literally shaking with emotion. "I know where you're coming from, and your ideas aren't welcome around here . . ." I let him have it with both barrels. After a moment of stunned silence, he replied, meekly, quietly, "Wow, I'm sorry. I just joined that group a few weeks ago. I had no idea that they were off the track. I've just blindly accepted everything they taught me. Thanks for telling me. I'll have to rethink everything they said." His humility, his teachability, his vulnerability made me feel ashamed for assuming the worst about him. Ironically, even though so much of what he said that night was weird and warped, and even though I still think the group he had gotten involved with is a destructive, spiritually toxic group, that night he demonstrated more humility than I did. I learned something about good faith from this very fellow whom I was so intent on straightening out. Just when we think we can write off the evil guy "over there," we find evil pretty close to home.

4. It's Okay to Not Know

Consider this. I don't know where my wife is at this moment. I don't know what she's thinking. I don't understand everything about her, even though we're closing in on twenty years of marriage. Just as I have some secrets she's never learned, I'm sure she has some facets unknown to me. Should I be anxious about this lack of knowledge?

No. It's okay, because I have enough knowledge of her to love her, to trust her, to build a life with her. The same is true with God. There is so much about God I haven't even begun to understand, but the little I do understand is enough for me to love, trust, and build a life with God.

Among these unknowns for me—how God will treat people of other religions, how things will be after this life for people who don't believe but who lived better lives than many who do, exactly how God balances our free will with a degree of divine control over the universe, how God plans to redress the injustices of this world of ours, whether God has created life on other planets, how the universe was created, and so on, and so on. If I know enough to do justice, to be kind to others, to maintain a humble relationship with God, I don't need to know these other things . . . or quarrel with those who have their own differing opinions.

PRACTICALITY KNOCKS

In sum, then, I believe the peacemaking attitude of pluralism is commendable, but as a friend of mine says, "An open mind is like an open window . . . you need a screen to keep the bugs out." If we honor the truth wherever it is found and honor the glory wherever it is found, if we honor people especially when we disagree and can accept the fact that it's okay to not have all the answers, then the window is open. But how do we get the right screen? What standard do we use to reject some ideas as false and dangerous, and admit others as true and healthy?

If we were abstracted minds floating in ethereal zones of timelessness, perhaps we could have the luxury of debating this screening question for a few billion years. But we aren't. We're real people, with bills to pay and diapers to change and grades to earn and contracts to fulfill and conflicts to resolve. Every day is a once-in-a-lifetime possibility. Every day lived is one less to live. Every day we live by some faith, good or bad, strong or weak, growing or stagnant or deteriorating. We need some practical tools to help us sort through the messages of various religions. We need some screening tools.

Here are four screening tools I have applied in my search, with good effect.

1. *Does the belief make sense?* Does it possess internal intellectual integrity and coherence? Does it fit reality as I know it? As a system of belief, does it hold water? Can I believe it, not just as comforting or pleasant or helpful, but more, as probable, as convincing, as believable?

2. *Is the belief workable and livable?* If everyone on earth held this belief, would the results be good? Does the belief lead to health and life and hope, or would it lead to self-destruction and despair?

3. *Do I want to associate with the people who profess this belief?* Does the quality of their community life tend to authenticate or undermine their message? Does their belief produce good fruit in their lives as individuals and as a community? Here I don't expect perfection, but I do expect honesty, forgiveness, love, unselfishness, acceptance, vitality.

4. *If I affiliated with this group, would I feel comfortable bringing an interested friend to visit?* I expect a healthy faith to be contagious, so I expect that I will have friends who want to visit whatever faith community I am part of—if it is indeed nurturing a healthy faith in me. Would they, wherever they're coming from, be as welcome as I am there? Would I be ashamed to bring them there, knowing the experience there would be for them incomprehensible, unwelcoming, offensive, or irrelevant?

WHAT ABOUT THE ORIGINAL QUESTION?

Don't all religions lead to God? Well, I wouldn't put it past God to be able to get through to people in (or out of) any religion. In my experience (more on this later), God is amazingly merciful, so I wouldn't be shocked at all if God's mercy extends to surprising lengths, in unexpected directions, to people you never would have guessed. If, like me, you take the story of Jesus seriously, you can't be too quick to claim to have everything figured out; he said the prostitutes sometimes had a better shot at entering the kingdom of God than the priests did!

But even so, please don't let that lead you to this unwise—I would even say *tragic*—conclusion: "It doesn't matter what you believe." The pluralists are right, I think, to have an aversion to the concept of a narrow, exclusive god who enjoys fueling petty religious squabbles. But God would be right, I think, to expect people equipped with state-of-the-art brains to care about the truth, to use their minds, to do their best to face reality and respond to it. An "I don't care—whatever" attitude toward the choice of one's path through life hardly seems the right choice, don't you agree? Do you remember what we said in this regard about good faith ... that the best way, perhaps, to a *right* faith (i.e. a faith in line with the truth) would be via developing a *good* faith, since a good faith will, by definition, be humble enough to admit it is wrong and self-correct, and active enough to keep pursuing truth and learning, thus leading over time to an increasingly accurate, truth-reflecting faith?

As we considered in chapter 2, it is uncertain how much certainty we humans can attain, but it is pretty clear that we ought to aspire to all the truth we can. How much truth we can grasp, and how firmly we can grasp it, is unclear; it is clear that we should always be reaching, reaching, reaching.

So it matters which path you choose, and it matters how you pursue your chosen path. All paths aren't all the same. Although all will no doubt yield some truth, they can't all be equally true, and so it's no use living in denial about the necessity of making choices, sometimes hard choices. In these pluralistic times, we have more live options than ever before—which presents us with opportunity and responsibility. We'll need both open windows *and* good screens.

A DIAGRAM

The following diagram has helped me to respond to this question, "Don't all paths lead to the same God?"

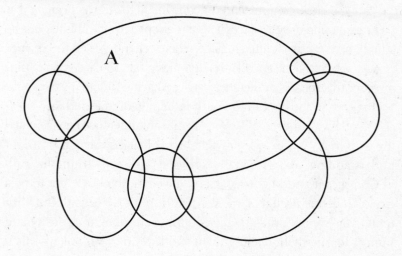

Imagine that Circle A represents the ultimately true religion, possessing all truth (and no falsehood) about God, life, the universe. If anybody claims to "have" this religion—in other words, if anybody claims to have captured the whole truth perfectly in his or her own mind—I think we are justified in laughing in his or her face. Whether he or she is proud or naive, either way, the laugh would be therapeutic.

Let the other five smaller circles represent various religions. One could be Buddhism, one Christianity, another Hinduism, and so forth. Or for that matter, each could be individual versions of one religion—the belief systems of five members from my church, or five Jewish rabbis, for example. (After all, no two of us has exactly the same religion.) As we would expect, each circle "covers" some truth, but not all, and each includes some misconceptions, misunderstandings, falsehood, and so forth. There is some overlap among them, but there are significant differences too. Clearly, each circle has something to teach and something to learn from all the others. In this light, instead of saying each religion is *equally valid,* we would be wiser to say that each religion has *real value,* conveying a viewpoint that can challenge and enrich the others and be challenged and enriched by the others.

Still, no circle comprehends or contains all the truth, meaning that no human mind or system sees it all and grasps it all. If this is the case—and it's hard for me to imagine any other scenario—then the essence of what we've called "good faith" becomes clear: To have good faith, I must see that there is a difference between having faith in my circle and having faith in the Big Circle, which is, admittedly, beyond me.

In other words, there is a very significant difference between having faith in *my religion* (i.e., my circle, my belief system, my current understanding) and faith in *God's religion* (i.e., God's truth, the truth as God sees it and knows it). Good faith has no choice but to be a circle, to define itself in some way, but it must do so with humility, tentativeness, openness to correction, even more, a curiosity and hunger for instruction and growth and learning. (Very likely, this is what Jesus was referring to when he spoke of our need to have the faith of a child.) It must not take itself too seriously. It must remain open to ongoing expansion, adjustment, and movement, so that it will become more and more "in sync" with the big circle of truth.

But how does one realign and redraw his circle? How does one bring it more in sync with God's truth, whatever that might be? How does one gather more data so as to enrich, adjust, move, and improve one's circle of understanding? The following chapters are intended to help answer that important question.

YOUR RESPONSE

1. I could/could not follow the critique of the pluralistic view which says, "All religions are equally true."
2. I affirm the following guiding principles for my spiritual search:

    Honor the truth wherever it is found.
    Honor the glory wherever it is found.
    It's okay to not know.

3. I affirm the following screening and affiliation tools from the chapter:

4. Here is my response to the "big circle" diagram:

RESOURCES

C. S. Lewis's wonderful children's stories, *The Chronicles of Narnia* (New York: HarperCollins), have much to offer to a spiritual seeker. The final volume, *The Last Battle*, depicts an interchange between the great lion Aslan and the follower of a patently bad religion that takes an unexpected turn. I highly recommend the whole series.

Steve Martin's film *Leap of Faith* explores similar territory.

PRAYER

God, far be it from me to judge people of other religions. I am not sure how you work in various religions, and how you evaluate each religion; that is beyond me, and I leave it to you. But I must evaluate the claims of the religious options open to me, and I must make choices. Please guide me in my choices, God. Don't let religion become a detour in my search for you, and in my desire to live in a way that pleases you. I don't want to trust in a religion instead of you, but rather, I want to trust in you and grow in my faith with the help of a religion, or better put, with your help through whatever religion is best for me. Again, please guide me, God. I don't want to lean on my own understanding.

PART 3

SPIRITUAL EXPERIENCE

CHAPTER 9 PREVIEW

How Might God Be Experienced?

This chapter introduces five of twelve ways in which people commonly experience God: ritual, nature, obedience, worship, and community. It includes a number of stories that illustrate each means of experiencing God.

WHO SHOULD READ THIS CHAPTER?

If you are interested in more than an intellectual approach to God, chapters 9 and 10 will be very important for you.

WHAT QUESTIONS DOES IT ADDRESS?

How can God be experienced through ritual? Why should we expect to find God through nature? How does doing what you don't necessarily want to do prove conducive to experiencing God? Why is worship more appropriate than analysis for experiencing God? Why is involvement with other people important in experiencing God?

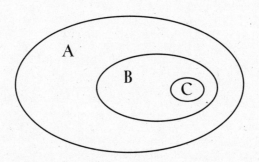

The birds ... became a key whereby I might unlock eternal things.

Roger Tory Peterson

—————

I say that this search for God was born not of reason but of an emotion because it was a search that arose not from my thought process—indeed, it was in direct opposition to my thinking—but from my heart. It was a feeling of dread, of loneliness, of forlornness in the midst of all that was alien to me; and it was a feeling of hope for someone's help.

Leo Tolstoy, *Confession*

—————

CHAPTER 9

How Might God Be Experienced?

Does God exist—one God, good and powerful and personal? Is God in any significant way "knowable"—not exhaustively, of course, but significantly, much in the sense a fellow human is knowable: able to be apprehended though not completely comprehended, touchable but not graspable? Is God really and truly "there" and yet not completely obvious, so that we must take some special effort to seek for God? If we have tentatively answered these questions affirmatively, then how might we best position, posture, or prepare ourselves to experience God, and how can we readjust our concepts of God to gain increasing alignment with what we learn of God? A survey of spirituality through history and around the world suggests to me at least twelve categories of answers, five of which are presented here in no particular order.

1. RITUAL

I'll begin here, because I've probably met more people who hate ritual than love it. I can't tell you how many times I've had people tell me they dropped out of the church or synagogue of their childhood because it was "just ritual." It's clear from their testimonies that ritual is never a foolproof means of experiencing God. But really, none of these means seem to be foolproof (and I'll resist any smart remarks about fools).

Yet I have met more than a few people who claim to have experienced God through ritual. They tell me that the familiarity and repetition of words or actions have become for them a kind of transparency, putting them in a frame of mind where the acts and words themselves become invisible, creating a "field" or "space" where God can somehow be experienced. In a similar way, perhaps, I find that when I really want to concentrate, if I put on familiar music or if I go sit in a fast-food restaurant with its familiar noises; in that unlikely setting, rather than being distracted, the act of shutting out the distractions helps me concentrate most fully. Perhaps in this way ritual creates space for solitude and reflection; one puts oneself in a place where a lot is going on—sights, sounds, candles, perhaps incense—but one is able to get beyond it and in that place concentrate on God.

Through, Not Just in Spite Of

That's not the whole picture though, because it is often through the ritual, not in spite of it, that people experience God. Take the Christian celebration of communion, for example. The ritual centers on eating a piece of bread and drinking a small sip of wine, while pondering the words of Jesus: "This is my body, broken for you . . . this cup is the New Covenant in my blood, which is shed for you for the remission of sins . . . as often as you do this, do it in remembrance of me." Isn't it possible that the act of eating and drinking, in a meditative frame of mind, can help one actually nourish himself or herself on God? Couldn't a person be helped in her experience of God by saying—with or without specific words—something like this? "God, I want to take you into my soul just as this food and drink come into my body? Just as the bread becomes part of my substance, and just as the wine carries its bittersweet heat down deep within me . . . I want you, God, to become part of my whole being."

Meanwhile, another person might also be experiencing God, along a line of thought like this: "God, Jesus said his blood was shed for the remission of sins. I think now of my sins, my wrongs, my lust the other day, that lie I told my coworker, the anger I had toward my wife, my hurriedness with my kids . . . Could it be,

God, that when Jesus shed that blood, he was feeling the ugliness and pain of these wrongs of mine, so they could be forgiven? God, just as I drink this wine, I drink in your forgiveness. . . ." And yet another might simply be saying, "I'm hungry for you, God. I'm thirsty for you. My soul is so empty. Fill me, God." Is it too hard to imagine how meaningful rituals like these could be means to experiencing God?

The Body, and Just Showing Up

Like communion, many rituals involve the body. Kneeling, fasting, feasting, bowing, singing, chanting, raising the hands, standing . . . no doubt they can be done in a perfunctory manner, in a way that helps little in experiencing God. But yet might these physical rituals also be undertaken in a way that says, "I'm not letting my body rule me right now. I'm not listening to my physical desire for a drink, my desire to take a walk, or my desire to fall asleep. I'm putting my will and my soul in charge of my body for this time, because I want my will and soul to reach toward God"? Even more—might certain movements of the body actually express and reinforce certain conditions of the soul, and of the spiritual relationship with God—as making love expresses and reinforces the love of husband and wife?

I suppose preaching could be seen as a ritual too. Few people remember much in the way of specifics after they hear a sermon (I say this with some sadness, as a preacher myself!). But perhaps that's okay. Perhaps just putting oneself in a quiet place, where the topic of conversation and contemplation is not just how to get rich, how to lose weight, or how to be more popular or successful, but rather where the topic is God and the spiritual life . . . perhaps just putting oneself in such a place puts one in a posture to experience God. Maybe it doesn't happen every week. Maybe it happens only one week a year. But most who have in any way experienced God would agree: The hope of that one "catch" makes all fifty-two "fishing trips" worthwhile.

Devotional Reading and Special Days

The same could be said for Bible reading, which is in a sense preaching to oneself, or letting the Bible preach itself to you. It is possible with the Bible, as with preaching, and as with any ritual, to become so preoccupied with the externals that one misses the deeper point, and in so doing, that one misses God. My grandmother used to say, in her wonderful Scottish brogue, that reading the Bible is like eating fish: Concentrate on enjoying the meat (the things that immediately speak to you) and put the bones (the things that make no sense to you right now) aside. Later on, if there's still time and you're still hungry, you can go back and work on the bones. Just taking the time to sit and read—or to join a Bible study class or discussion group—puts you in a place where God can be experienced.

The observance of holy days, sabbaths, and the like would also fit into this category. Again, setting aside one day in seven for the care of one's soul, for attending to one's search for God, for the nurturing of one's faith . . . that can't help but put a person in an appropriate posture for experiencing God. But then again, there's no guarantee. One can go to church or synagogue or mosque for all the wrong reasons. But if one goes for the right reasons, the ritual, the habit, the practice should increase the likelihood of one experiencing God. This is not, of course, because God is found in some buildings and on some days rather than others, but because we—if we don't take special care to set aside times and put ourselves in places where God is the priority—can forget to look and listen.

Ritual has a bad name. Perhaps we've forgotten how to enjoy it, how to profit by it. Perhaps we've never been instructed in how to profit by it, and so the ritual goes on without us. Perhaps we expect too much of it, that it will "work" too quickly, "deliver" too automatically, "function" in a foolproof way. But there, the real problem lies with our foolish expectations, doesn't it? I don't think we should give up on ritual. I don't think we should give up on any possible means of experiencing God.

2. NATURE

We've already spoken about seeing nature as creation, as a work of God, and therefore full of revelatory power about God. Nature is extremely important to me in my experience of God. But I must be honest. Nature is often like a ritual that is not working for me, sometimes saying little to me. Sometimes I take a walk in the woods and the flowers are just flowers to me, the dirt just dirt, the sky just sky, the wind just wind, my thoughts abuzz with worries like flies, or my mind and heart blank like white noise. Yet at other times, I feel that every bush has become a "burning bush," alive with the glory of God, that every breeze has a "still, small voice" speaking to me of God's presence and love, that running water and singing birds are God's voices to me of joy and comfort, that thunderheads shake me and bathe me and electrify me with the power and majesty of God. I make it my ritual to go into the woods and to walk by the streams often in hopes that, if I am open, today might be a day when each flower and leaf and bush are more than "just" anything, and like Moses in the old story, I'll realize that I'm on holy ground.

This experience of God through nature comes to me on many levels. There is an intellectual level. As I ponder the amazing intricacy of an organism, its perfect "fitness" for its environment, or the amazing ways the elements of an environment work together to make a self-sustaining system, I find myself saying, "God, what an amazing artist, engineer, scientist, inventor, and manager you are." The awe we feel when contemplating the intricacy of our own bodies (from our ability to leap and run, to the capacities of a strand of DNA) can be, in a real way, an experience of God. But there are dimensions that go beyond intellect too. One of the essential experiences of mysticism is an awareness of a glory hidden in all of creation, in every tree and blade of grass and speck of dust and grain of sand. That experience, I think, is an experience of the creator, coming through the medium of God's creation. (We'll return to this theme in chapter 15.)

3. OBEDIENCE/SELF-DENIAL

Oddly, saints and sages throughout history will tell us that God is often found through our doing things we don't want to do, or not doing things we want to do. We've already spoken of how fasting and other rituals (some call them spiritual disciplines, a more positive term, I think) can put one in a frame of mind and heart for experiencing God. But let's expand our understanding beyond things done in a religious service or holiday.

There are certain defining moments that can occur unexpectedly in our lives.

- A new coworker makes sexual advances toward you, and you are tempted to break your marriage vows, compromise your integrity, and put your whole family at risk through an affair.
- You are driving down the road, in a hurry because you're already late for an appointment, and you see a car broken down. Inside an old woman has her head leaning on the steering wheel, and it's clear she's crying.
- A relative has begun drinking too much, endangering his and others' safety when he drives and threatening to sabotage his marriage and career. Someone needs to speak sensitively but firmly to him about it, but everyone, including you, is too afraid. Or maybe the relative is you, and someone has just intervened and spoken to you, and you have a decision—to admit you have a problem and get help or to continue in your denial.
- Or maybe in each of the above situations, you made the wrong choice—and immediately after making it, another choice presents itself: to admit that you've failed and done the wrong thing, or to make excuses.

Choices, Wrong and Right

In these moments, we make choices. Too often, we'll all admit, we make the wrong choices. But people commonly agree that when they make the right choice (including the right choice of admitting our past wrong choices), a new experience of God often begins. There is a humility involved—realizing how vulnerable we are to doing wrong, to becoming bad people. There is also a kind of courage involved—to do the right thing even though our lust, our fear, our pride, our greed, or our laziness is crying out against it. Jesus said something fascinating in this regard. "If any person is willing to do God's will"—in other words, if a person wills to do what is right, even if it requires self-denial and personal sacrifice— "that person will know my teaching, whether it is from God." In another place, Jesus said that if a person loves and obeys him, he will disclose himself to that person, and God will "make his abode with him." Spiritual enlightenment in this way seems to follow doing what is right. Doing what is right doesn't earn enlightenment (as in "goods paid for services rendered"), but it rather becomes a medium of enlightenment, just as doing wrong would reinforce us in our "dis-enlightenment," plunging us deeper into experiences of alienation, guilt, and shame rather than experiences of God, goodness, and love.

4. WORSHIP/ART

I must put worship and art together, because in a real way, public worship is an experience of art, involving well-chosen words, music, architecture, perhaps sculpture, painting, film, drama, and dance as well. Sadly, too often public worship displays poor art, sloppy art, fake art—which may account for why many people find more distraction than help in their search for God at too many churches. But then again, often there's beauty, and sincerity, and best of all, in the best churches each attender is also a participant, helping make the music and say the words and use his or her gifts in the creation of something beautiful to celebrate the goodness of God.

I remember once being in Moedling, Austria, one of the places where Mozart lived. On a Sunday afternoon, my hosts took me for a walk there, a concert of Mozart's music was being held in the beautiful old medieval church there. We didn't have tickets, and we weren't dressed to enter anyway (it being a very formal event)— but I'll never forget the experience of standing outside and hearing the whole church vibrate with the grandeur of Mozart's choral music. There were dozens of violinists and singers making music inside, but from the outside, the whole church and all it contained seemed to be a single instrument filling the town with glory. It became a single, composite work of art—a multisensory, multi-media event of sight, sound, feeling. I thought, "This is what the church should be—an instrument vibrant with beauty and grandeur and glory."

The house of worship you attend may use Mozart and Bach on pipe organ, hymns on a piano, contemporary music with electric guitars and drums, or sitar or bagpipes or dijeridoo or the instruments and music of some other culture. The architecture may be gothic, Victorian, or Shaker—thatched roof or boabab tree—living room or school cafeteria. The liturgy (or format) may be ancient and formal or spontaneous and informal. But in just about every religious community, the experience of worship is intended at least to be an experience of beauty and glory. In that experience, you often can experience God.

Simple Prayers

Sometimes, the experience is very simple, and very subtle. I remember once, many years ago, when I was going through a time of real spiritual struggle. I was full of doubts and wondered if God was real at all. My father asked me to attend a prayer meeting at his church. Most of the men there (there were only men) were three times my age. I had long hair and a beard and was probably dressed in blue jeans and an old T-shirt; they were clean-cut, white-haired or bald, in suits and ties. They spoke with "thee's and thou's," a practice I never appreciated, and the tone of their prayers was somber, almost grave. It was an experience almost guaranteed to feel irrelevant to me. But

I experienced God with them that evening. "I am so full of doubts and confusion about you," I remember praying silently, "but these men are so sure of you, and that is where I need to be tonight . . . around some people with a simple, proven faith who are surer of you than I am at this moment." The simple piety of their prayers became for me a work of art that carried me closer to God.

Other times, the experience of God in worship and prayer can be much more dramatic. A few weeks ago, for example, I was in Sydney, Australia, at a conference for mission leaders. Each day, a gifted woman named Jennifer sat at the piano and led us in songs of praise and worship. Jennifer works in inner-city Chicago, so many of her chosen songs were old Negro spirituals or more contemporary gospel songs. There were contemporary choruses too, and some old hymns. On the last day, as she led us and we sang and clapped and pondered the words of the songs, I felt overwhelmed with the presence of God. Tears streamed down my face for over an hour as we sang and praised God. Some of you know exactly what I'm talking about, but this book is really for the benefit of those who don't . . . so I'd like to try to explain.

A Spiritual Reunion

Imagine a person whom you love a great deal—a friend, a spouse, a parent—but someone from whom you are frequently separated, or perhaps someone who has died. If that person whom you miss so deeply suddenly, unexpectedly appeared in front of you, you would no doubt embrace with unbridled enthusiasm and speak fervent words of your love . . . and perhaps cry too, for joy. Well, that's something of what I felt that day during a time of worship. God, whom I love but from whom I always feel some degree of distance simply because God is invisible (among other reasons), suddenly felt so near and real. It was as if God were standing right beside me, or even closer . . . right inside me . . . or even bigger, so I was right inside God . . . and I felt embraced, contained, filled, saturated by God and God's love.

I suppose if I experienced this constantly, I would eventually grow used to it, and it would become a normal level of bliss or ecstasy for my daily living. In one way, that would be wonderful, but in another way, there is something equally wonderful about the comings and goings of these experiences. The times of absence make the times of "reunion" all the more precious; I can't help but feel I would take God more for granted if it weren't for the feelings of absence at times—followed by these wonderful experiences of God's presence. (Similarly, if you lived in an art gallery every waking moment, wouldn't the paintings become mere furniture after a while, no more meaningful to you at any given moment than the calendar or whiteboard on your wall right now?)

Another Way of Knowing

In our society, the way we think we really come to know something is to doubt it, to question and test it, to dissect it (requiring us first to kill it), to analyze it by breaking it into smaller and smaller pieces—pieces that are smaller than we are, pieces we can control and feel we can explain. We will never know God this way, and I think you can see why without me trying to explain. The very opposite approach would be more appropriate, don't you agree? . . . to trust God, not doubt; to see God as big and whole, not in disintegrated pieces; to submit to God's superiority, not to try to feel (absurdly) superior ourselves; to recognize that we are fully understood by God, not to pretend that we ourselves fully understand . . . in short, to worship God.

Obviously, skepticism, analysis, dissection, and testing have their place. They are the tools of many trades, absolutely appropriate in the domain of shoppers, engineers, reporters, laboratory technicians, voters, and the like. But sometimes our tools take control of us, and they start using us rather than us using them. So far, we know of only one Being superior to ourselves (excluding angels, and assuming we believe in God), and it's hard to resist requiring God to climb on our microscope slides or testing apparatus as we require of nearly everything else. It's hard for us to even imagine "knowing" anything through any other means than critical analysis. Except when we fall in love. And perhaps that is how worship can best be defined: looking toward God with our hearts ready to be caught up in the thrill of love.

That is why, no doubt, many of us experience God in worship more predictably and intensely than through any other means. As we sing and think about God's goodness, as we hear that goodness expressed through the well-chosen words of sermons and prayers and readings, and as it is celebrated through dance and drama and music and other art forms, we sense a Presence drawing near us. In the experience of that Presence, we feel reunited not only with God, but also with one another in a new way. That brings us to the next means of experiencing God.

5. COMMUNITY

Those who seek for God generally agree that God is often found in other people, and more specifically, in the experience of loving and being loved by other people.

It hardly makes sense to try to describe this avenue of spiritual experience without telling some stories. Let me begin with an experience I shared with about 40,000 other pastors in 1996 in Atlanta, Georgia. A Christian organization sponsored the largest gathering of clergy in American history, and I must admit, I had mixed feelings about going. I have been to a lot of big events of this sort, and I often feel at least mildly uncomfortable with the hype. The first two days of the event, I struggled with those mixed feelings. The messages seemed to me okay, but on the whole hardly worthy of the expense and effort and opportunity of an event like this. The times of worship and singing were extraordinary, of course, as you would expect, with 40,000 voices filling the indoor stadium. The hype came at various times, with some speakers eager to "make an impact" and trying a bit too hard for my taste.

But on the last day of the event, two themes came out. The first theme had to do with reconciliation among denominations, and the second, with reconciliation among races. Representatives of North

American native peoples, Hispanics, African Americans, Caucasians, and Asians all spoke of their desire to break down the walls, and experience true unity and brotherhood in God's love; all expressed true sorrow for their own versions of racism and isolation. What happened that day is hard to describe. There were tears, there were embraces, there were cheers, there was repentance. It felt like a baptism of love. I kept thinking of Jesus' words: "Where two or three of you gather in my name, I am there in your midst." I also thought of the beautiful Jewish poem in the Old Testament: "Behold, how good and how pleasant it is when brothers dwell together in unity. . . . There the Lord commands the blessing." I felt I was witnessing a beauty that probably would not be written up in the history books—but that probably had been seen few times in history. In some way that I am sure I am failing to convey, God was made real there, and in that experience of mass-community, we experienced God.

FRIDAY NIGHT DINNER

I should balance that story with something more intimate and personal. I can go back to an incident several years ago. Two of our good friends at church showed up unexpectedly at our door one evening. They sat on our couch in an uncomfortable silence. Finally the husband broke the silence, as the wife cried quietly. A trauma had hit their lives and their marriage, a very personal trauma, and they had been bearing it alone. "We can't keep this from our friends any longer. We feel like hypocrites covering this up. We need your help and support."

Over the next few days, they spoke to two other couples, and a week or so later, on a Friday night, the eight of us, plus all of our kids, had dinner together at our home. We talked some, we prayed some, but mostly we were just together. And we kept getting together, every Friday night, for about a year. No agenda, just to be together because two of our friends were suffering in a difficult time and needed to not suffer alone. There were no great epiphanies, but I think all of us look back on those Friday nights and think, "God was in that. We experienced God in those times. We experienced God in our friendship."

Sometimes, often really, it's not as neat and sweet as that. I think of a situation in my church more recently, where somebody hurt somebody else's feelings, and told somebody else still, who took up the offense, and pretty soon a dozen people were mad at one another. I felt like I had taken my kids fishing and they had gotten their lines tangled in dozens of knots. In recent weeks, slowly people have been talking, seeing where they were wrong . . . seeing where they believed the worst instead of the best . . . hearing the other person's side of the story and seeing that they were doing the best they could, knowing what they knew . . . and forgiving one another. And again, although it's messy, although nobody would choose to schedule experiences like this, it's often through these ugly and difficult times that forgiveness flows, and love is deepened, God seems present in a very real way—in community.

I think of many experiences where individuals or couples have come to me in my office, to discuss some personal problem or confess some sin or seek guidance in some way, and I had no idea what to say or do to help them. But as I listened and tried to simply be there with love in my heart, open to God like a window open to a breeze, there was this sense, by now a familiar sense, that we were not alone, and that the two or three of us had someone Else in our midst. I can't imagine how impoverished my experience of God would be if not for these experiences of community.

YOUR RESPONSE

Go ahead and read chapter 10. Questions, resources, and prayer are combined for these two chapters.

CHAPTER 10 PREVIEW

How Else Might God Be Experienced?

This chapter completes a survey of twelve ways people commonly experience God: suffering, compassion, life-change, prayer, solitude, repentance, and joy.

WHO SHOULD READ THIS CHAPTER?

As in chapter 9, this chapter will be of special interest to people who want more than a conceptual approach to God and faith.

WHAT QUESTIONS DOES IT ADDRESS?

Does spiritual experience strengthen faith, or is it the other way around? Suffering drives some people away from faith—how can it strengthen the faith of others? How does it feel to experience God through serving others compassionately? Why do people with life-controlling problems often turn to and experience God? Would an answered prayer offer complete proof for God's existence? Why is solitude helpful for spiritual seekers? What is the relationship between repentance and spiritual experience? Why is joy a common doorway into the experience of God?

God wishes to be seen, and he wishes to be sought, and he wishes to be expected, and he wishes to be trusted.

JULIAN OF NORWICH, *JULIAN OF NORWICH: SHOWINGS*

Now faith is the assurance of things hoped for, the conviction of things not seen. . . . [W]hoever would draw near to God must believe that he exists and that he rewards those who seek him.

HEBREWS 11:1, 6 RSV

"For I know the plans I have for you," declares the LORD, "plans to prosper you and not to harm you, plans to give you hope and a future. Then you will call upon me and come and pray to me, and I will listen to you. You will seek me and find me when you seek me with all your heart. I will be found by you," declares the LORD.

JEREMIAH 29:11–14

CHAPTER 10

How Else Might God Be Experienced?

Which comes first, the spiritual experience or faith? Does faith create the spiritual experience, or does the experience create the faith? There's a parallel pattern seen in marital counseling, where many men tend to feel that sexual activity creates a feeling of intimacy, while many of their wives tend to feel that sexual activity expresses or celebrates or results from a feeling of intimacy that is already there, created through nonsexual means—conversation, tenderness, consideration. Imagine a husband and wife who just had an argument, and now they have resolved it. The husband, wanting to strengthen their bond, gets a sparkle in his eye suggestive of sex—which is, at that moment, the very last thing on his wife's mind. An argument ensues: Does sex create intimacy, or the other way around?

Of course, they both are right. Sex can both create and express intimacy. Similarly, spiritual experiences can create and strengthen faith, and yet they require some measure of preexisting faith to occur. So these categories of spiritual experience shouldn't be seen as formulaic prescriptions to achieve faith, as in, "engineer these experiences and faith will follow." You could as accurately try to guarantee that sex will engineer intimacy. Understand that the relationship between spiritual experiences and faith is more complex than a simple, linear cause and effect.

6. SUFFERING

In suffering, people often feel abandoned by God. They cry and pray for relief, and relief doesn't come, and the questions just echo . . . why? why now? why me? why him or her? For many people, it's suffering that drives them to atheism or agnosticism.

Yet to be fair, there are many others who say the opposite. I think of an older woman who told me this story. She had a heart disease and pneumonia, and she was in the hospital. One night, she was having great difficulty breathing, and the thought hit her for the first time: I may die before daybreak tomorrow. At first, she felt a panic, which only made her more desperate for breath and threatened to throw her into a frenzy that could perhaps kill her. "I've got to calm down," she told herself. "What can I do?" And then the thought came to her, "I'll pray." And as she prayed, she told me a peace came over her—a peace she had never experienced before. The fear of dying left her. She eventually drifted off to sleep, and each time she awoke, she asked herself, "Is the peace still there?" And each time, it was. "Brian," she told me, "I've always heard people tell stories like this, but I never experienced anything like it myself. But since that night, I've known that God is real—real in a way I never imagined I could know."

One of the benefits of finding a faith community (as we'll consider more deeply in a later chapter) is that you surround yourself with people who have stories like this to tell. And one of the benefits of continuing to search for God in the midst of suffering (rather than assuming God has abandoned you) is that eventually you will have some stories of your own.

Opposite Responses

As I said, though, sometimes suffering drives people from faith. My friend Larry Culp edits a newsletter called *Network*. It links the community of adult sufferers of cystic fibrosis (CF), of which Larry is a member. He devoted a recent issue (April 1997) to religion and CF, and the essays it contained conveyed powerfully the variety of responses to this horrible disease. Consider this collage of quotes from that issue (CF Network, Inc., P. O. Box 204, Dublin, PA 18917–0204):

> I had always believed in God and then my health began to seriously deteriorate. . . . When I finally had to receive a liver transplant, I had had enough and was through with God. . . . I was very ill and though I prayed every day to get better, I only got worse. . . . I was appalled and seriously pissed at God. . . . Everyone always says that I should thank God that I am alive, and part of me wants to. But the other part of me thanks myself, and the people who love me, for wanting to fight to get better.
>
> JENNIFER, 21

> Today I am not bitter, but at peace with having CF. Through my suffering, I've been able to grow and contemplate life in ways many people my age have not. . . . My mind and eyes have been opened to God's glory through my struggles with CF. I have been blessed.
>
> CAROLYN, 23

> I had cystic fibrosis and I was gonna have to learn to deal with it. Maybe that's when I started to think in terms of the *physical* world, for lack of a better term, as being the only world that I would live in. . . . I majored in biology. . . . I took these teachings as my new "religion," having learned to have faith in the scientific method. The "miracle" of life, which some say is God's gift, now seemed nothing more to me than a complicated set of chemical reactions. Very complex, surely . . . but requiring the Hand of God? I saw no such need for such hocus-pocus. . . . I do not feel the need for a grand master plan put forth by some omnipotent being, nor do I feel that there is such a

being watching over us every day, acknowledging us and our prayers. I don't believe any more.

KENNETH, 39

...The door slammed shut and I was in the dark again. I don't have the key anymore ... and I will never trust in God again. I will never pray again either because I prayed ... every day and my prayers were never answered.... I try and take each day as they come, along with the pain and loneliness, but I know that only time can heal that, and not God.

JENNIFER, 22

As I read these powerful and poignant stories for the first time, I wondered how Larry himself was dealing with his illness and integrating it with his faith. Editing all these intensely personal essays must have only intensified his own struggles, I thought. Then I came upon his own piece near the end of the newsletter:

I have been through most of these dark, emotional places, places familiar to many who have CF. Even today, it's easy to regress.... My faith teaches me to look *in* and to look *out*. To look *in* at what's wrong with me, and to look *out* to serve others. This is against my typical proclivity to look *out* at what's wrong with others, and look *in* to serve myself.... I don't know why God allows horrible things to happen in this world.... In my own small way, I can do my part to make sure I'm not part of the world's problems, but part of the solution.... I try not to allow CF to color my view of God, but try to allow God to color my view of CF.... I don't know where I'd be without God in my life.

LARRY, 37

The same variety of responses to life, paradoxically, is present among those who are healthy, rich, free, privileged, advantaged. It's odd. Like Larry, there's a lot I have no idea how to explain. And like Larry, I make no editorial comment at all on those whose suffering has driven them from faith, or faith from them. All I can say is "God bless them all," and hope, like Larry, that I can somehow be part of the solution wherever I can, including being of some help or comfort or encouragement to these dear people.

7. COMPASSION

The suffering of others can indeed pose even greater challenges to faith than our own suffering. But when we leverage ourselves into the situation in the right way, even the suffering of others can open for us experiences of God, especially as we are taken up into being part of the solution to their suffering. In our anger or frustration, we might pray, "God, why do you allow this? Why don't you do something?" And at that moment, God has every reason to say something like this to us: "I *have* done something: I've placed you in the situation with a compassionate heart and the ability to help. Now you can become an expression of my concern." Obviously, few of us ever hear these kinds of messages directly from God, and most often, we only realize the significance of our involvement in retrospect.

Where Was God?

A friend of mine has been deeply troubled by history's atrocities—Hitler, Pol Pot, abortion, the Plague, and so forth. His conclusion: If God exists, God must be dispassionate, incapable of feeling any compassion, uncaring, apathetic. Someday I want to explore this thought with him: Might my friend's own compassion, his outrage, his deep feeling itself be a reflection of the care of God? In other words, if God were dispassionate, how could God create beings with compassion? Perhaps at least a partial answer to the question, "Where was God during the Holocaust?" is this: God was and is in every person feeling compassion and outrage. If no one felt any compassion or any outrage, then we would have reason to believe in a dispassionate God. And perhaps the answer goes even further: God was in those being tortured, mistreated, killed—suffering and dying with them. Perhaps this will help my friend. Probably not. Probably there is no answer to make this problem more tolerable; probably our best response is not to try to devise an intellectual system that accounts for suffering, but rather to feel the outrage and compassion and be driven by them to action.

Sometimes we see God in the caring faces of those who care for the suffering. Sometimes we see God in the agonized faces of those who suffer themselves. Jesus alluded to this kind of experience when he told the parable about the naked and homeless, the destitute, the imprisoned criminals, the shut-ins with chronic diseases who had been visited by his followers. To those who had shown compassion in various ways to their needy neighbors, God says, "As you have done it to the least of these, you have done it to me." In other words, we can experience God *in us* as we show compassion, and we can also experience God *in the person who receives our compassion.*

A Lone Shoe on a Sheet of Ice

This must sound very mysterious and theoretical, but it is really quite poignant and down-to-earth in experience. I remember one morning my wife and I were driving in our neighborhood. It was a cold winter morning, and on a side street something unusual caught my eye as I drove past. It was a single shoe on a patch of ice in the middle of the road. I took a second glance and saw on one corner a young boy near tears, and on the other corner, an old man, legs splayed on the sidewalk, lying there in bare feet! We stopped, turned around, and got out of our car. It was a pathetic sight in this typical suburban neighborhood. The gentleman, African, unable to speak English, was reaching out to us with both hands, terror in his eyes, speaking a mile a minute. On the other corner, the boy, his grandson as it turned out, was screaming, "Please help us. Please help us."

The boy explained: "This is my grandfather. He is from Ethiopia. He just arrived yesterday. He has never been in the cold before. He wanted to walk me to school and then he fell on the ice. He is not used to walking in shoes, and he never before saw ice. His shoes fell off when he fell and he says he can't walk, and I think I'm already late for school. . . ." We got the boy in the front seat, and gingerly helped the old man into the backseat. It was clear his leg was broken badly. He was in a lot of pain.

We took the boy to school and then took the man to his son's home. His daughter-in-law, an immigrant whose English was quite good, came out, and the three of us got him inside. We made sure she knew how to get him to a hospital, and as we left, the man— his face full of a mixture of pain and relief—wouldn't stop talking to us, obviously thanking us although we couldn't understand his words. The whole episode took less than fifteen minutes, but it brought with it an experience of God that lingered for days—and that is with me now as I retell it.

It hits me on multiple levels. On one level, I think, "Here was a man who was in real need. People kept driving by, and he was cold and afraid, and it seemed that no one cared. But God cared about him, and God made sure Grace and I came along, noticed him, and helped him. What a privilege to be instruments of God's love, agents of God's compassion!" On another level, I think, "God, you were in that old man in need. When I came to him, I found you there. In showing love for that man, in simply being his neighbor, I was given the privilege of finding you in a new way, in a new place . . . and even more, I was given the honor of in some small way showing love for you."

True, it's possible to experience "compassion fatigue," where we become so overwhelmed by the needs and suffering of others that we lose any sense of God in the middle of it all. But it's also true that some of the most poignant experiences of God come in these very situations. As we do good to others, we find God is there, with us, even in us.

8. LIFE-CHANGE

Have you ever attended an Alcoholics Anonymous (AA) meeting, or any similar meeting (NA, CDA, and so on)? You'll better understand this means of experiencing God powerfully if you attend a few meetings with a friend in recovery some time soon. At nearly every meeting you'll hear a true story from someone whose life had gone out of control due to some form of addiction. This person realized that he was completely powerless over his addiction, and eventually reached "bottom," a point where he despaired of his own ability to change his own unmanageable life through his own willpower. At that bottom point, he reached out to God—a Higher Power outside of himself of whom he admittedly had little understanding—and in the days, weeks, and months that followed, he found that this outside power was restoring him to sanity. Over time, he learned more about this power. For example, he learned that God was morally good and that part of God's healing process involved not only release from addiction, but release from moral anarchy; the person will tell you about how he engaged in a searching moral inventory, identifying his wrongs and seeking, wherever possible, to make amends to those he had hurt.

He also learned that this Higher Power cared about others, and so he began to dedicate himself to carrying the message of a caring, restoring God to others in similar pain. In addition, he learned that he would very easily relapse unless he sought to maintain constant conscious contact with God through prayer and meditation, and to practice moral discipline in all of his daily affairs.

Story after story you will hear, and even though the room might be filled with cigarette smoke, and four-letter words will likely be as common as "amens" and "hallelujahs" are at church, you will sense the presence of God. At least I know I have.

The Only Idiots

I'll not forget my first AA meeting. Before entering ministry, I was a college English teacher. I taught at a small college in Washington, D.C., for a while, and one day, I arrived at the school only to find the lights off and no one there. My first thought was, "Is this the day when the clocks are changed? Am I here an hour early?" But it wasn't the last week of October, so I was still mystified. I walked down to the office, and I knew something was strange when I saw the coordinator's door open . . . and one of my colleagues (not the coordinator) seated in her chair with his feet on her desk. He motioned for me to come in and laughed: "So you and I are the only idiots who didn't know that classes were canceled today." We discussed the fact that everyone else had, apparently, been notified that there would be no classes that day due to some major renovations in the building. I got ready to go home. Then Bill said, "Hey Brian, can I ask you a personal question?"

Bill, I should tell you, had a Ph.D. in philosophy and was a very bright, very cynical atheist who had been ribbing me somewhat good-naturedly ever since he found out I was a committed Christian. So I wasn't surprised when he asked, "What's a nice guy like you doing in a disgusting religion like Christianity?" I laughed and said, "What kind of question is that to hit me with at 8:00 on a Monday morning?" Then this cynical guy seemed to get tears in his eyes.

"Brian," he said, "can we talk for a minute?" I nodded, and then there was a pause, then this: "You know me. You know I have a real problem with this God thing. Well—and you're the first person I've told this to—two weeks ago I admitted that I have an alcohol problem, and I've been sober for two weeks—the longest period of sobriety I've had since I was about thirteen. When I got here about a half hour ago, I was terrified. I thought—oh no, I have a whole day on my hands with nothing to do—and I felt the urge to go out and drink. AA keeps telling me about this Higher Power bit, but I don't buy it yet. But then I prayed anyway, and right after that, you walk in the door. Kind of spooky, huh?"

We went out to breakfast, and he told me his story, and we hung out together until the day's first AA meeting in the area, which I attended with him. Both of us felt we had experienced God in a real way, in the process of Bill's life-change.

9. PRAYER/INTERVENTION

Bill's answered prayer was definitely an experience of God for him—even though he wasn't sure whether he even believed in God or prayer yet! And I can tell you so many stories from my own life where I have felt the direct intervention of God—plus, as a pastor, I am in contact with hundreds of people each with dozens of stories of their own. Put together, those stories are pretty compelling evidence for God's existence and involvement in our lives. I have to admit, though, that the stories have a problematic edge to them.

Take, for example, the story of Tim Dyer, who lives in Tasmania, Australia. Once, he and his wife were traveling from Melbourne to Sydney for a conference. They had left their children with friends in Melbourne and were traveling in a friend's car. It's a long drive, so they left at about 5:00 A.M., and most if not all of the passengers were soon asleep. At about 7:00 A.M., the driver fell asleep at the wheel, and the car flew off the road at a high speed and flipped end over end down a steep hill. It landed—almost as if placed there by a huge hand—upside down in a gully, the gully just being deep enough so that the cab of the car was not crushed. Other drivers saw the accident and jumped out, assuming the worst because they couldn't see the cab-sized gully beneath the car below them. Nobody even tried to come down to the wreck, because it looked obvious that no one could survive such a crash. The car appeared flattened to them.

Meanwhile, the passengers were all hanging upside down in their seat belts, and one by one, they managed to unlatch themselves, fall to the ceiling, and crawl out the broken windows. Imagine everyone's surprise when every one of them, driver included, emerged with no broken bones, no serious injuries, just bruises and scratches.

A Dream and a Prayer

Three weeks later, Tim and his wife were back in Tasmania and they got a letter from a good friend, a woman living in India. She wrote because three weeks earlier she had had a terrible dream of her friends being in an accident. The dream was so alarming that it awoke her from a sound sleep at 4:00 A.M., and she felt compelled to get out of bed, get on her knees, and pray for her friends' safety. The next morning, she thought there must not have been anything to the dream because the car in her dream was bright red (and she knew their car wasn't red) and because the children weren't present (and this couple was seldom separated from their kids). She was just writing to make sure they were okay.

Imagine Tim's surprise when he realized, yes, the car they had been in was bright red, and that, accounting for the time difference, their friend had awakened at exactly the same time as their accident. A remarkable story (and, I assure you, a true one from a credible person, not some superstitious kook who likes to tell exaggerated or fabricated tales). But, of course, the story raises a lot of questions. What about all the accidents where cars don't conveniently find life saving gullies to land in? Did God care less for those people? And wouldn't have God saved these people if no one had prayed? Why give this woman this dream? What role did her prayer have in the whole thing?

I tell the story—and include the problematic edges—because I think that prayer, whether answered or unanswered, isn't as simple a subject as many of us preachers make it appear to be. Prayer certainly doesn't work like a scientific experiment that can be repeatedly validated under controlled conditions. But having said that, if you're ever on the receiving end of one of these miraculous "coincidences," you have this strong feeling that, problematic issues notwithstanding, you have experienced God. Many of you know what I mean.

10. SOLITUDE

It's funny about solitude—for introverted people, solitude feels like a vacation, but for the more extroverted, it feels like a punishment, as in solitary confinement. But extroverts and introverts alike will agree that there is something to be said for getting away from other people for extended periods of time—half a day, a day, a weekend, a week, even more—to have a time where the only companionship available for your soul is the presence of God.

One value of solitude is seen in the beautiful parable about the lost (or prodigal) son, told by Jesus and recorded in Luke 15. A runaway boy squanders his wealth on wine, women, and parties. When he has spent all his money, not surprisingly he finds he has also lost his popularity. Destitute, he gets a job feeding pigs (a deplorable job for a good Jewish boy). And nobody will talk to him. It is in that forced solitude, the story goes, that the boy "comes to himself." And this coming to oneself then opens him to the possibility of coming home to his father and his true home.

Recollecting My Ghost Images

Solitude has a similar value for me. In my busyness, in my many roles, in the context of many demands and projects and goals, it is easy to lose touch with myself. And when I am out of touch with myself, it's hard—perhaps impossible—to get in touch with God. Why? Because there's no solid "me" to bring into contact with God. I'm a composite of ghost images, like an out-of-focus TV. But in solitude, I recollect all of these out-of-sync selves and we are reconstituted into a more solid me . . . and that reconstituted me is the person who can "come home" to God.

Again, I don't want to raise unrealistic hopes. There are times when I try to draw away for solitude, and rather than having a great experience of God, my mind is filled with more confusion and turmoil, or I am plagued by worry or lust (hardly a great spiritual experience) or a feeling of spiritual dullness in which God's absence rather than presence feels accentuated.

The Spiritual Side of Fishing

It seems strangely fitting to me, in this regard, that many of the first followers of Jesus were fishermen. I am an avid fisherman myself, and this whole search for God has many similarities to fishing. In my office hangs a framed picture given me a few years back by my staff members (who know how I spend my days off), which contains this quote in beautiful calligraphy: "The charm of fishing is that it is the pursuit of what is elusive but attainable—a perpetual series of occasions for hope." And I suppose that is how it is with solitude and the other means of experiencing God we are considering. One can put oneself in the right place in the right frame of mind, and then one must wait, but not passively—rather, actively, as a fisherman waits with his line in the water, or as a farmer waits after he has planted his crops—leaving the outcome to God. That's where faith comes in . . . believing that there will be a tug on the line or that the fields will come to life and in time bear a harvest.

11. REPENTANCE/GRACE

Repentance is an essential part of the coming to oneself that is in turn an essential part of solitude. And it is in the context of repentance that many people find their initial experience of God. Repentance literally means to give something a second thought, to think again, to see life and oneself in a new light, to turn a corner, to "do a 180." Repentance is like exercise or dieting in some ways: Just about everybody needs it, but it is amazingly easy to avoid.

If someone else comes to you telling you that you need to repent, there's a good chance you'll react defensively: "Who are you to judge me? You have plenty of faults of your own. I'm not so bad. Why focus on my few faults and ignore the many good things about me? There are plenty of worse people than me for you to pick on!"

But there are times in life when nobody has to tell us—we're telling ourselves: "I haven't got this right. I don't like what I'm becoming. There's something wrong in the way I'm living. And it's not just outward behaviors either; those outward behaviors are fueled by something inside me . . . and that's where the problem is. Something deep within me is broken, sick; it needs to be fixed, healed." We might have specific data to deal with, telling us we're broken inside—another broken relationship, another broken marriage, another broken promise, another broken dream. Or we might just have this nagging feeling of guilt, a sense that we've taken the easy way, the path of least resistance . . . that we've gone with the flow and in some way lost our souls in the process.

Humble Beginnings

That kind of reflection—where we see ourselves and think again about what direction we want to take in the future, sure that it is a very different direction than we've taken so far—often puts us in a frame of heart and mind where we experience God. Why is this? Here's my guess: At those moments where we freely admit our wrongs, we are as close as we ever get to being truly humble. At those moments there is a response that comes from God, a personal response so natural and strong that it can't be stopped, like a hand instantly reaching out to a companion who falls, or like a mother's instinctive turn when she hears her child's cry. The words the theologians use for this pure, spontaneous response is "grace"—amazing grace.

Grace is what a father feels (and a son receives) when he catches his son doing something wrong, and the boy (instead of defending himself or blaming his little brother or making an excuse or telling a pathetic lie to cover it up) bursts into tears and says, "I'm sorry." Punishment seems unnecessary; a stern word even seems out of place. The father takes the boy in his arms and simply says, "It's okay. I love you."

When we experience the grace of God in this way, it can be one of life's most significant events.

12. JOY

Sometimes the search for God is activated by peak experiences of joy. My contemporaries might remember a gravely-voiced musician from the 60s named Barry McGuire, best known for his hit "Eve of Destruction" and his work with The New Christy Minstrels. One summer, I played backup guitar for another musician (Scott Wesley Brown), and I was fortunate enough to be Barry's trailer-mate at a large outdoor music festival. I'll never forget a story Barry used to tell in his concerts. . . .

One of his nonmusical jobs was working on a fishing boat out of a little town called San Pedro, California. One day, after a long day of fishing, a school of dolphins swam up alongside the boat. Barry leaned over and admired their beauty through the clear Pacific water as they swam just beneath the surface, keeping pace with the boat. One dolphin in particular seemed to look up at him. Barry felt this crazy impulse, this wild urge to somehow make contact with the animal. But how? Almost without thinking, he grabbed a towel from the deck, tied a knot in the end, and leaned over the edge of the boat. The next time the dolphin surfaced, Barry swung the towel and whacked the dolphin playfully. To his surprise, the dolphin seemed to like the game, and for the next several minutes, Barry was laughing and "yahooing" and whacking dolphins, as more and more surfaced and seemed to playfully imply, "Hit me! Me too!" The play lasted for some time, and then the school moved away from the boat.

A Gift

In the silent moments that followed, as the exhilaration calmed to a peaceful contentment, Barry says he felt something . . . a sense that this experience was a gift, a gift from his creator . . . and he felt in the experience of joy a certain call, a homeward call, a call toward God. The great scholar and writer C. S. Lewis described similar experiences in his autobiography, *Surprised by Joy.* In each pure experience of joy was a hint of something more, a call to find an even greater joy, a joy of the spirit, a joy of being connected to God. My friend Michael Kelly Blanchard expresses it well in one of his songs, called, "Thanks Be to God." As life's pleasures and joys come our way, the sense that there is someone to thank is, in a real way, an experience of God. These experiences really are a gift, and if a gift, then there must be a giver.

Who do you thank at the gate of the dawn as the hounds of the
   night back away?
Who do you thank for the morning's new song, sung by birds
   as they play?
Who do you thank for the sermon of sun
Preaching the hope of a new day begun,
Testifying that love's light has won?
Who do you thank for this kingdom come?
. . . . Who do you thank for this mural of life,
the savor of senses sharp as a knife,
the privilege of poignant, the honor of right?
Who do you thank for delight? . . .
Who do you thank for the treasure of home, wrapped in the
   real of routine,
The blessing of knowing your own flesh and bone, and watch-
   ing them wake from your dream?
Who do you thank for the structure of souls,
tied to each other from infant to old,
beauty so human, so holy to hold?
Who do you thank for such gold?

"MERCY IN THE MAZE"

After completing his interviews and research for a fascinating
book on prayer, radio host Larry King (a self-described agnostic who
doesn't [yet, at least] "sign my name to God's starting roster") was
surprised to feel the same nudge toward gratitude that Blanchard so
beautifully celebrated in his song. King recalls a conversation with
the rabbi who had been his advisor in the writing project:

> "I can't give up on you, Larry, I'm a rabbi. . . . I can't
> make you pray, Larry. Nobody can do that. The answer's
> right in front of you. It's right inside you. But it's something
> you have to want to find. I can only point the way. In the
> end, you must take the final steps of the journey alone."

. . . I watched his black yarmulke disappear into the morning crowd. When I could see him no longer, I headed in the opposite direction, toward Central Park South. As I crossed the street it occurred to me that I didn't have to be anywhere for another hour, so I decided to meander. . . . Today I made a point of looking at the city with fresh eyes, listening to the sounds of the street and smelling the fresh spring air. At Columbus Circle, waiting to cross into Central Park, I remember saying quietly, "Thank you." I suppose it was for the blessings of being alive, finally having a fabulous wife, feeling wonderful, being surrounded by a vibrant, vital city—all of that. I can't honestly say to whom that "thank you" was directed, but I know I wasn't talking to myself. (Larry King, *Powerful Prayers*, 1998)

A small step perhaps, but a step of faith nonetheless.

THIS LIST IS INCOMPLETE

We've considered a number of means by which God might be experienced by us. Please don't try to make this an exhaustive list. The whole point is that there is not just one or just two or even just twelve ways in which God might speak to us, make contact with us, become experience-able by us. Perhaps you've heard the story about Saint Augustine, before he was anything close to being a saint. He was a womanizer, a partier, with little concern for God or morality. One day, outside his window some children were playing. They had a little chant they said as part of their games: "Take and read, take and read." It seemed to Augustine that God was speaking to him through those children . . . to take up a copy of the Bible and read it. He did, and he experienced God. Which category in our list would that experience fit under?

God seems to be amazingly creative in finding ways to connect with us. For me, a few words of a conversation sometimes have struck me with the force of revelation, or a scene in a movie seemed to be "meant" for me at that time, or the line of a song, or even the music itself, seemed to be inspired for me in a particular life situation. And so at unexpected moments, these serendipitous experiences of God come, as C. S. Lewis said, by surprise. Perhaps the experience of God is far more common than we had realized, but we have been numb to it, wrapped up in this or that trivial pursuit. What a tragedy to go through life never waking up to the possibility of experiencing God!

One of my favorite quotes comes from George MacDonald. He said, "The Spirit of God lies all about the spirit of man like a mighty sea, ready to rush in at the smallest chink in the walls that shut Him out from His own, walls which even the tone of a violin or the smell of a rose is sometimes enough to rend."

A WISE RABBI

I remember hearing the story of an old Jewish rabbi who was approached by a young agnostic. "I can't see God anywhere," the young man explained. "Can you help me?" "I don't think so," the old rabbi answered, "because I can't identify with your problem. You see, I can't *not* see God." And of course, in this way, simply by sharing his experience, the old rabbi did help the young man. Perhaps when we're old, and when we're farther along on our search, and when our eyes are better trained, we'll be like the old rabbi. And perhaps we'll be able to remember what it was like before we had experienced God, so that we can understand those who are as we used to be.

So, how might God be experienced? We have considered many ways. Which ways have you explored? If all of them are new to you, which ones should be your starting points?

YOUR RESPONSE

1. I have experienced God in the following ways. . . .

2. I am interested in further pursuing the following ways of experiencing God in the future:

3. Here is how I plan to pursue these ways of experiencing God:

RESOURCES

Two books by Roman Catholic Henri Nouwen might be helpful: *Life of the Beloved: Spiritual Living in a Secular World* (New York: Crossroad, 1996) and *The Return of the Prodigal Son* (New York: Doubleday, 1994).

Greek Orthodox Archbishop Anthony Bloom has written a very helpful book, *Beginning to Pray* (New Jersey: Paulist Press, 1970).

As for the profound subject of experiencing God in pain and suffering, five writers stand out. C. S. Lewis's *The Problem of Pain* (New York: Macmillan, 1962) has helped thousands, including me. Peter Kreeft's *Making Sense Out of Suffering* (Ann Arbor: Servant, 1986) builds on Lewis's more philosophical work, and to a degree personalizes it. Philip Yancey's *Where Is God When It Hurts* (Grand Rapids: Zondervan, 1977) and *Disappointment with God* (Grand Rapids: Zondervan, 1988) are also excellent. Many have criticized Rabbi Harold Kushner's *When Bad Things Happen to Good People* (New York: Avon, 1981) for theological imprecision, but on a popular level, it has also helped thousands. And Joni Eareckson Tada's books, beginning with her autobiography *Joni* (Grand Rapids: Zondervan, 1976), speak from the vantage point of a woman who has suffered the pains and deprivations of being a quadriplegic. You also might want to find Amy Grant's song, "Somewhere Down the Road" too, on *Behind the Eyes* (A & M records, 1997); in 5 minutes and 9 seconds, it says a lot and says it well.

Those with a background or interest in psychology and counseling might benefit from the writings of H. Scott Peck, or Paul Tournier (whose books are hard to find, but are worth the search). Tournier's integration of hard science (he was a medical doctor before becoming a counselor), social science (psychology and psychiatry), and spirituality is rich, and has helped me greatly. See, if you can find it, *The Adventure of Living* (trans. by

Edwin Hudson, New York: Harper & Row, 1965. Check www.interloc.com for help in finding out-of-print books).

As for artistic explorations of the experience of God, the films *The Color Purple* and *Chariots of Fire* depict dramatic and poignant experiences, as do the wonderful ramblings of Garrison Keillor (in his enchanting Lake Wobegon books and tapes). As a preacher, I'd have to say that Keillor's stories are better at simply conveying grace than 90 percent (maybe even 100) of the sermons I have preached.

Why not listen to Bach or Mozart, or Handel's *Messiah*—not just as a student of their music, but as a seeker for God? A trip to the art gallery in this spirit could also be very productive. I wish you could catch the spiritual zest of my friend Bob Jackson's paintings, which flow from a faith-enriched vision of life. Or perhaps there are cathedrals, chapels, or other structures designed for people of faith nearby for you to visit, to see how the art of architects can help you in your spiritual quest.

PRAYER

God, thank you for the ways in which I feel I have experienced you or some aspect of you (grace, love, beauty, justice, purity) already in my life. It is not enough to say that I am open to experiencing more of you; I desire that experience . . . I am hungry and thirsty for it. Like a child asking a parent for food and drink, protection and love, I ask you to reveal yourself to me, and to help me to truly experience you. I can not trump up or manufacture this, God. I can only ask you to help me.

I would like to tell you, God, what I currently understand you to be like. (Continue on your own, using the adjectives that you believe are descriptive to God. You can simply say, "I believe you are . . . .") I am sure all of my understandings are partial; I ask you to deepen my understanding of you. If any of my understandings are wrong or misguided, please guide me and redirect my thinking. I want to have an accurate understanding of you, and a closer and closer relationship with you.

CHAPTER 11 PREVIEW

Can God Be Experienced Through Doubt?

This chapter looks at times when faith is stretched or shaken as necessary steps in the development of a mature faith, and offers a perspective for seeing even doubt as a channel for more deeply relating to God.

WHO SHOULD READ THIS CHAPTER?

This chapter should be especially helpful to people whose faith is being undermined because of emotional or physical pain, or who simply don't "feel" close to God.

WHAT QUESTIONS DOES IT ADDRESS?

What is the difference between doubting "against" and "with" God? Why does anger at God actually reveal a level of faith and commitment to God?

I stretch lame hands of faith, and grope,
And gather dust and chaff, and call
To what I feel is Lord of all,
And faintly trust the larger hope. . . .
There lives more faith in honest doubt,
Believe me, than in half the creeds. . . .
That which we dare invoke to bless;
Our dearest faith; our ghastliest doubt;
He, They, One, All; within, without;
The Power in darkness whom we guess—
. . . . No, like a child in doubt and fear;
But that blind clamor made me wise;
Then was I as a child that cries,
But, crying, knows his father near;
And what I am beheld again
What is, and no man understands;
And out of darkness came the hands
That reach through nature, molding men.

ALFRED, LORD TENNYSON, "IN MEMORIUM"

CHAPTER 11

Can God Be Experienced Through Doubt?

We've been talking about many "positive" ways of experiencing God, but there's another side to the story—a side we may be more familiar with than we wish. The great mystics through history tell us of "dark nights of the soul," of the "absence of God," of spiritual dryness and depression, of times of anger with God, of the experience of spiritual abandonment—where God feels distant, silent, nonexistent to the very person who once felt so near, so secure, so sure in his relationship with God. It is surprising to me that these great spiritual leaders have these experiences. I don't know whether to feel encouraged (that I have these experiences in common with them) or depressed (that there is, apparently, no escaping them). What is even more surprising to me, and wholly more encouraging, is this: That these spiritual pioneers tell us that in the end, these "negative" spiritual experiences have drawn them closer to God and strengthened their faith.

I used to feel very worried—even guilty—about the episodes of doubt or spiritual depression that came my way. Gradually now, I'm starting to realize what the great mystics of the past knew: God can be experienced through doubt and other spiritual "diseases." So, I am learning more and more to doubt *with* God, instead of *against* God. Let me explain this important distinction by telling a story.

DOUBTING WITH GOD

Paul was one of my best friends growing up. We were adventurous boys and rowdy teenagers together—and we both became committed Christians during the same time period too. We got married the same weekend and stood in one another's weddings (his wedding was on Saturday, mine on Sunday, which delayed his honeymoon—so his was the greater sacrifice by far!). We had kids around the same times, and both of us had children with some serious health problems: A few years before my third child was diagnosed with cancer, Paul's oldest child needed open heart surgery.

I remember visiting Paul and Josh in the ICU after surgery. Paul was bent over the bed, his face just a few inches from Josh's face. Josh was hooked up to all kinds of technology via tubes and wires. Josh was crying, groaning, screaming with a hoarse voice—his chest hurt so bad. And as I came closer, I could see what else Josh was doing: He was pounding on his father's chest. His fists were pounding out a message his little mind couldn't yet articulate: "You're my father! You're supposed to protect me! You're not protecting me! This is your fault! I'm in pain! I'm angry at you! I hate you! I think you must hate me to put me in this hospital and subject me to this pain! You're a bad father! I must punish you! I don't trust you anymore! I don't love you anymore!"

EMPATHY FOR GOD

Poor Paul. I can only imagine what he must have felt. Driving home, I felt empathy for Paul, an empathy that would be intensified a few years later as I had to hold down my crying, writhing son while he got spinal taps and bone marrow tests as part of cancer treatment. But that day, driving home, I not only felt empathy for Paul, I also felt sorry for God, if I can put it that way.

I saw how my doubts are often much like Josh's little fists—trying to express my pain, my rage, my terror, at being in situations I don't want to be in, difficulties I can't understand, predicaments I can't solve. And there God is, loving me so much that he draws even closer so I can hit him all the harder . . . because he understands that's what I need to do. I read the book of Job in the Old Testament, and I think of Josh and Paul there in the ICU. These are stories of doubt, but also of faith, don't you agree?

FAITH IN A FIST

So I am learning also to see faith in Josh's fists. After all, he doesn't lash out at the nurses. He doesn't cry to the doctors. He doesn't punch the nurse's aids. He doesn't expect anything of them. It's his very connection to his father that makes him express his furious doubts to him. It's his very love for his father that forces him to say, through his fists, "I hate you." And, I am learning, it is my faith in God that forces me to sometimes doubt him.

They say that the opposite of love isn't hate; it is rather indifference. And I have to think that the same is true of faith. Doubt isn't a spiritual danger sign nearly as much as indifference would be.

DOUBTING MY FAITH VERSUS DOUBTING GOD

There's something else I have learned. Doubting my faith isn't the same as doubting God. My faith is my own creation—a worldview, a paradigm, a map for life, a set of guiding principles—that I am assembling and reassembling from what I read, who I know and respect, what I experience, and so forth. My faith isn't perfect, and it isn't static. It is guaranteed by my finitude to be incomplete, inaccurate in many places, out of proportion, in need of continuing midcourse corrections. Therefore, it deserves to be doubted at times—doubted so it can be corrected (as the "big circle" diagram illustrated in chapter 8). If I didn't doubt my faith, I would protect it, not correct it; defend it, not amend it.

So I'm learning that when I doubt my faith, I don't have to doubt God. In fact, doubting my faith can be an opportunity for increased faith in God. A proverb in the Old Testament says as much: "Trust in the Lord with all your heart. Do not lean on your own understanding. In all your ways, acknowledge him, and he will direct your path." As we saw in chapter 8, there is a difference—subtle but very significant—between having faith in my faith (i.e., faith in my intellectual concepts about God—another way of saying "leaning on my own understanding") and having faith in God. There is a corresponding difference between doubting my faith and doubting God.

When I doubt my faith (in other words, my own understanding of God, life, the universe, etc.), when I can't lean on it because I'm not sure it will hold my full weight, then I can paradoxically more fully lean on God with my whole heart. At those times, my prayers sound like this: "God, I don't understand anything very clearly right now, including you. My certainty and confidence levels are low. But I still believe you are good—better than my best flawed understanding of you. So I am reaching out to you, calling out to you, asking you for your help, in the middle of my doubts. I feel like I'm walking in the dark, and I don't want to stumble or wander from the good path. Guide me in the path, Lord. Direct me."

HELD IN A GRASP STRONGER THAN OUR OWN

Those kinds of prayers don't feel very full of faith. They feel desperate, weak, pitiful. But I wonder, from God's perspective, if they aren't the expressions of the greatest faith of all ... like a person hanging over a cliff, holding on to a saving hand, who reaches a point of saying, "I can't hold on anymore. I am trusting you to hold me. It's your grip on me, not my grip on you, that will rescue me. It's all up to you." Can you see the faith in those words? You might say, "It's an unrealistic situation, though. I've never been hanging from a cliff." But, of course, you have. Part of being human, it seems, is the awareness that we are hanging over a precipice, susceptible to the horrible gravity of despair or greed, lust or laziness, ambition or addiction, hedonism or nihilism. (For a vivid description of this experience of hanging in space, see Tolstoy's dream in the final pages of his *Confession* [New York: Norton, 1983].) In our times of strength and confidence, we say, "I can save myself." There's no faith in that, really. It's only when we feel utterly incapable of saving ourselves that faith becomes relevant. (Of course, "relevant" is a gross understatement at those times.) We hate those times of weakness, but I can see why life would be engineered to bring us to them; without them, we might never learn what faith is at all. Someone has said that you never know if your faith is real until it's all you have left.

OLD FRIEND IN A NEW WAY

Several years ago, I had a falling out with a very good friend and coworker in the church. We represented two different forces in the church, and those forces were in tension, and so our friendship nearly snapped under the strain. We were still committed to one another, because in principle, as Christians, we believe in reconciliation. But our relationship didn't seem much like a friendship anymore, and it was more a source of discomfort to both of us than of pleasure.

A few days ago, we met for breakfast. Even though we have been somewhat awkward with each other, we have tried to keep getting together—not nearly every week, as years ago, but every few months, just out of commitment to our belief in reconciliation, just out of stubborn refusal to let go and call the relationship over forever. Our breakfast the other day was one such meeting. But it was different. Somehow, we felt that we had both gotten beyond our differences, and this time, instead of feeling it was hard work to keep the conversation going, laughter flowed, and vulnerability flowed, and we found ourselves asking for one another's advice and prayers and help. We dropped our empty coffee cups and bagel crumbs in the trash can and left that little restaurant as old friends again . . . old friends in a new, deeper way.

When I got in the car, I didn't know whether to laugh or cry. I actually cheered. I praised God for this reconciliation, and thanked God for this friend. And now, as I write, I realize anew that our relationships with God go through similar phases sometimes. We aren't comfortable with each other. The conversation doesn't flow as well. We aren't sure we can trust as before—or we aren't sure we can be trusted as before.

At those tough times, I've learned that there is a lot to be said for just hanging in there. For keeping on going to church. For saying your prayers. For keeping the communication lines open. For sustaining your relationship on pure, stubborn commitment when all the warm feelings of affection seem gone forever. That kind of willpower, I am learning, is one of the purest forms of faith—a kind of faith you just don't develop until you are forced to, when your relationship with God seems to have gone bad. Sometimes, faith means believing that doubt is just a stage, a rotten mood that will pass, and that in time, by the grace of God, you'll get over it, and be old friends again in a new, deeper way.

YOUR RESPONSE

1. In what ways do I currently doubt *against* God?

2. In what ways do I currently doubt *with* God?

3. Write a plan for dealing with times of spiritual struggle:

PRAYER

There are times, God, when I struggle in my faith. I may even become angry at you at times. It is childish, but I sometimes feel I need someone to blame for things I do not like, and you become the target for my anger. Help me not to become trapped in my anger. Thank you for the freedom to be honest about it. Thank you for being like an understanding parent to whom I can open my heart. I believe, but when I doubt, help me doubt with you and not against you, God.

PART 4

HELP FOR THE SPIRITUAL
SEARCH

CHAPTER 12 PREVIEW

Why Is Church the Last Place I Think of for Help in My Spiritual Search?

This chapter frankly acknowledges some of the difficulties in connecting with a church (or other faith community) for help on the spiritual journey. It suggests that there are three types of churches: Type 1 for "finders" or insiders only, Type 2 for "seekers" or the unconvinced only, and Type 3 for both "seekers" and the already-convinced. Finally, it suggests ten ways to get the most out of church.

WHO SHOULD READ THIS CHAPTER?

If you feel intimidated by or alienated from the church, this chapter is especially for you.

WHAT QUESTIONS DOES IT ADDRESS?

Why should I consider connecting with a church, and what kind should I look for? How can I get the most out of church?

Two are better than one, because they have a good return for their work: If one falls down, his friend can help him up. But pity the man who falls and has no one to help him up! Also, if two lie down together, they will keep warm. But how can one keep warm alone? Though one may be overpowered, two can defend themselves. A cord of three strands is not quickly broken.

ECCLESIASTES 4:9–12

And let us consider how we may spur one another on toward love and good deeds. Let us not give up meeting together, as some are in the habit of doing, but let us encourage one another. . . .

HEBREWS 10:24–25

No scientist could deny the importance of working within the conviviality and tradition of a community, from which he or she has learned the tacit skills of research through an implicit apprenticeship and to whose judgment the mature work is to be submitted for approbation or correction.... Those who speak of our being in a "post—modern" era frequently cite as one of its characteristics the recognition that community plays an important role in constituting our being.... These considerations provide a contemporary setting hospitable to the idea that ... the Church ... should find a place....

JOHN POLKINGHORNE, *THE FAITH OF A PHYSICIST*

Because of piety's penchant for taking itself too seriously, theology—more than literary, humanistic, and scientific studies—does well to nurture a modest, unguarded sense of comedy. Some comic sensibility is required to keep in due proportion the pompous pretensions of the study of divinity. . . . This comes from glimpsing the incongruity of humans thinking about God. . . . The most enjoyable of all subjects has to be God, because God is the source of all joy. God has the first and last laugh. The least articulate of all disciplines [theology] deserves something in between.

THOMAS C. ODEN, *THE LIVING GOD*

Postmoderns are not less interested in religion than ever before. Indeed, they are exploring new religious experiences like never before. The church has simply given them a less interesting religion than ever before.

LEONARD SWEET, *QUANTUM SPIRITUALITY:
A POSTMODERN APOLOGETIC*

CHAPTER 12

Why Is Church the Last Place I Think of for Help in My Spiritual Search?

Philip Yancey tells the story of a woman, a prostitute in Chicago, who found herself in "wretched straits, homeless, sick, unable to buy food for her two-year-old daughter." She came to a friend of Philip's:

> I could hardly bear hearing her sordid story. . . . At last I asked if she had ever thought of going to a church for help. I will never forget the look of pure, naïve shock that crossed her face. "Church!" she cried. "Why would I ever go there? I was already feeling terrible about myself. They'd just make me feel worse." (*What's So Amazing About Grace*, Grand Rapids: Zondervan, 1997, p. 11)

As a pastor, of course, I wince to hear these words, but I know she was right. Millions of people stay away from churches every week because they know that many if not most churches will more likely set them back than help them progress in their spiritual journey. Many of us are doing what we can to change that situation, but the fact remains: Church is often the last place people think of for help in their search for faith.

CHURCH NAMES

You can learn a lot about churches by studying their names. (In this chapter, let me use church to mean any house of worship . . . synagogue, mosque, temple.) For example, I was driving through the coastal plain of North Carolina a few days back and saw this huge sign, in a script reminiscent of the fireworks signs you also see in that part of the country: "Victry and Holiness Church of Our Lord Jesus Christ." The VAHCOOLJC church building itself appeared to be a converted Texaco station with a really bad paint job (white paint here, red paint there, all peeling, so you couldn't tell which came first). There were a few heroic plastic geraniums scraggling in oil drum planters (painted white) on the concrete islands where gas pumps once stood. It looked like the old garage was now the sanctuary, with the old office area serving as fellow-ship hall and Sunday school classroom. I assumed the rest rooms were still rest rooms.

The juxtaposition of the huge "Victry and Holiness" sign and the dwarfed, peeling, ramshackle Texaco station could probably become a metaphor for not just the VAHCOOLJC, but for every church of every denomination in every place. Because every com-munity of faith—whether First Baptist, Fourth Presbyterian, Saints Andrew and Peter Roman Catholic, Beth Shalom Synagogue, or Fire Baptized Pentecostal Holiness Tabernacle—has high ideals and ethereal aspirations that make its actual accomplishments look by comparison like . . . a run-down North Carolina gas station.

We all sneer at churches for how poorly they do in contrast to their high ideals. Love God? They can't even paint. Love one another? They can't even get together to plant real geraniums. Spread a saving message to the world? They can't even spell "victory." And we can go on and on—about how they spend money on cathedrals and neglect the poor, about the shameful way they treat homosexu-als, about their racism and sexism, about the terrible way they for-got Uncle Bart when he was so sick and nobody even called or came to visit, and above all, about their bad taste in interior design. Sure, they have a few redeeming features. I'll bet you could get one heck of a potluck dinner at VAHCOOLJC, for example. And if you have to die, there's probably nobody better than the VAHCOOLJC choir to sing "Amazing Grace" at your funeral. But in spite of these small virtues, most of us find it easy to sneer at churches.

ENOUGH SNEERING!

Until you do what I did, that is. I got sick of myself and my friends sneering about churches, so we got together and started one. And guess what we found out? It's a whole lot harder than it looks. It's hard to raise money, and to get the musicians to show up on time, and to keep the Sunday school teachers getting along, and to remember to turn on the air-conditioning an hour early so the room is cool when everyone arrives (for hell hath no fury like overheated worshipers), and to keep the hand-clappers and the non-clappers from launching their own inquisitions against one another, complete with fiery tortures and heroic deaths. And if you succeed in doing those things—necessary things, if you want to have a church—you're run so ragged that it's hard to remember why you started the thing in the first place!

Here's what you find out: You find out that the higher our aspirations, the grander our ideals, the more sincerely we dream great dreams ... the more paltry and pathetic our actual best accomplishments seem, grimy with old Texaco grease, faded like fake, sun-bleached geraniums.

THE OTHER SIDE

And here's what else you find out: As paltry and pathetic as we seem, at least we try! At least we don't give up and live for the next sale at Kmart or Nordstrom's! At least we keep the dreams alive! At least we try to get together, and get along, and grow in faith, and love each other, and honor God—even if it means we have to use the old Texaco toilets and sit on cold folding chairs! So, I salute the VAH-COOLJC! At least your sign stands big and bold! At least you hold your dreams! At least someone tried to spruce up that old shot Texaco station! At least someone had some vision! At least someone thought about and cared about victory and holiness, as opposed to mediocrity and sleaze! I'd rather attend your grimy geraniumed garage than a beautifully landscaped country club with this sign out front: "Gathering of Comfortable, Apathetic People Who Stopped Dreaming and Growing and Who Feel Good Enough Just as We Are, Thank You."

WHY YOU SHOULD FIND A CHURCH

That's why, in spite of the notable failures of all our churches, I think you should find a community of faith if you are a sincere spiritual seeker. You are developing some spiritual dreams and aspirations of your own now, and you should band together with others who share them. Sure, you'll have to put up with a lot. (And if you're human like the rest of us, you'll give other folks some things to put up with too!) But perhaps that's one of God's tricks in the church. Just staying involved humbles us and teaches us patience, and those are good things for spiritual seekers to learn.

Now when I say this, some of you are probably thinking, "Wait. I'm not ready for this yet. I'm not even sure what I believe. You must be assuming I'm farther along than I really am." No, I mean what I say, and I make no assumptions about where you are, as long as you are a sincere spiritual seeker. But I understand your concern. There are some kinds of churches that aren't ready for you, and you aren't ready for them either. That's why I recommend you find a community of faith that is a "Type 3."

TYPE 1 GROUPS

Type 1 groups are what we could call "finders only." The only people welcome there are people who already believe, who already agree, who already have found whatever it is that the current members have found. If you come in, not already agreeing, not already believing, you'll be like a blue-jeaned and T-shirted teenager who shows up at a ritzy black-tie dinner party (or even worse, a middle-aged, tuxedo-clad, Bach-loving gentleman who shows up at a teenage bash). You—and everyone already assembled—will immediately know that you don't belong.

Type 1 churches are not bad, but they may be bad for you. How do you know if a house of worship is Type 1? Sometimes the name will tell you. If you can't figure out what the sign out front (or the ad in the Yellow Pages) means, it could be a sign that this place isn't right for you. (Sometimes, though, the sign out front hasn't changed, but the people inside have, and they will provide a warmer welcome for you than you might expect.) Better still, talk to someone who attends there. Ask, "Is this the kind of place that a person who doesn't already agree or believe will be welcome? Are you user-friendly for spiritual seekers?" People are surprisingly honest about this sort of question, and very often, rather than invite you into a disaster at their own church, they will graciously refer you elsewhere.

TYPE 2 GROUPS

Maybe you thought that all churches are Type 1, but fortunately, that is not the case. There are also Type 2 churches, which we could call "seekers only" churches. Type 2 faith communities are filled with people who are spiritual seekers of a sort. They would never sport a bumper sticker on their car that said, "I Found It!" or "Jesus is the Way!" or "Pray the Rosary!" or "Read the Koran!" or "Eat Kosher!" Type 2 churches attract the kind of people who are turned off by that kind of Type 1 dogmatism.

That is the strength of Type 2 churches—that anyone is welcome: atheist, agnostic, pantheist, monotheist, convinced, unconvinced. They are generally great places to go for intelligent discussion, freedom from dogma, open dialogue. But that can sometimes be their weakness too. If you are a spiritual seeker and you find something—if you begin to develop a more defined commitment to something or Someone specific, you may find yourself increasingly out of sync with a Type 2 faith community. The whole idea of these places is to be open to any ideas, and so any kind of significant closure and commitment can seem as unwelcome as the lack thereof would seem in a Type 1 group. In fact, Type 2 groups tend to attract people who have been burned in Type 1 groups. As such, they allow participants to keep up the social rhythms of church life—gatherings, music (even potluck dinners!), discussion on topics of ethics and spirituality and social justice—without the encroachment of anything too dogmatic.

Concerns

A Type 2 place would probably be more comfortable for you than a Type 1, but my main concern about a Type 2 is that it can easily turn your search into a destination. It can turn you from a seeker who is trying to find something to a seeker who is subtly pressured not to find anything. My additional concern with Type 2 groups is that you may not find much help there. If you're looking for a place to talk, to air your questions and frustrations, to dialogue, you'll probably find that. But if you're looking for people who have themselves found something, people who have something going on in their lives beyond what you already have . . . by definition, they may be hard to find. Even if they're there, they may be hesitant to talk openly about what they've found, because Type 2 churches generally aren't about finding. That's certainly not always the case. Some of the best-read and clearest-thinking people I've met belong to these kinds of faith communities. But the seek-and-don't-find problem is still worth monitoring.

TYPE 3 GROUPS

Type 3 groups, or "seeker-finder" groups, have the advantages of Type 2 churches—an accepting environment for people who don't already agree with their beliefs, morality, and so forth. They understand part of their mission as being there to help people like you in your search, and often they are very fluent in the language of your questions, doubts, objections, concerns, fears, hopes, and aspirations as a spiritual seeker. After all, many of them have just come down the same path you have as a sincere spiritual seeker.

Type 3 groups also have the advantages of Type 1 groups. Advantages? Yes, there are some. The challenge of explaining those advantages is one of my most difficult tasks in writing this book—difficult because I must use two despised words: tradition and dogma. I must try to convince you that tradition and dogma are not the same things as restriction and dogmatism. Here goes. . . .

Imagine You're God

Let's imagine for a minute that you are God (silly, I know, but play along with me). And let's imagine that you (God) care a great deal about a sincere spiritual seeker by the name of _____(insert your name here). And let's imagine that you care no less for this spiritual seeker than you have for millions of others through the years. Let's imagine that your care is fatherly, motherly, which entails two things: first, that you don't have favorites, that you don't love one more than another qualitatively or quantitatively; and second, that you want your children not only to love you, but also to love one another.

In other words, imagine that your goal as God is not just to have individual, exclusive relationships with each of your children, but also that each of your children will have relationships with his or her siblings. Your goal is not to have a large number of isolated client relationships, but rather to have one interactive family relationship.

Let's imagine some of the reasons for desiring each seeker to be part of a larger family or community. First, since you (as God) are so much greater than each of your individual children, and since they are so limited, no one of them can know more than a sliver of you. But if they each share their unique perspectives, all can gain a broader experience of you. Not only that—but they'll have a lot of fun together too.

Furthermore, there are many people in the family who have been seeking much longer than the new seeker. They would be equipped to help him find answers to many of his questions. They would also know better than the new seeker the spiritual pitfalls that all spiritual seekers face over time (and there are, as you probably have already found out, pitfalls aplenty). These more experienced family members would thus have much to teach the new seeker.

Now, still imagining you are God, you would have another concern. There are many spiritual realities that the new seeker has no idea of. He has no language for them, no experience of them. Take, for example, humility. The new seeker may know about humiliation, or self-effacement, or poor self-esteem ... none of which have anything in common with true humility as a spiritual virtue. Or take, for example, spiritual love, or charity. The new seeker may know about erotic love, friendship, affection, or team spirit, but spiritual love (which sees a stranger, or even an enemy, with the same tenderness as a lover) is a reality he only has the faintest concept of, if even that. He may have Ph.D.'s in biochemistry, awards in sales, credentials in CPR, and trophies in long-distance running, but in humility and charity he is a kindergartner, no, an infant.

And to make matters worse, he doesn't know how little he knows. He hears the words and thinks he knows, but he is ignorant even of his ignorance. If you are God, what do you do for him? He doesn't even have the language to learn what you want him to know. Might you want to put him into a community of people, into this family, which has been learning and preserving these virtues of humility and charity for centuries, so that he can see them demonstrated in real people, so he can see what he doesn't know and then begin to learn?

Now, still imagining you are God, let's extend the community even farther. What about the people who were part of this family a hundred years ago, a thousand years ago, and more? Would you want the wisdom and experiences of the past to be forgotten with each generation, or would you want them to be preserved in the family and passed on from generation to generation? In other words, would you want the new seeker to learn not only the lessons of his contemporaries, but also the accumulated wisdom of his forerunners through the centuries? Wouldn't the family history be important for him to learn and be a part of, for his benefit and also so that he can pass it on to the new seekers of tomorrow?

One more imagining: What if, through the centuries, the family has had some problems, some arguments? What if they developed misconceptions of you (as God) at times, imbalances, distorted images? And not only that, what if they developed some bad spiritual habits along with good ones at times, bad habits that needed to be corrected and avoided in the future? Wouldn't you want each new seeker to gain the benefit of the lessons learned from the mistakes of those who have gone before? Wouldn't you want him to know the skeletons in the family closet as well as the stories of the heroes and explorers?

A New Definition of Tradition and Dogma

Well, those accumulated stories, lessons, conclusions, embarrassments, celebrations, and memories are known as tradition and dogma. I know they have a bad name, and no doubt, it is one of the family embarrassments that people like me (pastors, preachers) have given them a bad name. You hear the words, and because of many people like me, you think: dogmatic, exclusive, unwilling to listen or dialogue, rigid, harsh, backward, outdated, arbitrary. But it doesn't have to be that way. To enter into the stories and lessons and heritage of a faith community can be exhilarating, exciting, liberating, educating.

Learning Math

Think about other things you have learned. Remember learning math? I remember the most terrible mistake I made in my math education: I got sick for two weeks with bronchitis when the class learned negative numbers. All of my education, I was taught, "You can't subtract a larger number from a smaller number." It was drilled into my head. But then, I was absent for two weeks, and when I came back, kids were at the blackboard, squeaky chalk in hand, breaking the rules—and the teacher didn't seem upset at all. It drove me crazy! Who was lying, the old teachers or the new one? Who changed the rules?

Eventually, my outrage calmed down. I realized that I had been given a provisional rule ("You can't subtract a larger number from a smaller one") that had been appropriate for a beginner like me, but the fact that I had obeyed it, as well as the other elementary rules, now meant that I was ready to graduate to a new set of rules. (Then came the letters. Why are they putting x's and y's in with those numbers? Then came the Greek letters. What are those S's and Q's doing here?)

No Independent Study

If the teachers had just given me a book and sent me off for "independent study," I couldn't have learned these new concepts on my own. For English, for social studies, I could do it on my own, but for math, I needed the teachers. Like my fellow students, at first, with each new concept, I didn't get it. I just did the problems, followed the instructions, listened to the explanations, blank-faced, brain-dead. It was all rote, memory, mechanical imitation, devoid of "getting it." But then, one by one, the concepts became my own; the lights came on. I "got them."

That's the real goal of tradition and dogma: not to impose a bunch of meaningless rules on you, not to oppress you or make you feel stupid, not to put you through meaningless exercises or assign "busywork" to keep you out of trouble, but to help you learn. The goal is for you to get it for yourself, so the lights will one day come on, so you can do work of your own: Balance your own checkbook (negative numbers come in very handy there), figure out how much carpet to buy for your living room (how do you convert to square yards again?), build a bridge, design a spaceship to explore Mars.

A similar analogy could be made to learning music or painting or football. To learn, you must enter the tradition (Bach, Rembrandt, Vince Lombardi). You must master the dogma (key and time signatures, perspective, offensive strategy). You must associate with those who know more than you (music teachers, art teachers, coaches). The goal is not that you become a clone, but that you become a creative participant in the tradition—playing and composing and creating with your own style, contributing, receiving, and giving. You associate with the teachers and other students so that you can learn, know what they know, become like them, maybe even teach others someday, passing on the tradition and dogma yourself.

Tragic Failure

Sadly, many teachers of faith are even worse than the worst teachers of math, piano, painting, sports. How many kids hate math, despise piano, avoid art, have humiliating memories of sports because of those obnoxious "teachers" who should have been doing something else? The failure of religious educators is all the more tragic because the subject is so much more important. That's why (getting back to our main point) I think it's worth the effort to find the right community of faith. And that's why I think a well-led Type 3 group is the best to go for.

The search for God is in many ways a solitary search, but it cannot remain solitary. There comes a time to put down the books (including this one) and return from the lonely trail in the forest and meet the family, join the class, meet the teachers, join the community, learn the stories and lessons, past and present.

Where to Look

The greatest downside of Type 3 faith communities is their rarity. You can find them in nearly all denominations. (I won't say all, because some groups are firmly committed to a Type 1 or 2 approach.) I'm glad to say that the number of Type 3 groups seems to be increasing. It is less a matter of the label on the front of the building and more a matter of the leadership (and hence the mission) of the individual community. But the problem remains: How do you find the Type 3 group that is right for you?

Here's a suggestion. Of all the people you know, think of the two or three whom you respect the most. Call, write, or e-mail them, and explain to them: "I've begun some spiritual searching, and I'm looking for a group that will help me in my search. Do you have any recommendations?" It might take some research. It might take several visits that are "no-go's." You might become so desperate that you'll even pray and ask God to help you find the right group. (On second thought, don't wait until you're that desperate. . . .)

WARNINGS

I can't go further without offering you some warnings. Although I believe you need a community of faith for your spiritual search to be authentic and effective, some churches will hurt your search more than they will help it. For example, some churches work like pyramid schemes, like the worst kind of network marketing, where there is a kind of euphoria each time a new "prospect" is brought in, and where everything seems to be done "for" the new prospect. But really, the new prospect is almost like food or fuel for the organization. Watch out for groups like these. If you are not wanted (as in many Type 1 groups), that's bad. If you are welcome and wanted (as in good Type 2 and 3 groups), that's good. But if you are *needed*, that's bad again.

Secondly, some groups, intentionally or unintentionally, can seek to impose a higher degree of pressure than is good for anyone, especially a sincere spiritual seeker like yourself. The pressure is counterproductive. On the one hand, if you yield to it, you develop (as we have seen) bad faith. On the other hand, if you resist it, you are both seeking and holding yourself back at the same time—an uncomfortable and frustrating posture to maintain for any length of time. Encouragement is good. Pressure is not.

Finding a good faith community is indeed an important component to finding good faith; just be sure to value the word "good," because an unhealthy group can be worse than no group at all. My quip a while back about praying for guidance in this regard is more important than it may have seemed. I have to believe that God will lead you to the group or groups you need, if you sincerely ask for guidance, knock on some doors, and enter the doors that are opened to you.

GETTING THE MOST OUT OF CHURCH

Once you're inside the door, I have several suggestions to help you get the most out of church.

1. *Keep your expectations low.* Don't expect to go from not getting negative numbers to getting calculus in one visit. Be realistic.

2. *Keep your sense of humor.* Reread the quote from Thomas Oden in the Chapter Preview, and remember VAHCOOLJC.

3. *Expect to see weirdos.* I visited a church with a friend recently. Wouldn't you know it, a fellow with an obvious mental illness— and an aversion to bathing—came and sat next to me. Through the whole service he mumbled to himself and smelled bad. My friend who invited me was, I think, quite embarrassed. I'm sure my friend wanted to say, "Believe me, not everyone here is like the guy who sat next to you! This is actually quite a fine group of people!" And, of course, I knew that. The fact that they lovingly accepted this fellow showed me how fine they were. (There are a thousand other churches that talk about caring for the homeless, the needy, etc., etc., but have never actually made a smelly or mentally disoriented person feel as welcome in their midst as this guy clearly felt.) If churches are truly accepting, loving places, shouldn't we expect the rejected and unlovable to flock to them?

4. *Expect to see hypocrites.* In other words, expect the other people there to be about like you—imperfect, learning, with a long way to go, possessed by "victry and holiness" aspirations and achieving Texaco and geranium results.

5. *Don't expect to like everything.* The music might not match your tastes, and the speaker might have on an ill-fitting suit, and the carpet color may not match the curtains, and the lighting may be all wrong, and the pronouns may not be gender-inclusive. But that's not why you came. Try to get beneath all of that.

6. *Listen to the words*—the words of the songs, the sermon, the prayers—and plumb them for meaning. And be sensitive to the intangibles too: Do you feel anything special there? Do you get the feeling God shows up in this place?

7. *Meet some people.* Find some people you can relate to and ask for their names. Invite them over for coffee, or out for tennis, or something, anything, so you can build some relationships. Tell them exactly where you're coming from, why you're there: "Look, I'm not a Christian (or Jew, or Moslem, or whatever) myself; I'm on a kind of spiritual search, and I'm hoping to find some help in my search here at your church (or synagogue, or mosque, or whatever)."

8. *Ask them questions, direct questions:* "Tell me about your spiritual background. Have you ever experienced God? Why do you believe as you do? What are the most important beliefs you hold? What advice would you have for someone like me? Would you pray for me?" Why beat around the bush? There are so many places where it's not "polite" to talk about religion or politics; take advantage of this place where religion is a safe topic! If they can't handle your questions, ask someone else, and if you can't find anyone at that church to help you, find another church.

9. *Observe their relationships and lifestyles.* Is it "good faith" that you're observing? Do the people love each other? Conflicts are inevitable with maturing, healing people like ourselves, so don't be surprised by conflicts—but do you see signs of grace: forgiveness, reconciliation, patience, understanding?

10. *Get involved.* Find a place you can volunteer. Don't just take: Give.

11. *As you are able, participate* in worship, prayer, service, fellowship, outreach. Obviously, you can't fake it. But as it comes, let it.

AS IT COMES, LET IT

I have often wondered about the church, "God, couldn't you have done a better job than this? Couldn't you have suppressed hypocrisy more, allowed division and disunity less, edited (or prohibited) late-night religious television more, inspired better music and shorter sermons?" And the answer comes to mind: "Yes, but there would be no room for people like you." If God is going to let people like me in the church—people who learn slowly, who get manipulative when things don't quickly go their way, who lose their patience too quickly and too often, who have a lot to learn and a long way to go—then what's amazing isn't how many problems there are in churches, but rather that churches exist and function at all. It's amazing that all of our grit doesn't clog the gears; it's amazing that all of our viruses don't bring down the whole network. The farther along I go, the less I'm surprised when things go wrong, and the more I'm surprised when they go right for very long. It's a miracle, really.

These days I seem to be less scandalized by the distance between our reach and our grasp, between our idealistic signs and the faded, peeling realities they often represent. I find myself a little quicker to see the beauty, the wonder, the grace, and the genius in bringing people together into a humble community of faith where they need each other and where together they need God. Again, as that experience comes to you, let it.

YOUR RESPONSE

1. I would/would not like to find a faith community to help my search.
2. I would like to find a Type 1/2/3 faith community.
3. Here is a list of faith communities I would like to visit or revisit:
4. Here are the people who have most earned my respect, whom I might consult for referrals to a good faith community.

5. Here is how I plan to get the most out of my involvement with a faith community:

RESOURCES

A good source for leads on Type 3 Christian churches is the Willow Creek Association, accessible via the internet at www.willowcreek.org. If you are interested in how churches can and must revitalize, you may be interested in my first book, *Reinventing Your Church* (Grand Rapids: Zondervan, 1998).

PRAYER

God, I can't expect any faith community to be perfect. If it were, I couldn't join it without spoiling it. I do ask that you guide me to a faith community where you will help me grow and where you will use me to help others. I recognize that there are lessons I can learn and benefits I can receive in a faith community that I can gain nowhere else. I also feel a certain fear, because I am aware that I can become entangled or misled in many negative ways too. Again, in faith I ask you to guide me, and I will pursue involvement in a faith community with a posture of dependence on you.

CHAPTER 13 PREVIEW

Why Is the Bible the Next-to-Last Place I Think of for Help in My Spiritual Search?

This chapter acknowledges the difficulties faced by a modern reader approaching the Bible. It offers reasons to make use of the Bible as an important resource for spiritual growth, and then presents a brief summary of the Bible. It considers and rejects two common ways of approaching the Bible, and recommends a third approach.

WHO SHOULD READ THIS CHAPTER?

This chapter is especially for people who have never "gotten into" the Bible before.

WHAT QUESTIONS DOES IT ADDRESS?

Why is the Bible so difficult for modern readers? Why does it come to us in the form it does? How can its problems actually be seen as advantages? What is the basic story of the Bible? How can the Bible be interpreted and applied intelligently today?

The Bible is not a kind of divinely guaranteed textbook in which we can, without any trouble, look up all the answers. I find the notion of the "classic," rooted in its own age but possessing through its underlying universality the power to speak across the centuries to other ages, to be the category which best contains my own understanding of the spiritual power of scripture.... It is the power of ... the Bible ... to speak freshly to each generation of its readers, revealing further truth, which becomes available, not by a process of alien imposition, but by the continuing elucidation of the profundity of the text.

JOHN POLKINGHORNE, *THE FAITH OF A PHYSICIST*

***

Every part of Scripture is God-breathed and useful one way or another—showing us truth, exposing our rebellion, correcting our mistakes, training us to live God's way. Through the Word we are put together and shaped up for the tasks God has for us.

2 TIMOTHY 3:16–17 (THE MESSAGE)

CHAPTER 13

Why Is the Bible the Next-to-Last Place I Think of for Help in My Spiritual Search?

A CONFESSION

I have often wondered about the Bible, as I have about the church: "God, couldn't you have done better than this?" If God were trying to give us a holy book, a self-revelation, couldn't God have made it clearer, less controversial, more universal, less vulnerable to cultural irrelevancy? Couldn't there have been, instead of a collection of varied genres and wildly different writers living and writing in vastly different times and cultures, a single individual or committee inspired to give a coherent, chronological spiritual primer?

Instead of historically rooted books like "First and Second Thessalonians," "Psalms," or "Nehemiah," with mixtures of poetry, history, legislation, personal letters, and fiction, couldn't there have been clear, expository, timeless prose, with titles like, "First, Second, and Third Books of Theology," "The Truth About the Trinity," "How to Have a Good Marriage," "A Clear Guide to the End of the World," or "Seven Easy Steps to Cure Greed and Lust"? Couldn't God have anticipated every heresy, schism, problem, and controversy and made clear, unarguable, foolproof, preemptive strikes through some inspired chapter of a divine textbook?

What could God possibly think we gain by having a collection of holy Scriptures in this seemingly disorganized, patchwork form, if indeed they come from God at all?

ON SECOND THOUGHT

After my mind follows this train of thought for a while, I begin to ask a different question: How else could it be? If God is indeed having a real story unfold through history, then of course, the story has to "happen" with freedom, and the reports of it have to come to us in their raw, unedited forms, warts and wrinkles, bizarre twists and unpredictable turns. And even if God were to edit the stories into a more "acceptable" form, for which audience would God edit them? For scientific, college-educated rationalists? For the wild-eyed artists and poets? For rice farmers in the East, fishermen in the North, hunter-gatherers in the South, or philosophers in the West? For gender-egalitarians from the West (guaranteeing it wouldn't be read by more patriarchal folk from some other places), or vice versa? Would it really be better for us to have the story rehashed and "sanitized" so we like it more readily and accept it more easily? Or is there some benefit to getting it gritty, breathless, and warm from the lips of those who were there, told in their idioms, through the lenses of their cultures—leaving the job of interpretation and application for our myriad and dynamic settings up to us?

IF GOD

If God wants us to interact personally with the story, to go deep with it, so that it captivates and inspires and transforms us, then of course, it must offer challenges, mysteries, amazements, bafflements—not just journalistic clarity or technical precision. If it describes astounding, shocking realities (visions, miracles) experienced only a few times in history, how could there be easy language and common metaphor that would render the unexplainable as explainable, the uncommon as pedestrian? No wonder parts of it are unheard-of, bizarre. If God wants it to be a book that interests and challenges people around the globe for their whole lives, that guides us into life's deep mysteries, that trains us to see the world from diverse points of view and in so doing, stretches us to not be so limited by our own inherited point of view, then of course it can't be like the phone book, a government code, or a high school biology textbook—easy reference, fully indexed, conveniently formatted for quick, easy use.

Nor can it be a one-read book, after which we say, "The Bible? Oh, yes, I read that years ago," implying that we'll never need to look at it or think about it again. If God wants the book to be an authentic medium of spiritual enlightenment and instruction, then how can it be a book that we feel we can fully grasp, have control over, take pride in our knowledge of, feel competent in regards to? Mustn't it be an untamed book that humbles us, that entices us higher up and deeper in, that renders us children rather than experts, that will sooner master us than we will master it?

If the book isn't only to be about God, but also about us . . . not only revealing the Creator, but also contributing to the formation of a family, a movement, a heritage, then mustn't it have our fingerprints on it, showing us not only God but ourselves in relationship with God and one another? And if God is interested in recording an unfolding story in such a way as to foster its continued unfolding, without so explaining and clarifying it that the story is spoiled, bled of its drama, de-plotted, demystified . . . then wouldn't the book you would expect look very much like the book we actually have?

CANTANKEROUS FORM

Might its cantankerous form tell us that there are things more important in life than a good, logical, linear outline? That we are more than brains . . . that we have imagination, passion, fury, hope . . . and that God is as interested in converting and informing these as our conceptual selves? Might it tell us that all contact with God (at least for us humans, and for now) must be situational . . . that there is no way for us to know God except in the ways that people in the Bible story did: in the middle of feast and famine, good and bad governments, changing economies, disappointing marriages and dysfunctional families, poignant moments and exhilarating victories, deep friendships and bitter betrayals?

And might it have a built-in security system, so the insincere or halfhearted find nothing, so the prejudiced find exactly what they were expecting, and so those who are hungry and thirsty for God find a spiritual feast?

So, I complain less about the Bible these days, and appreciate it more, without asking it to be something else, which would, I now realize, be something less. And I encourage everyone I can not to bypass the Bible, but rather to dive into it with gusto, for it provides amazing resources for those on a spiritual journey.

THE FIVE-MINUTE BIBLE SURVEY

If you're not familiar with the Bible, let me offer this brief overview. The Bible is a collection of ancient "books," or documents, which together become the basic library of monotheism on planet earth. The thirty-nine (or twenty-four, depending on which are grouped together) documents that comprise the Hebrew Bible cover a period from roughly 2000 B.C. until about 450 B.C. To them are sometimes added fifteen more documents (or thirteen, depending again on which are grouped together) which are often called the "Apocrypha," and which cover the period from about 300 B.C. to 100 A.D. Christians include twenty-seven more documents, together called the "New Testament," covering a period from just before the birth of Christ to about 65–90 A.D.

These documents include history, poetry, prophecy (messages from God in specific situations, sometimes, but not all that often really, predicting the future), and personal letters. Within these genres, there are numerous clear examples of fiction—parables, dreams, and so forth. Sometimes, it's hard to tell exactly what a passage is intended to be—history, poetry, fiction, nonfiction.

All of these documents combine to communicate a story, a beautiful story, a haunting story, a nearly unbelievable but, to many of us, ultimately believable story. Let me try to summarize it for you.

THE STORY

Before the beginning of everything we think of as "the universe," there was God—a creative (as God was soon to prove), intelligent, conscious, communicating, dynamic, caring entity whose magnitude goes beyond our limits both of perception and imagination. God created the universe, using time, space, matter, energy ... and something more. When God created our planet and populated it with life, God chose to insert something of his own self into the mix: Into human beings, God would breathe his own "breath of life," his very Spirit, his own image.

This mysterious endowment was a great ennoblement, but it brought with it a certain burden, a responsibility unknown to granite or paramecia, mushrooms or sequoias, bog turtles or crocodiles, seagulls or sparrows, otters or gorillas. That unique endowment and responsibility made the first humans—and us, today—capable of freedom, wisdom, creativity, love, communication, civilization, virtue; it also made them vulnerable to rebellion, pride, foolishness, destructiveness, hatred, division, and vice. They, as we, too often fell to the latter.

So, being neither robots nor prisoners, these free human beings early on failed to fulfill the full promise of their primal innocence and natural nobility, and with the development of the first civilizations it was clear that human beings had a self-destructive bent. One feature of their self-destructiveness was their tendency to lose contact with God, to live life without reference to God, to throw away their spiritual compass and get lost. That didn't mean they became irreligious; in fact, they seemed incurably religious, incapable of numbing or obliterating their spiritual faculties, at least not for very long. Rather, their estrangement from their Creator meant that they innovated as best they could, developing religions as varied as their cultures and their landscapes. In fact, by about 2000 B.C., each social entity on earth had developed its own religion to explain its mysteries, solve its problems, bolster its power, vilify its enemies, and so on. The assumption on planet earth was that there were many gods, each having power over certain territories or certain natural phenomena (the sun, the moon, fertility). Some of their forms of worship were no doubt beautiful and honorable, but many became base and degrading—including horrific human sacrifice, sexual exploitation, and the like.

A FAMILY WITH A DESTINY

Into this situation of religious pluralism, with a welter of religions mixing beauty and horror, truth and misunderstanding, God communicated with a Semitic shepherd living in modern-day Iraq, then known as Chaldea. The man's name was Abram, later known as Abraham. Abraham was given a sense of destiny, that he would be the father of a great family, and that his descendants would bring spiritual blessing and enlightenment to the whole world. Key to this enlightenment was this revelation: *There were not many gods, but only one.* And this God could not be adequately represented by any of the standard images (idols), but was greater than the stars and the sea, more majestic than the sky and the mountains, because all things were created by this God. Not only that, but this God was deeply concerned about the ethics, morality, social justice, and personal integrity of human beings, himself being ethical, moral, just, and pure. (What a contrast to the capricious god-concepts of Abraham's neighbors, gods whose vices were as exaggerated as their powers!)

These were radical ideas, though they may seem commonplace to us (which is proof of Abraham's influence!). They took generations to accept. But God was patient; these creations were made to be free, so they could not be pushed or forced. They had to learn at their own pace, so direct intervention (via some extraordinary spiritual experience—a vision, a voice, a dream) was always delicate. Additional interventions came, though, at critical times, to Abraham's son Isaac, Isaac's son Jacob (who was later renamed Israel, this name becoming the "family name" of the Jewish people to this day), and Jacob's son Joseph. The family was guided to a land of their own just east of the Mediterranean, where this new understanding of God could be nurtured in relative peace and stability. Eventually, the clan grew quite large, and God apparently planned a difficult experience to solidify their identity and more deeply root these new beliefs in this family of people, and through them, in the human family as a whole.

UNITED IN SUFFERING

God used a famine to drive them from their land to Egypt, where they would either assimilate into Egyptian culture and squander their destiny or intensify their distinct family identity as refugees, and not only as refugees, but eventually, as an oppressed, enslaved minority group as well. These shared sufferings did their work, and after about four hundred years in Egypt, their identity was strong, their spirit was still (barely) unbroken by their hardships, and their unique faith in one supreme God was embedded deeply within them. God intervened again, calling a uniquely prepared man named Moses to liberate these special people from their oppression and enslavement and return them to their homeland, which had been unseen by them for four centuries.

The return took much longer than one might expect, because God did not want the land resettled by halfhearted followers. It was essential that they maintain a vigorously distinctive identity and vibrant spiritual vitality as they reentered their homeland. During this difficult but formative time, the family wandered as nomads in the harsh wilderness between Egypt and Palestine. It was during this nomadic period (called the Exodus) that formal public worship of God began. Additionally, the moral standards of this community of faith became codified during these years, most notably in the Ten Commandments. No wonder Moses is remembered as such an important figure in the family history of the Jewish people, since he led the people through this amazing passage.

CONQUEST, CONFEDERACY, AND KINGDOM

A generation later, a reinvigorated younger generation completed the conquest (because other tribes had moved into the land during their absence) of their homeland. The extended family now consisted of twelve clans, and they formed a loose confederacy that was frequently challenged by neighboring nations, sometimes overcome, and subsequently reformed several times over the next several hundred years.

Eventually, this loose confederacy evolved into a rather short-lived monarchy, a development about which later biblical writers were ambivalent. Their first king, Saul, was a disappointment. Their heroic second king, David, initiated their "golden age," around 1000 B.C. His son Solomon was another disappointment as a king, and Solomon's son was such a weak and insecure ruler that civil war broke out, and the nation was divided into northern and southern kingdoms.

DETERIORATION, EXILE, RETURN

Into this deteriorating situation, God repeatedly intervened. Sometimes, God gave people strong dreams to get their attention. Other times, they had other spiritual experiences. Occasionally, remarkable miracles occurred. Some people were given a special sensitivity to God and became spiritual leaders called prophets. Their writings in the Bible record the context and content of the messages they received from God and passed on to the people.

In this divided and weakened condition, the descendants of Israel became an easy target for rising empires to their north. Eventually, from about 700 to 550 B.C., both the northern and southern kingdoms were conquered. Many survivors from the south were deported to Assyria where they became servants in various capacities. Seventy years later, two leaders, Nehemiah and Ezra, gained permission to repopulate their homeland and led the refugees (most of whom had been born in exile) back to rebuild their capital city, Jerusalem.

Through all these hardships, these people never completely lost faith. Nor did they allow their faith to lose its distinctiveness. Of all people in the world, they alone believed in one supreme, good Creator, and they sought to remain faithful to that vision. The era of the great Hebrew prophets ends with the story at this point, about 450 B.C.

A NEW CHAPTER

During the next 450 years, the Greek empire flourished and the Roman empire rose, subjugating the Jewish people as they did the whole Mediterranean world. The Jewish people showed inspiring courage and faithfulness to God during these times of political and religious persecution. Many stories of their courage and faith are contained in the Apocrypha, which comes from this period. Into this milieu was born Jesus, later to be called the Christ, meaning the Messiah or Savior or Deliverer. After thirty years of obscurity, Jesus came into the public eye, presenting himself as an itinerant Jewish rabbi . . . with a difference. The religious world of his day was polarized—much as ours is—with the rigid religious conservatives on one side (the Pharisees) and the more lenient religious liberals on the other.

Jesus refused to be slotted anywhere on their continuum. He said that a time of change had come, a new chapter was beginning, a whole new era in the spiritual life of the human race was being launched. With the memory of the great golden age of King David far behind them (far, but not forgotten), and with the oppressive grandeur of the Roman kings around them . . . Jesus announced a new kingdom, the kingdom of God.

UPSIDE DOWN

Everything about this kingdom was upside down. In it, the poor and meek were winners, not the rich and aggressive. In it, some prostitutes and tax collectors were far ahead of many priests and Pharisees. Children and women were given unheard-of status, and God was brought nearer than ever before: Jesus said that in this new era of the kingdom of God, God could be known as a loving, caring, compassionate father . . . and that even rebellious runaways would be warmly welcomed home.

The crowds flocked to hear this message. Reports of miraculous healings were commonplace, although Jesus himself tried to keep them quiet. Naturally, the religious establishment felt threatened, and so they conspired with the Roman authorities to have Jesus arrested and killed. Their plot succeeded through the help of an insider, one of Jesus' twelve prime students (called disciples), and one Friday afternoon, Jesus was crucified and buried.

SURPRISES

Three days later, reports began to spread that the grave was empty, and that Jesus had risen from the dead. At first, not one of the disciples believed these rumors, but in the coming days, one by one and in larger groups, they claimed to have encounters with the risen Jesus. Then came perhaps the strangest event of all.

Remember: For two thousand years the descendants of Abraham had guarded their faith, kept their distinctiveness, monitored their faithfulness, resisted all pressures to intermarry or adopt the religious practices of other nations or in any way allow their unique commitment to monotheism to be polluted or diluted. Isolation, separation, distinction were at the core of their being. And now, the disciples report, Jesus is telling them to bring the good news of this new kingdom to the entire world, to every nation, every religion, every culture, every language. Further, they came to understand that Jesus' death had not been a colossal accident, but rather was part of God's plan: In some mysterious way, as Jesus suffered and died, he was absorbing and paying for the wrongs of the whole human race. Now, the whole human race could receive forgiveness and reconciliation to God; it would be as simple as asking, seeking, and entering an open door.

STILL UNFOLDING TODAY

If Jesus was right, the one true God wasn't just for the descendants of Abraham anymore. Belief in, relationship with, and experience of the one true God was to permeate the whole world, like yeast slowly rising in bread, or like seeds subtly planted in the soil. The time had come to open the doors to everyone. There would be a thousand problems, Jesus said. It would be messy, with plenty of mistakes and no shortage of opposition. It would take time, a long time. But they should not give up until every person hears the "good news"—that God loves them all, wants to welcome them into his family, and wants to involve them in the ongoing spiritual story of the human race.

The New Testament concludes with the story of the spread of that message and the creation of faith communities all over the Mediterranean world. And that story continues to unfold today. Perhaps, as you read and I write, we are part of its unfolding even now.

INTERPRETING THE STORY

Now when it comes to interpreting this story, when people read the Bible and try to discern what it means to our lives and situations today, there are two common approaches, neither of which I will recommend to you.

1. *The literalist approach* requires us to take the Bible literally from beginning to end. If by *literally* we mean, literally "paying attention to every letter," well, okay. That's what good readers do anyway. But if by *literally* we mean unimaginatively, without regard to the genres and cultures of the original writers, treating the whole thing like a code of law or textbook on science, prying the Bible out of its milieu, pretending to unjustified levels of certainty . . . I'm sorry, I can't recommend that.

2. *The liberal approach* rightly, I believe, distances itself from the wooden reading of the worst literalists. But I believe many liberals overreact. They do not wish to be bound by the outmoded worldviews of the past—whether from Abraham's time, David's time, or Jesus' time—so they take the Bible and subject it to the worldview of our own time. Whatever seems distasteful to contemporary ears doesn't pass through their grid. Uncomfortable elements (e.g., stories of miracles, or limitations on sexual behavior) are explained

away; we're given permission to ignore them, avoid them, ridicule them as primitive and silly. What's left is a domesticated Bible, a "nice" Bible, a tame Bible that, I fear, presents a God and world redesigned in our image. In so doing, we become slaves to our contemporary culture (which, a hundred or thousand years from now, will seem as backward and silly as any past worldview seems to us). That leaves us just as parochial as any literalist, we stuck in the worldview or plausibility structure of today, they in their alternative worldview from the past.

A THIRD OPTION?

Could there be a third approach? I think so. Let me outline it like this:

1. Let's begin by accepting the idea that God wants to speak to us through the Bible. It contains the story of the romance between God and humanity, and our fellow spiritual travelers for centuries have felt that it is profitable for our spiritual health and development. To lightly discard it would be at least unwise, and probably arrogant too. We would soon find ourselves in deep weeds indeed, without it.

2. Let's continue by acknowledging that we need the Bible. We need to know the story, we need to learn from the sages of the past, we need the benefit of their experiences and mistakes, we need the inspiration. We need the corrective perspectives given in the Bible, vantage points from outside our contemporary culture (which is so natural to us that we are unaware of how it may distort our perceptions), foreign vantage points from which to view ourselves, distant fulcra upon which to get leverage to move ourselves in better directions.

3. Let's also frankly acknowledge that certain things in the Bible present problems to us. For example. . . .

 A. Does the Bible really require us to believe that the earth was created in 144 hours, something less than 10,000 years ago?
 B. Does the Bible allow only male-dominated social or ecclesiastical structures? Is patriarchy the only biblically permissible mode for society?

C. Does the Bible recommend sanctions against homosexuals, and if so, what sanctions, and why?

D. Does the Bible require us to believe that anyone who doesn't believe it in its entirety is going to hell after death, and if not, which parts can one be ignorant of or skeptical about, and why?

4. Let's avoid the responses of both literalists and liberals, the one refusing to reconsider their interpretations of the Bible in light of contemporary experience, and the other refusing to reconsider contemporary biases and "certainties" in light of the Bible. In other words, let's try to practice good faith in the Bible, refusing to deny either our own experience on the one hand or our respect and need for the Bible on the other. Where we can't reconcile contemporary experience and the Bible, we can honestly admit that we just don't know, having confidence that we will be led in time to better understanding. We can live in that dynamic tension, make the best of it, and be gracious to one another in the meantime.

5. Let's spend a minority of our time and energy on the controversies, and concentrate fully on the biblical teachings that are clear and compelling without debate. Mark Twain said as much: It wasn't the parts of the Bible that he didn't understand that bothered him—but the parts he did understand. For example, it's pretty darn clear that what is most important in life is for us to love God with all our heart, soul, mind, and strength, and to love our neighbors as ourselves. Our personal spiritual health and the contemporary unfolding of the biblical story will both fare better, I think you'll agree, if we concentrate for the next twenty-five years on those simple, clear basics. Somehow, I can't help but think the other issues will fall into place over time. Jesus chided the Bible scholars of his day for "straining out a gnat and swallowing a camel." Ironically, whether liberal or literalist, we could easily do the same thing, concentrating so on the minor controversies that we miss the big picture.

MY EXPERIENCE WITH THE BIBLE

I am a pastor, so every week of my life I am interacting with the Bible in my own personal thinking and in preparation for the next week's sermon. Well over forty-five times each year, I prepare and present a message from the Bible for the church I serve. People often ask me, "Don't you ever run out of things to say?" I tell them, "No, I wish I could preach several times each week. There's always more to say. This book is so rich!" Week after week, year after year, I see the relevance, power, resources, and wisdom of this book. It really is amazing.

Many of the people who come to the church I serve (which, as you probably have guessed, is what we earlier called a Type 3 church) don't believe in the Bible when they come. They're skeptical. I don't tell them they have to believe it. I just try to present it. I try to be honest about the parts that confuse me. I try to focus on the parts that are abundantly clear and profitable (and I am quite certain that my lifetime will end before I reach the last of those things!). And over time, I notice that people come to share my respect for and trust in the Bible—as a needed, dependable, enlightening, unique, challenging, fascinating resource for spiritual seekers . . . a book with God's fingerprints all over it and his breath behind the words.

YOUR EXPERIENCE WITH THE BIBLE

There are many ways you can interface with the Bible. You can read it on your own. You can use a self-study guide. You can join a Bible study group or class. You can attend a church where the Bible is the basis for the sermons. There are Internet chat rooms oriented to Bible study and telephone hotlines where you can call with your questions. You'll find several resources in the appendix to help you get into the Bible in a productive way.

POINTING OUTWARD

As wonderful as the Bible is, it doesn't seem to intend its own function to be like that of television: *Watch more and more, stay on the couch for another thirty minutes, never turn it off, why go outside? Don't change that channel; don't go away!* No, the Bible seems to keep sending you away ... to think, to live, to feast, to fast, to meet, to serve, to stand firm, to back down, to confront, to apologize, to worship, to teach, to learn, to love. And before long, you have new reasons to come back, new questions, new predicaments, new needs ... through which you'll find new adventures into which you'll be sent away, and so on. It's the life that counts, not the reading about it. The book is there to thrust you into life, again and again chasing you off the couch, challenging you into new adventure.

YOUR RESPONSE

1. I would describe my experience with the Bible as
   nonexistent
   negative
   positive
   mixed
2. My approach to the Bible will be
   literalist
   liberal
   third alternative
   other
3. I would like to
   begin reading the Bible on my own
   join a Bible study group
   other
4. I will be reading the Bible for the following purposes, or to find answers to the following questions:

RESOURCES

Many people these days have benefited from getting the Bible on audiotape, so it can be listened to during commutes, exercise, other activities.

Several films depict Jesus' life, with more or less accuracy. The *Jesus* film produced by Campus Crusade for Christ is one of the best, as is *Jesus of Nazareth*.

If you are one of the many people put off by the Bible and its vocabulary, you shouldn't miss Kathleen Norris's *Amazing Grace: A Vocabulary of Faith* (New York: Riverhead, 1998). Norris tackles what were to her offensive bibical and theological words like *sinner, salvation, blood, dogma, and orthodoxy,* and shares how she got through the offense to meanings that have enriched her faith.

Many churches offer Bible study groups. As you get involved in a community of faith, these can be an excellent resource.

If I were to recommend a short syllabus of Bible reading, I'd recommend Genesis 1–3, selected Psalms (1, 8, 19, 23, 27, 32, 51, 95, 150), Isaiah 40–53, the gospel of Luke, and Romans 1–8.

PRAYER

God, I would be arrogant and unwise to shun the insights of sages and leaders from the past whose reflections on having a relationship with you have been authenticated through the ages. So I do not want to ignore the rich heritage of monotheism on planet earth found in the Bible. But God, I confess that the Bible is often difficult for me; I feel so far removed from the ancient world, its languages, customs, and culture. Help me bridge these gaps and not be distracted by secondary matters; help me to see the truth you have for me in the Bible. Let it be a mirror to help me better see myself and a light to help me progress on this path of spiritual searching and growth. I don't want to just keep learning and thinking; I want to put my faith into practice in my daily life.

CHAPTER 14 PREVIEW

What If I Lose Interest?

This chapter faces the real possibility of losing interest in the spiritual search. It uncovers a factor in many if not all people that may sabotage the spiritual search. It summarizes both costs and benefits of staying with the spiritual journey long term. The chapter concludes with a brief consideration of hell and heaven as ultimate factors in a cost-benefit analysis.

WHO SHOULD READ THIS CHAPTER?

Anyone planning on long-term spiritual growth should give this chapter a careful reading.

WHAT QUESTIONS DOES IT ADDRESS?

Why might we be tempted to suppress the truth or in other ways sabotage or abandon our own spiritual search? What are the costs and corresponding benefits that will make persevering worthwhile? What are the purposes of the horrific imagery of hell and the beautiful imagery of heaven in religious literature?

But even as hope died in Sam, or seemed to die, it was turned to a new strength. Sam's plain hobbit-face grew stern, almost grim, as the will hardened in him, and he felt through all his limbs a thrill, as if he was turning into some creature of stone and steel that neither despair nor weariness nor endless barren miles could subdue.

J. R. R. TOLKIEN, *THE RETURN OF THE KING*

CHAPTER 14

What If I Lose Interest?

Grace and I have four children. In 1990, Trevor, our third child, was six years old . . . a wonderful, thoroughly normal (and thoroughly extraordinary, too, of course) kid. Then he got cancer.

His regimen of chemotherapy kept his immune system next to nonfunctional. This immuno-compromised state meant that any infection was potentially life-threatening. Seven times in the first nine months of treatment, he would spike a fever, we would have to rush him to the hospital, and he would spend a few days or weeks there on intravenous antibiotics.

TURTLES

One of his infections was identified as salmonella. That was a haunting diagnosis for me to hear, you see, because I have an unusual hobby: I keep and breed rare turtles and tortoises. Turtles and tortoises commonly carry salmonella. The natural question: Did my son catch this infection from my animals? If the antibiotics couldn't fight it, and (perish the thought) Trevor died, would my hobby have cost my son his life? How could I forgive myself? How could my wife forgive me?

Of course, the infection could have come from other sources, and we never found out the actual source. Early on in treatment, Trevor developed a craving (another side-effect of his chemotherapy) for eggs, and several times we found him in the kitchen in the middle of the night scrambling or poaching some eggs: "I was just hungry, Mom and Dad. I didn't want to wake you up." Perhaps he got salmonella from the eggs—from undercooking them, or from failing to wash his hands after touching the raw eggs. But the possibility was there that his infection was from the turtles, and therefore *my fault*. Can you imagine how this thought haunted me during his entire hospitalization?

PRESSURE-TREATED LUMBER

Not only that, but another fear plagued me. When Trevor was younger, I had built a loft bed for him and his big brother. The only problem was this: I used pressure-treated lumber to make the bed. I was basically ignorant of the danger of the chemicals in the wood at the time. Some time later, I learned that this lumber should never be used indoors, or anywhere it will have frequent contact with human skin—because the chemicals used to treat the wood can be carcinogenic.

Even then, when someone told me of the danger, it took me several months before I got around to dismantling the bed and disposing of the wood. Cancer seemed like such a far-off risk. There was no urgency.

Looking back, I'm horrified and deeply ashamed of my carelessness on both counts—choosing the wrong materials and taking my time about removing them. The results could have been fatal. Some months after Trevor's diagnosis, I remember the thought sending a shiver up my spine: "I may be the cause of his disease, his suffering."

"You didn't mean it," you might say. "You weren't trying to give him cancer. It wasn't intentional." True, but carelessness is carelessness, and unintentional carelessness can kill as effectively as intentional malice. In my own soul, I know this is true. I shouldn't have taken any chances with my son's health, in the first case with letting that bed stay in the house for even one night after I heard that it was dangerous . . . and in the second case by allowing in our home a possible threat of needless infection for my immuno-compromised son. I am ashamed to have to admit these failures, but they happened.

WHY DREDGE THIS UP?

Thank God, Trevor survived all his infections—including salmonella—and he has been cancer-free for seven years now, as good as cured, the doctors say. Why am I dredging up these terrible memories, then? Everything turned out okay, so why not drop the whole thing?

Because of this: In both cases, I was strongly tempted to suppress this truth. I am also ashamed to have to admit this, but I didn't want to let the doctors know about my turtle hobby, and I didn't want to admit the possible role of the loft bed in causing my son's disease. I wanted to let everyone assume it was chicken eggs, or to know nothing of pressure-treated lumber in the house. I wanted to protect myself. I wanted to deny any possible culpability.

TWO IMPLICATIONS

My desire to suppress the truth, to protect myself, to cover up my mistakes—if it has some corresponding reality in you, and if it is in fact indicative of a problem common to all of us—has at least two frightening implications regarding our search for faith and for God:

1. We may not really want to find God.
2. We may not want to find the real God.

In other words, we need to acknowledge that just as there are spiritual hungers and thirsts in us, moving us along in our search, there are contrary forces and fears that will vote every chance they get to back-burner the search, abandon it altogether, or in some other way compromise its integrity. For that reason, it's wise to ask ourselves some questions.

FAKE SEARCHING

What if deep inside, we know that God is all about truth (the whole truth)? And what if we feel guilty about things we have done, are doing, or would like to do? What if we would like the truth about ourselves—our carelessness, our deceit, our worst secrets—to be suppressed? Wouldn't that give us every reason to not want to find or face God? Might it tempt us to conduct a false search, where we pretend to want faith, but really are just going through the motions—so as not to look guilty? Wouldn't that state of affairs make God the enemy, paradoxically the one we seek *and* the one we seek to avoid?

What if we have some cherished vices? What if we nurture secret lives that we are deeply ashamed of, dark sides to our psyche that would scandalize everyone we know if they were known? What if there are sexual affairs, secret perversions, shady business practices, well-covered addictions, or sweet bitternesses embedded in our hearts like thorns in our thumbs? And what if, partway through our search, we begin to sense that God wants to deal with those things . . . that coming to him will require us to come to ourselves, come into the light so to speak, come clean about these secrets? Will that fear tempt us to abort our search? When pushed to the wall, will we decide we love shadows rather than light, our pet pleasures more than spiritual authenticity? Will we conveniently lose interest right at the point we most need to press on?

RESPECTABLE

It might not be such ugly things. It might be more "respectable" things—like respect itself. Maybe people think of you as a certain kind of person . . . logical, independent, fiercely nontraditional, iconoclastic, rigorously logical, cool, detached. Maybe they respect you for those qualities. To "come out of the closet" as a person of faith would blow that image, force you to eat some of your skeptical words of the past, require you to admit that you were wrong before, humble you to admit that you needed something beyond yourself after all.

I remember this feeling. I was a teenager when I went through a critical phase in my spiritual journey. I remember feeling, with some excitement, "It's happening! My faith is coming alive! God is really real after all! This is wonderful! I can't wait to tell people about this!" Then a wet blanket descends: "But I'm already the president of the church youth group. What will they think if I tell them it's just coming together for me? Will they think I've been a hypocrite? Well, actually, they would be right. But do I want them to know it? Maybe I shouldn't admit this transformation I'm experiencing. Maybe I should just pretend that this newfound faith had been there all along. . . ."

COUNTING THE COST

Do you see the trap? If I capitulate to the fear of losing people's respect, if I begin to pretend, if I perpetuate a fraud, then I turn my good faith into bad faith, and I basically guarantee that I'm not going any further in the development of good faith. This search for faith ends up being pretty costly.

I need to be straight with you in this regard. I need to repeat that previous statement: Faith . . . good faith, real faith . . . can be pretty costly. A person finding faith sooner or later has to count the cost. He'll either lose interest and turn back at that point or forge ahead. Generally, as you'd expect, the greatest breakthroughs often follow those decisions to pay the price and plunge onward, in spite of the cost.

COSTS

Let's assess some of the costs that often accompany spiritual growth:

1. *Pride.* At some point, no, at many points, you'll have to learn how deep your pride's roots go. Like a gardener facing a weed-choked flower bed, you'll feel the agony of uprooting egotism, arrogance, conceit, selfishness. Probably all of the following debits in our "cost of faith" list are simply line items in the pride account.
2. *Judgmentalism.* Good faith requires you to face your own failures, which increasingly makes it seem morally obscene

to be so hard on other people. Good faith requires you to say good-bye to judgmentalism and all her clones: racism, sexism, agism, classism, holier-than-thou-ism, and all of their arrogant ism-counterparts, because faith requires you to acknowledge (not just to say, because nearly everybody says this without really meaning it) that you're ultimately no better than anybody else.

3. *Vices.* In the past, you could always judge yourself by other people, and there were always copious quantities of worse people around who, by their very badness, inadvertently did you the favor of helping you feel superior. As you move into faith, though, you stop comparing yourself favorably to others, and start comparing who you are to the person you could be, the person God wants you to become. Indulgences you used to allow yourself now seem cheap, beneath you, dangerous spiritually, dangerous to others even, because of the negative example they set. It's not that you're being forced to give up anything; it's that certain things don't fit anymore, like last decade's styles (wide ties, narrow ties, paisley socks, polyester, whatever . . .)—you could wear them, but they're just not "you" anymore.

4. *Imbalance.* Without good faith, you can afford to be a workaholic or a slacker. You can obsess on golf or sex, antiques or danger. You can be a rabid Republican or a demonic Democrat. You can be a miser or a prodigal, flighty or stodgy, overdose on privacy or parties. Choose your extreme; choose your imbalance . . . anything is open for you. But as good faith becomes more part of your life, as God becomes more part of your life, you start to desire balance.

5. *Apathy.* Apart from faith, you can indulge your apathy by saying, "Why try anything new? Why work for a better world? Real improvement is impossible. What difference can I make anyway?" Enter faith, and a whole new factor

enters the equation. Words like "impossible" seem out of place. Despair and cynicism feel like insults to God. Hope grows, and love, and therefore motivation to care, to give, to act, to try, to dream, to risk.

6. *Greed.* "What's mine is mine, and I want to keep it," we say before we have faith. We might even go further: "What's yours is mine, and I want to take it . . . and who's going to stop me?" After faith, we change: "What's mine is really God's, and so I want to use it as God would want me to use it—for my needs, for others' needs, as God wills."

Obviously, our list could extend well beyond these six, but they fairly represent the kinds of costs that go along with faith, costs you must sooner or later assess and decide to either forego or pay in full. Don't face them, and you'll lose interest in your spiritual search.

FREE BUT NOT CHEAP

"The best things in life are free," the saying goes, and it is true of faith. But even though faith is free, it isn't cheap. Like love, it presents itself as a gift that you cannot buy, but rather must reject or receive . . . and if you receive it, it costs you nothing—except the status quo. That's a price some people will not pay. How about you?

"But if faith costs me the status quo, if faith requires me to be open to change, what will I gain in return?" you ask. A fair question, but a hard one to answer . . . at least, a hard one for one person to answer on paper or in words. The best way to find an answer is to observe the gains that have come to other people because of their faith. No, that's the second best way. The best way is to experiment yourself.

GAINS

If you experiment with faith, if you observe the impact of faith on the lives of others, you'll find that the flip side of each cost represents a beautiful gain. Let's consider our previous six examples:

1. *Humility (Pride)*. In spite of how little I know about humility, I do know this about pride: Pride is tiring, a cruel taskmaster, a complicator, a destroyer. Humility, in contrast, relaxes, refreshes, relieves, simplifies, renews. To the degree that becoming childlike includes becoming humble, humility releases childlike play, laughter, sleep, smiles, fun. Our pride forces us to take ourselves so seriously, which leads us to take others less seriously and God less seriously still. Humility prompts the reverse (note the etymological link between "humility" and "humus" and "humor" and "human"), bringing us down to earth (humus) and letting us have a good laugh at ourselves (humor) for who we are (human). Everything depends on you when you're proud; you're indispensable. That brings a lot of pressure. When you're childlike, humble, down-to-earth, small . . . the pressure is gone. Losing pride is like going to the dentist with a root canal. It's scary and it hurts. But it feels so much better when the damned thing (I mean that literally, not as a vulgarity) is out!

2. *Community (Judgmentalism)*. If I've been worshiping at the altar of pride, it's rather hard to convince others to kneel down with me for very long. They have their own idols to worship, and besides, mine doesn't look all that good to them anyway. Remove that obstacle, and two things happen. First, I can simply enjoy other people without judging them, which tends to attract them a bit more than before. Second, I find a new and special kinship with other people of good faith, a kindred spirit often called "fellowship." This fellowship, when grounded on good faith (as opposed to other kinds of faith), creates an inclusive community spirit, breaks down barriers, and brings people together.

3. *Virtue (Vices)*. There's an old story about a preacher who was interrupted one day by a heckler. "I challenge you to a debate on God versus atheism," he shouted. The preacher responded, "I'll gladly have such a debate, under these con-

ditions. You bring two people whose lives have been transformed by their belief in atheism, and I'll bring two people whose lives have been transformed by their belief in God. This way, our debate can explore not only the content of our beliefs, but also the effects of our beliefs." The heckler declined the offer. The story illustrates the fact that wherever you find faith—from an AA meeting to a youth group, from an inner-city storefront church to a remote monastery, you'll find people struggling (with God's help) for self-mastery, striving (with God's help) to become better people, aspiring (with God's help) to be freer of vice and fuller of virtue. Was it Martin Luther King, Jr., who said, "I'm not the man I would be, or the man I should be, but thank God Almighty, neither am I the man I once was!"?

4. *Balance (Imbalance).* Faith gives life a center point around which to balance life's competing demands, opportunities, enjoyments. Faith gives life a reference point around which to proportion life's components. Faith gives life a reason to be lived gracefully and well.

5. *Passion (Apathy).* It's sad—the image of the anemic, callow, thin-skinned, atrophied, weakling, insipid, petty, inconsequential, pathetic saint persists. How different from the vibrant reality of a tough and resilient Mother Teresa, a steady and bold Billy Graham, a wild and crazy youth group leader, a daring and innovative mission leader. Speaking personally, nothing could have made me work as long, hard, consistently, and sincerely as faith has these last twenty or so years—not money, not guilt, not pressure, not fame—only faith. Good faith launches more volunteerism, nurtures more love and neighborliness, inspires more social action, impassions more social justice, engenders more personal growth, and fires more virile visions than any other force on earth. The world is still in too short supply of these assets, you say? Yes—a fact which calls for more good faith!

6. *Generosity (Greed).* There is something in life so much better than getting: giving. The joys of generosity exceed the joys of consumption and greed in both quantity and quality, not to mention intensity and persistence. Good faith always flowers into generosity in its many forms . . . hospitality (generosity with my home), patience (generosity with my time), liberality (generosity with my funds), empathy (generosity with my emotions). Perhaps you've heard the play on the old question: "What do you give to the person who has everything?" Answer: *generosity!*

Again, as with the costs, these six gains are representative of a much longer list we could create. But any list of this sort, in a big way, misses the point. There is another gain, so obvious it's almost embarrassing to mention. Through faith (good faith, that is), you gain God.

LUNCH WITH KARL

I had lunch the other day with a fascinating fellow. Karl was a pastor for many years, very successful by all normal standards. But during his second pastorate, he lost something—energy, hope, perspective, maybe even faith. Exhausted, burned out, sick and tired, he left the ministry. (This kind of story is far more common than you might think.)

What does a washed-up pastor do with his life—especially one with a family to support, a mortgage to pay, college tuition to anticipate? He got a job in finance, and worked his way up the ladder in a large investment firm. He hated the work, but he needed money. Eventually, he was hired on in a large retirement facility, and a year later his well-developed people skills won him attention as a candidate for the job of executive director—a position not unlike being the mayor of a town of several thousand senior citizens. A pretty good-sized "congregation"—with better-than-pastors' pay too, no doubt.

We had a really enjoyable lunch together. He looks very happy; he clearly loves his work, and is good at it. The whole place reflects his positive, upbeat attitude—residents and staff alike. (I was treated with extraordinary courtesy by everyone from the guard at the front gate to the waitress in one of the many cafeterias!)

ELEVEN YEARS LATER

During the meal, we shared our stories. As the waitress cleared our dishes, our conversation went a level deeper. "When I left the ministry, my faith was devastated," he said. "Now, eleven years later, I cringe when I think back on many of my sermons. They were so abstract, so disconnected from real life. It was like I was in this little box, and things that seemed so important in that box seem so insignificant in the big world out here.

"I have a lot of questions now. There are a lot of things I was sure about back then, but now, I just don't know. Maybe some of it is midlife; maybe some of it is cynicism; maybe some of it is wisdom." After a pause, he continued, "But there was one sermon I preached at the very end, when I was so burned out. I could preach that sermon still today, because in spite of everything I've been through, I still know that sermon is true."

I asked him the title of the sermon. It came from a passage in the Old Testament: "I am my beloved's, and he is mine." The sermon had two parts, he said. Part 1: I am my beloved's. I belong to God. I am in God's care. I am one of God's children. Part 2: God is mine. God has given himself to me. He has entered my life, entered into relationship with me, connected with me. God is mine.

And that says it better than anything else could: What is the ultimate benefit of faith? Being able to know and feel what Karl knows and feels ... that no matter what, I am God's, and God is mine ... that we have a connection; we have a relationship. Faith in your life brings God in your life. That's why losing interest is so dangerous— so much is at stake; the consequences are so significant.

CONSEQUENCES: HELL? HEAVEN?

Some of you are wondering at this point: "Is he about to threaten us with hell if we give up the search? I knew there would be fire and brimstone sooner or later. . . ." Rest assured, there's no fire and brimstone planned here. Nevertheless, it is worthwhile at this point to realize that the horrific biblical imagery of hell and the enticing imagery of heaven must be intended for this very purpose: to magnify and intensify for us the significance of the consequences of losing or keeping interest in the spiritual search.

Of course, it's next to impossible to have a serious discussion about heaven or hell these days: The topic is so emotionally charged as to be radioactive. How can one enter into the controversy without losing one's balance and missing the point, suffering radiation burns in the process? Let me get just close enough to this dangerous subject to raise a few simple questions:

1. Does it matter *to you* whether you lose interest in your search or persevere in it?

2. If you lose interest and give up your search, what negative consequences would *you* expect?

3. If you persevere in your search, even when it is difficult to do so, what positive consequences would *you* expect?

4. Could we call the consequences of #2 above "hell," and the consequences of #3 "heaven"?

5. Could we also assume that there may be additional consequences, both positive and negative, beyond what you've foreseen?

6. May we assume that whatever is meant by heaven and hell is meant as an encouragement not to lose interest—an encouragement to weigh the negative consequences of losing interest as so undesirable and the positive consequences as so wonderful, that you will not want to abandon your spiritual quest, no matter the difficulties? In other words, may we assume that the real point of the concept of heaven and hell is to impress upon us how *consequential* our spiritual decisions are?

7. And may we assume that you'll make your own free, adult decisions about losing or maintaining interest in light of the

relative importance *to you* of those expected consequences? In other words, may we assume that you can't be pushed or pressured into meaningful decisions about such important matters, but that you must make your own free, uncoerced decisions? In fact, may we assume that if someone puts too much pressure on you by raising the "radioactivity" of the rhetoric too high, the pressure will be counterproductive?

THE CANDLE MAY FLICKER, BUT IT WON'T FLICKER OUT

I know the search is hard at times. I know the candle of faith flickers. For reasons we have considered, and others as well, it is tempting indeed and all too easy to let the candle flicker out. I wonder how I can encourage you—knowing full well that I can't pressure you—not to let that happen. Perhaps sharing some more of my personal story is the best thing I can do. That's what the remaining chapters will offer.

YOUR RESPONSE

1. What costs do I anticipate in pursuing faith? Which have I already experienced?

2. What gains or benefits do I anticipate in pursuing faith? Which have I already experienced?

3. Under what circumstances might I be tempted to abort my search, and how might I avoid aborting my search?

RESOURCES

Many people have been helped by embarking on a thirty-day experiment of faith. The idea is simple: for one month, you attempt to live as if God were real, even if you are not yet convinced of that. Each day, for these thirty days, you attempt to live what we could call the "Four G's":

A. Golden Rule: You try to "do unto others as you would have them do to you."

B. Gratitude: You try to thank God for every blessing you can, beginning with life, shelter, food, safety, health . . . down to minute by minute pleasures and experiences.

C. Generosity: You try to give to others—time, hospitality, money, empathy, respect. You live with liberality, not miserliness.

D. Going: You determine to attend religious services for this month—to go faithfully.

You also might find it helpful to make prayer and Bible reading a daily habit during this time. Reading (or rereading) this book or books recommended in this appendix could enrich this time as well. If your findings are inconclusive after thirty days, sign on for another thirty.

PRAYER

God, I must admit a certain ambivalence I have about you. While part of me is drawn to you, part of me is afraid of you or even resentful of you. I feel you pose a certain threat to me—at the very least, to my ego (since with you around, I'm no longer Number One), and more practically, to my behavior (I am becoming aware of many shabby features of my life that need changing). I find that I need humility and courage as well as faith to continue this search, and I ask you for the humility to admit my needs and my faults, and the courage to be willing to change. I believe the changes you have in store for me will be for the best, but I find it hard to let go. I want to surrender my often stubborn will to you, God. Help me to do this even now. I believe that what I gain will be so much greater than what I lose. I want to let go of all I must let go of in order to have empty hands to receive all you want to give me. I believe that you love me. And one more thing: I am sorry for the many wrongs I have done. I would like to come clean with you about them whenever they arise, and rather than justify myself or make excuses or blame others, I would like to freely admit my wrongs and ask for your forgiveness and power to change.

PART 5

MILESTONES IN MY SPIRITUAL JOURNEY

CHAPTER 15 PREVIEW

Tadpoles on the Kitchen Table

This chapter attempts to convey my delight in finding God in creation.

WHO SHOULD READ THIS CHAPTER?

This chapter will be of special interest to nature lovers like myself, as well as those who feel that science and faith are enemies.

WHAT QUESTIONS DOES IT ADDRESS?

How can nature be seen to reflect God? How does a faith approach to nature differ from a strictly scientific approach?

Just as science has found the power of the sun itself to be locked in the atom, so religion proclaims the glory of the eternal to be reflected in the simplest of elements of time: a leaf, a door, an unturned stone.

HUSTON SMITH, *BEYOND THE POST-MODERN MIND*

CHAPTER 15

Tadpoles on the Kitchen Table

Here's what I remember about Olean, New York, where I was born. We had a big backyard—big in the eyes of a little boy, anyway (Have you ever noticed how everything about your childhood home shrinks when you return as an adult?)—where you could find toads and leopard frogs. We had a rock garden where you could catch garter snakes and red-bellied snakes under the flat slate. We had a little brook next to the driveway, where the rocks had fossils in them, and under the rocks you could find crayfish and dusky salamanders. And across the dirt road there was a field with an electric fence (scary!) that was full of big cows, and sometimes you could see deer and maybe even a red fox in the early morning mist.

If you walked up the hill behind our house, you'd come to Eiser's Pond, owned, no doubt, by the Eisers, whom I never actually met. I remember my dad taking me up there on a spring day. Frogs! Big ones! Jumping into the water from the bank! And there, in the cattails, little black dots, perfect, in the clearest jelly, a mass, floating like a cloud of bold periods. Dad had boots on, and he waded in, scooped down with the plastic bucket, and came up with the frogs' eggs.

Back home, we put them in a goldfish bowl and put the goldfish bowl in the center of our kitchen table. (My parents loved my brother and me, indulging our boyhood interests to heroic degrees, as you can see.) Days passed in the mysterious way they do for children, not slow, not fast; they just passed. The little black periods turned into commas, and after some days, the commas wiggled!

Soon the jelly melted away, and the little tadpoles became free swimming, and Dad must have put lettuce in the water, something to feed the little guys, because they grew.

At breakfast, I'd ask, "How are they doing?" At lunch: "Are those little legs I see forming?" At dinner: "How much longer until they're frogs?" Thus began my love for nature, a love that still grows today.

WRONG WORD

I'm uncomfortable with the word "nature" in the last sentence, because I actually believe it would be truer to say, "Thus began my love for God." "Nature" feels like too autonomous a term, too much of a stand-alone, too disconnected from the Creator. Even as a boy, in every metamorphosing tadpole, every deer standing ears-erect in the mist, every white pine tree hiding a perfect robin's nest in a niche among its branches, every red-winged blackbird calling from a cattail, I could sense a taste of something so fine, something *more*, a precious treasure, a subtle clue, an enticing scent, a delicious hook. Now, though not then, of course, I see these as signs pointing to God. When I would lift a fossil-pocked rock in the creek bed by my house, uncovering a crayfish who would invariably wave its pincers defensively (like the old robot in *Lost in Space*—"Danger! Danger!"), its bulbous eyes finding me, its antennae held back like tiny horsewhips, I wasn't just seeing a "thing," a crustacean with some Latin name, I was seeing a piece of God's handiwork. A little funny, a little scary, but (in the words of a boy) "totally cool," its very coolness part of God's signature.

Imagine being five and crouching with me beside the cinder block foundation of my house. I would pull the grass back from the gray blocks, barely breathing, concentrating . . . a gray pill bug, a black field cricket, a tiny brown toad, a striped baby garter snake, a red eft. A red eft! Have you ever seen one? What could be more beautiful than the delicate brick-orange back, the lighter yellowish underside lightly peppered with black dots, highlighted along the spine with two neat rows of red dots, each ringed in black. Such a beautiful creature, and so harmless. If you traveled thirty light-years to a distant solar system and emerged from your spacecraft to find delicate, colorful, benign creatures like this, you would travel home and tell your friends that the trip was worth it just to see such an amazing life-form! And here it is in my own backyard.

Who can assign a value to these creatures? Who can deny the existence of a Creator when viewing such wonders? Who can help but love these creatures, and in loving them, who can doubt that his or her love wants to reach through and beyond the creatures to their Creator?

A SONG FROM COLLEGE YEARS

Long before I began writing prose, I wrote songs, and many of my old song lyrics express my wonder and love for God-in-creation better than I now can in prose. This one was written while I was in college:

Your Majesty

I love to see your high white clouds sailing, Lord,
    like a fleet of mighty galleons on the blue,
and watch white seagulls dive and glide among them.
    Your Majesty, they make me think of you. . . .
The rhythm and the roar of ocean breakers,
    like great dark pages they turned as the tide withdrew.
They curled and they crashed and they pounded the surf in the
       white foam.
    Your Majesty, they make me think of you. . . .
I love to watch the dark gray clouds as a storm's approaching,
    and see the willow branches sway as the wind blows
       through . . .
see the flash of lightning, hear the rumbling of your thunder.
    Your Majesty, they make me think of you. . . .
Upon a tall and mighty mountain, with a valley spread below
      (so beautiful)
    I lean into a strong fast breeze and deep inside I know,

that all of creation joins in majestic declaration, from a single
   leaf and flower of clover to a burning yellow star to show,
Your Majesty, how wonderful you are!
Your salmon spawn after fighting up fast river currents.
   Your geese migrate each season as you taught them to.
Your great sea turtles return to the beach of their birth.
   Your Majesty, they make me think of you. . . .

Years later, this song expressed a similar sentiment:

The Glory of God

There's a farm that I know, as a child I would go, and run in its
   fields below.
Near a barn on a hill stood an old windmill, and in the afternoon sun it would glow
. . . with the glory of God, the glory of God, the glory of God
   shining through.
And I pray for you that you'll see it too, for this life is a search
   for the glory of God. . . .
There are people I've met whom I'll never forget, full of laughter, some young and some old.
Sometimes on a face, this mysterious grace seems to smile out
   and shine out like gold.
It's the glory of God, the glory of God, the glory of God shining
   through.
And I pray for you that you'll see it too, for this life is a search
   for the glory of God. . . .
There are moments that come like a gift from someone who
   loves you, but you hardly know.
They bring a tear to the cheek, and a catch when you speak,
   and the meaning you seek seems to flow . . .
with the glory of God, the glory of God, the glory of God shining through.
And I pray for you that you'll see it too, for this life is a search
   for the glory of God. . . .

NOTHING BUTTERY

Everyone who knew me as a boy was certain that I'd grow up to be a scientist of some sort, given my love for all things natural. I remember in eighth grade, looking forward so much to taking biology—a chance during school hours to indulge a personal delight—for fun and credit! But I also remember a huge disappointment as I realized that science studied animals in every way except the way that counted most to me: simply as living beings, full of fascination and wonder. It renamed creatures as organisms, dissected organisms into systems, and reduced systems to chemistry, chemistry to physics, physics to mathematics. I've heard this reduction process called "nothing but-tery." That red eft? That's nothing but a larval stage of the primitive vertebrate amphibian *notophthalmus viridescens*. That sunset? That's nothing but light being refracted through humid atmosphere. That house finch singing? That's nothing but a territorial organism's defense call.

EIGHTH-GRADE BIOLOGY

Eighth-grade biology taught me that I would rather pursue my interest in the natural world on my own, having been thoroughly turned off by scientific reductionism, where everything is "understood" when it has finally been reduced to a numeric equation or a Latin name of some sort. It's amazing any sense of wonder survives that kind of education. It strikes me now, looking back, as a kind of sick brainwashing, a kind of secular fundamentalism that is too proud, rigid, and closed-minded to admit a sense of awe, to acknowledge the mystery beyond the rim of mathematical orthodoxy. I guess that's why I decided to pursue literature and music instead of science; they allowed me to explore and celebrate the very things that science seemed determined to explain away as "nothing but. . . ."

I think things have changed a bit even since my childhood. I sense that secular scientific fundamentalism is softening. Just the other day, while reading an article about spirituality in a local publication called

The Washingtonian, I came across a new term. Our postmodern world was referred to as a "postsecular world," and I thought, "Yes, how fitting. Secularism is running out of steam. People are finally coming to realize the bankruptcy of an approach to life that claims to explain everything by little equations." The poet William Wordsworth complained in the early 1800s about the scientific approach that would "murder to dissect"—and nearly two hundred years later, the rest of us are finally seeing some wisdom in Wordsworth's indictment.

DOUBTING SECULAR FUNDAMENTALISM

Let's pause here a little longer. Think about your scientific education. It was based on an unspoken, hardly recognized assumption—a dogmatic tenet of secular faith, really: that everything is completely explainable by our going back and understanding its causes or by tearing it apart and understanding its parts, as if the parts were the cause of the whole. Cause-effect thus becomes the key to everything. As you read these words, you might say, "Of course. What else is there?" That reaction, I think you'll see, proves how well we've been taught a certain secular orthodoxy . . . an orthodoxy that is crumbling as we progress to a postsecular world.

Now you might expect me to say, "But if we trace all cause-effect chains back far enough, back billions of years, we come to the Big Bang, and since that cause itself can't be explained within a closed system of cause and effect, there must be a God." I could say that, and I actually do believe that, but that's not my point here at all. Rather, I want to help you see something much bigger, something I've only come to see in recent months and have never tried to articulate until today.

There is another way—an equally valid perspective—to try to understand things, a way that is not opposed to the cause-effect approach but rather encompasses it and enriches it, a way that in fact reinjects the sense of wonder and awe into the secular nothing-buttery approach by cracking it open to new light and fresh air. We could call it the purpose approach. Cause-effect looks back and asks, "What caused this?" Purpose looks up or ahead, and asks,

"And why was it caused? For what purpose? For what end?" Cause-effect looks for a force pushing events from behind. Purpose looks for a pattern or design or intention or meaning pulling events from ahead, guiding them from above, enriching them from within.

SEEING THE ABSURDITIES

My secular education taught me—never directly, of course, and perhaps all the more convincingly because of its subtlety—that any approach other than cause-effect was superstitious, primitive, backward. It never proved that assertion; its only argument was to ignore questions of purpose, or if they arose, to scoff at them, call them belittling names. Hardly a scientific approach! The rejection of purpose in a tight, closed, cause-effect system is, upon further investigation, at least ironic and at most downright absurd. There's certainly no logical requirement to so limit our inquiry. Here's how I summarized the absurdity in my previous book:

> ... Freudianism says that all beliefs and behaviors flow out of certain psychosexual complexes ... all beliefs except, of course, Freudianism, and all behaviors except, of course, the behavior of expounding Freudianism. Evolutionism says that all characteristics, including the development of thinking brains, are selected naturally to favor survival ... not necessarily the apprehension of truth; this belief suggests that the very organ which conceives of evolution is oriented to produce useful theories, but not necessarily true ones. Marxism and Skinnerian behaviorism alike suggest that individual human behaviors are determined ... whether by class-struggle or pain-avoidance mechanisms ... conveniently excluding the behaviors of the theorists themselves, who speak and write as if their theories were generated in the vacuum of a pure search for truth rather than in the mechanism of their own socio-economic or intrapersonal dynamics. And radical [pluralism] rejects the universal

truthfulness of every other belief while assuming its own position as the only universally true one. (*Reinventing Your Church*, Grand Rapids: Zondervan, 1998, pp. 171–72)

Do you see the irony? The very people who claim to have explained everything by their cause-effect system can't explain themselves or their own quest for truth—which is an act of purpose, not merely of cause and effect.

EYEGLASSES

In many ways, we're like farsighted people who are understandably and legitimately thrilled by how much more detail we now see because of our new eyeglasses (secular science) than we ever saw before without them. The problem comes when our being thrilled with our new clarity of vision leads to being overly impressed with ourselves, our progressiveness, our advancement, our technology, our great vision—so impressed, that we become unwilling to have our vision examined again. We have become unwilling to accept the possibility that our current prescription—given to us by the modern, secular, scientific world—has blinded us to some big things even as it helped us see other littler ones, distorted and blurred things at some distances even as it sharpened things at others, made some things disappear even as it brought others into focus.

Now, as we enter the postsecular age, perhaps we'll be able to see that as wonderful as our scientific education has been, it's time to drop its rigid, fundamentalistic dogmatism and open our eyes again to see the parts of life that can't be fully explained by cause-effect (though they certainly can *partially* be so explained). Then, the wonder will begin to return, as we recognize that purpose, design, meaning, and pattern have a place after all. This new vision is the finding of faith.

Obviously, as a boy, I had no language to articulate this kind of discomfort with the predominant worldview I was being educated in. In fact, I was caught in a double bind. My religious world gave me one version of fundamentalism that refused to be open to the insights of science, while my secular world gave me this scientific fundamentalism unwilling to see anything brought to the table by faith. In other words, science forbade me to see anything in the universe other than nails, equipped as it was with this one hammer of cause and effect. But I do remember a kind of enlightening moment that came during my college years—almost silly in its simplicity, but perhaps you will be able to relate, because you've probably had similar experiences.

THE ENTOMOLOGICAL ARGUMENT

I remember doing homework at a picnic table when a tiny bug landed on my shirtsleeve. It walked this way, then that. It reached up its front legs and took hold of its left antenna, bent it down, and washed it in its mouthparts. Then it walked around a bit more, then repeated the washing procedure with the right antenna, and then flew away. An inconsequential event. But I remember thinking, "That tiny bug. Why did it decide to land here, walk there, and wash its antennae now, not later? It's not enough to tell me about its evolutionary development or its biological drives for food, comfort, and reproduction. No, this little creature really is alive! It really makes choices! It's not just a mathematical equation, a totally determined organism in an environment. It really is alive and lives with its own purposes!" And the train of thought continued: If alive and purposeful, then there is something in the universe called life and purpose, and if life and purpose, then there must be a source of life and purpose. Aquinas and Anselm (great theologians who posited powerful intellectual arguments for the existence of God) must make room for this newest proof—the Entomological Argument for the Existence of God—"If there are living, purposeful bugs, there must be a God." The wonder returns!

THE OLD BOX IS TOO SMALL

That wonder has been for me through the years an increasingly powerful apologetic (an argument for the existence of God). I know that some folk out there can attempt to "nothing-butterize" the sense of wonder itself, but I also know that I would be denying my truest sense of how things really are to go along with them. I can't squeeze everything back into the cause-effect box anymore. Purpose, and along with it design and pattern and meaning, won't fit its narrow confines. It's not enough to feel smug about naming elements in a cause-effect chain—especially if the chain itself is part of something bigger, something with pattern, meaning, design, and purpose.

As I said before, evolution doesn't bother me. If you tell me that God created the earth "by hand" in six days some thousands of years ago, I'm impressed. If you tell me instead that God set a whole cosmos in motion some billions of years ago, a cosmos perfectly calibrated within the narrowest of margins to produce at least one planet where life would be developed through cause-effect chains that were designed into it by a purposeful Designer . . . I'm no less impressed; in fact, I may be even more impressed. The "how" and "when" of it all seem almost inconsequential to me compared to the "what" and "why" which lie beyond cause and effect.

UNCHANGING

I'm in my forties now, but you'll still find me crouching down to see a red eft hiding in the moss, whenever I get the chance. Whenever I can, I head up to a stretch of the Potomac River a couple of hours from here, for a five-mile walk that I have taken in various seasons, under varying weather conditions, over many years now. The mountains change as the seasons change, from grays and browns to palest greens, to bold emeralds to bright crimsons and blazing yellows, to fading ambers and darkening rusts. . . . The river changes through floods and droughts, sometimes opaque butterscotch brown, sometimes so clear you can see the wood turtles scrambling and bounding along the rocky bottom like astronauts on the moon.

The vegetation changes, the birdsongs change, the insects change, and everything changes, everything but this: As the psalmist said, "The heavens declare the glory of God, and the whole earth displays God's handiwork." To me in my forties no less than at five, the world rings like a struck bell with this resonance: There is a God, and God is alive, and God is good, and God is beautiful. There is cause and effect explorable by science, but the very chains of cause and effect are linked in a purpose and pattern and meaning that goes beyond anything secular orthodoxy can explain. I guess you could say that in my experience, science keeps leading me to faith, ever since tadpoles wiggled like lively commas on my kitchen table in Olean, New York.

YOUR RESPONSE

1. In what ways does nature/creation enrich your faith?
2. Where can I go in the coming week or month to enjoy some facet of creation, and in so doing, enjoy the Creator?

RESOURCES

Annie Dillard's *Pilgrim at Tinker Creek* (New York: Harper-Collins, 1988) offers musings on creation that are enriching to one's faith. And, of course, there are many excellent nature guides to help you learn to appreciate the rich endowment of species of plant and animal life that surround us.

PRAYER

God, I thank you and honor you for your artistry in creation. It is truly amazing and awe-inspiring. In particular, I want to thank you for . . . (Complete this prayer with your own thoughts.)

CHAPTER 16 PREVIEW

Jesus Anonymous

This chapter explores the role of Jesus in the spiritual search, acknowledging the sad failure of Christians to represent him very well.

WHO SHOULD READ THIS CHAPTER?

People who are unsure what to make of Jesus.

WHAT QUESTIONS DOES IT ADDRESS?

Why are some people turned off by the word "Jesus"? Are there reasons to push beyond these turnoffs?

After a sampling of ten negative images many people associate with Jesus, the chapter explores some more positive and hopeful associations.

Jesus of Nazareth has been the dominant figure in the history of Western culture for almost twenty centuries. If it were possible, with some sort of super magnet, to pull up out of that history every scrap of metal bearing at least a trace of his name, how much would be left?

JAROSLAV PELIKAN, *JESUS THROUGH THE CENTURIES*

For they concur with the thought John Donne put poetically in his sonnet on the Resurrection, where he says of Christ,
He was all gold when He lay down, but rose
All tincture....
Donne was referring to the alchemists, whose ultimate hope was to discover not a way of making gold but a tincture that would transmute into gold all the baser metals it touched. A Christian is someone who has found no tincture equal to Christ.

HUSTON SMITH, *THE WORLD'S RELIGIONS*

CHAPTER 16

Jesus Anonymous

No one has had a greater influence on my life than Jesus. But I have to confess: I have a love-hate relationship with "Jesus." I mean, of course, the name, the word—not the person. To be sure, I keep growing in love for the person behind the name. But the name makes me squirm sometimes.

Maybe you feel the same way. It's hard, here, at the beginning of the twenty-first century, to say or hear the name "Jesus" without thinking of some or all of the following:

1. A big-haired lady caked with too much makeup, or a toupeed man whose face moves way too much when he talks, staring DIRECTLY into your eyes through the television screen, with an intensity so overdone as to defy all interpretations of honesty or sincerity, entreating you to believe in Jesus. They are telling you, yelling at you, that they see—*RIGHT NOW! AT THIS MOMENT!*—a tumor of exactly the kind you have recently been diagnosed with— being COMPLETELY HEALED in the name of JESUS! (Never mind that the show was prerecorded, so that "right now" has little meaning. Also never mind that your tumor is not healed, or that even if it is, thousands of others aren't.)

2. "Jesus saves" graffiti, common from highway abutments in Philadelphia to roadside signs posted on trees in Georgia to bumper stickers seen at all points south and west. What exactly the graffiti is supposed to communicate remains unclear . . . and why anyone would think that

vandalism-evangelism would be more helpful than hurtful to travelers who read it is anybody's guess.

3. Overlong, boring church services, where things like "Jesus is God" or "Jesus is Lord" or "Son of God" are said so often and with such familiarity that it seems inappropriate to ask what they mean . . . even though you realize that you have next to no idea. If you do ask, it becomes embarrassingly apparent that the person whom you are asking has never been asked this question before, or, if he has, still hasn't figured out an answer that you can understand.

4. Any one of many movies about Jesus in which he nearly always (choose any three of the following): (a) speaks with a British accent; (b) has unquestionably Anglo-Saxon (and therefore non-Semitic) features, including but not limited to wavy brown hair, creamy white skin, and/or dreamy blue eyes; (c) pauses a little bit too long between . . . sentences and . . . phrases as . . . if . . . to . . . suggest . . . that he is really tuned in . . . to another frequency than . . . the . . . rest . . . of us; (d) walks "floatingly," as if he just got off roller skates, or else has a bad back; (e) never seems to smile or laugh, and therefore hardly seems like the kind of person children or fishermen (not to mention wine-imbibers and prostitutes) would have enjoyed being around.

5. The Jesus Seminar . . . an ongoing scholarly inquiry into how Jesus can be liberated from the straightjacket of first-century myth and prejudice. Unfortunately, too often immediately following his liberation, he is then reinserted into the even more confining modern straightjacket of nineteenth- and twentieth-century myth and prejudice (just in time to be outdated for the twenty-first century).

6. The slogan "Jesus is the only way!"—which seems to you frightfully narrow-minded, exclusive, arrogant, and insulting. This slogan is repeated incessantly by many of Jesus' most ardent followers, and the more you question what is

meant by it, the louder it is repeated back to you. (Granted, those who repeat the slogan most ardently intend it as neither frightful, narrow-minded, exclusive, arrogant, or insulting. It is, rather, a sincere way of saying that they really believe in him. More on that later.)

7. People who seem to show up at your door just as you're trying to leave (or sleep), or slide up beside you on an airplane just as you're trying to read (or sleep), or confront you on a sidewalk just as you're trying to get away from them, and ask, sometimes smiling but more often nervously, "Do you know Jesus personally?" or "Are you saved?" or "Are you born again?"

8. Some of the schmaltziest and weirdest music you've ever heard, played on seven out of eight radio stations in certain parts of the country, in between which preachers vary their pronunciation from "JAY-zuss" to "GEEzis."

9. A pink, well-fed baby featured in nativity scenes and on Christmas cards, almost always eliciting the cry, "Ahh, how cute"—probably the last words anyone would have actually said about the actual Jesus.

10. The holocaust, slavery, the rape of the environment during the Industrial Era, the subjugation or annihilation of native peoples and/or their cultures, oppression of women, opposition to free speech, politically inflammatory rhetoric (such as "We're gonna take back this country for JAYzuss!" etc., etc.), the bombing of abortion clinics, the reckless calling down of damnation on anyone and everyone, witch hunts, inquisitions, suppression of scientific inquiry, and any one of a dozen other horrors done or defended by somebody somewhere in the name of you-know-who.

IF IT WEREN'T FOR THE CHRISTIANS

It pains me to write these things. But twenty centuries of Christianity have led many people (including Friedrich Nietzsche) to say,

"It would be a whole lot easier to believe in Christ if it weren't for the Christians."

If Jesus were to reappear among us today, I wouldn't be surprised if he'd call himself Mike or Sue or Abdul or Nikita or George or Carol. Or more likely, he might remain completely anonymous—anything to distance himself from the image believers like me too often create for him. We Christians have, I am brokenhearted to admit, succeeded after twenty centuries at turning the name "Jesus" into an obscenity for many people in many places around the world.

A THIRD-MILLENNIAL BIRTHDAY GIFT

I say "we Christians" because I too am part of the problem, far too often. I often think that one of the greatest gifts we Christians could give to Jesus at the two-thousandth anniversary of his birth would be to just shut up about him for twenty-five years or so, during which time we would try to come to terms with what a mess we've made of the simple path that he introduced to planet earth (and which we quickly complicated, confused, and corrupted), during which time we'd simply try to practice what he preached, especially the parts about loving God and loving our neighbors, during which time we would stop producing Jesus-junk (pencils, T-shirts, computer screen-savers, bumper stickers, plastic mugs, refrigerator magnets, and the like, with his name embossed upon them, which successfully merchandise and therefore cheapen his name) and try to rediscover some sense of reverence, dignity, and good taste.

After twenty-five years of that, perhaps we could say his name again on rare occasions and it wouldn't sound so frivolous, so stained, so obscene. And perhaps we wouldn't then embarrass him so much. (Having said that, I realize he must have a level of security, virtue, and maturity that put him far beyond embarrassment . . . qualities I evidently lack, since I can't understand how he puts up with our shenanigans.)

I CAN'T BE SERIOUS

Let me indulge this fantasy a little more. I am a preacher. Maybe for the next twenty-five years, no sermon preached by my colleagues and I should be permitted to go beyond four minutes in length, as a way of admitting that we know next to nothing of Jesus, so we should say next to nothing for a change. Maybe we should declare a twenty-five-year moratorium on all baptisms; after all, since we seem to have forgotten what being a Christian is all about, how can we induct others onto the path with any confidence? Maybe apologetics (the reasoned defense of one's faith) should actually spend the next twenty-five years apologizing—for all the things thoughtlessly, roughly, stupidly done with either misguided zeal or unguided apathy. Maybe the Billy Graham of the twenty-first century should reverse the method of Jesus, and not call sinners to repentance, but rather should call religious people to repentance, since they've become the best excuse for sinners to keep sinning and for the cynics to remain jaded. Obviously, I can't be serious. Or can I?

Serious or not, I can't finish this book on finding faith without telling you, as sincerely as I can, what a crucial role this unnamed person has had in the finding and formation of my faith. But as you can see, this is awkward for me ... not because I am ashamed of the real Jesus, but because I am so ashamed of what we Christians have made of him to people like you. I have no authorization to do this, but I'll bet a million Christians would add their hearty amen if they heard me say this: *I want to apologize to you, a person sincerely seeking faith, for the mess we Christians have made of Jesus and his whole enterprise. I'm so sorry.*

Thankfully, there are still a few stars sparkling in this dark sky. Let me tell you about one of these brighter examples.

SISAVANH'S STATEMENT

For several years back in the eighties, I taught English as a second language to adult refugees and foreign students here in the U.S.—Cambodian, Vietnamese, Laotian, Chinese, Ethiopian, Iranian, Afghan, and others. What wonderful memories I have of these splendid people! I remember one day, we were having a somewhat free-ranging discussion about the cultures represented in our class. One student, a Lao, talked about being Buddhist. Then, with characteristic respect, he asked me, "Teacher, what religion you?" (Obviously, I hadn't done too well yet teaching the verb "to be.")

"I am a Christian," I said. And this fellow, I believe Sisavanh was his name, said, "Oh, Teacher, we love all Christian. When I escape my country, the communist want to kill me, and I go to refugee camp in Thailand. I go there, and I don't know nobody. I have nothing, no money, no food, no family. But Christian people there, they give me everything. They give me food, clothing, medicine, blanket, place to stay. They teach me a little English. I never forget them for that. That why I love all Christian. Very good, very good."

WONDERS

As Sisavanh spoke, so energized, so sincere, dozens of heads were nodding in agreement. At refugee camps around the world— in Thailand, Pakistan, Greece, the Philippines—these people had felt a touch of love that came through people motivated by Jesus Christ. That, I thought, must make Jesus proud. True, there are far too many embarrassments said and done in the name of Jesus. But there are also many wonders.

I don't know what you think of Jesus. I hope you have met at least a few people who impressed you as those missionaries in the refugee camps impressed my students. I hope the other kind of impressions—the bombastic, the insensitive, the disrespectful, the rude, the arrogantly narrow-minded—haven't completely alienated you. If you think about it (I hope I'm not trying to make excuses here), the bad behavior of Christians tells you less about Christ than it does about human nature. After all, what other raw material does Christ have to work with? If he tried to exclude anyone who might embarrass him, whom would he be left with? (Certainly not me.) Perhaps we shouldn't be surprised that we flub things up so grandly.

BUTTERFLIES, LIGHTNING, WIND, SPRING

I don't want to make it sound like I have Jesus all figured out. I don't. Nearly every Sunday for almost fifteen years I have preached about Jesus and his teachings. That means that every week I have pondered Jesus and his message for hours on end. I have read hundreds of books about Jesus and his message and his ongoing mission on earth, and I have done some writing myself. But still, I must confess that Jesus in many ways eludes me, even as he attracts me.

Behind the pages of the gospels—the four accounts of Jesus' life included in the New Testament—I find someone really there, someone substantial, too real, too vigorous, too alive, too robust to be reduced to a quick formula or set of principles. I push, and he pushes back. He won't be domesticated, mastered, outlined, packaged, shrink-wrapped, or nailed down (at least, not for long). That's frustrating at times. But it's also quite wonderful.

DEAD OR ALIVE?

After all, it's only the dead butterflies that you can put on pins and display in glass cases. Live ones require you to enjoy their beauty in quick, stolen glances, iridescent here on this clover, swaying there on that goldenrod, pausing over there for a few moments for a drink beside that puddle, soon up again dazzling and skipping along on the breeze. Similarly, lightning can't be captured in a bottle; the wind can't be conveyed via propositions; springtime can't be unleashed on demand. I have found Jesus to have the same elusive but blazing vibrancy and reality. This is why I have come to believe in God as I have, and why I believe in Jesus. You, of course, may disagree or remain unconvinced, and I certainly understand that. As I've said, we Christians on the whole haven't made it easy for you.

YOUR RESPONSE

1. What are your impressions and beliefs about Jesus?
2. Which aspects of Jesus' teaching do you agree with, or disagree with?

3. What people seem to you to reflect the spirit of Jesus?

4. What do you wish to learn about Jesus, and how might you do this?

RESOURCES

Three modern books on the life of Jesus stand out in my opinion: *The Jesus I Never Knew* by Philip Yancey (Grand Rapids: Zondervan, 1995); *The Lord* by Romano Guardini (Washington, D.C.: Regnery, 1996), and *The Case for Christ* by Lee Strobel (Grand Rapids: Zondervan, 1998). A wonderful book on the teachings of Jesus is Dallas Willard's *The Divine Conspiracy* (HarperSanFrancisco, 1998). Of course, even more important would be to begin reading one of the four gospels (short biographies of Jesus) on your own. Luke is probably the most accessible and rewarding for modern readers; Mark is the shortest; John is a bit more philosophical and actually focuses on the issue of faith; and Matthew shows the most connection with the Jewish roots of Jesus' teachings. To return to the theme of chapter 12, I would also recommend connecting with a Type 3 faith community to put your explorations into a relational context.

PRAYER

God, if Jesus is truly from you, I want to know it. If what he says about you is true, I want to understand it, believe it, and live it. If following Jesus is the best way for me to grow closer to you, that is what I want to do. Help me, to get a true glimpse of Jesus. Reading this book has been a start for me, or a new step in my spiritual search. But I don't want to stall in my journey. I want to keep moving ahead. Guide me in the next steps I should take to continue to nurture this relationship with you. I hear stories of other people whose lives have been touched by you and transformed by their faith in you. God, I look forward to the unique relationship I will develop and experience with you. Give me a faith that is not only good for me, but is also a positive example for others who need faith.

CHAPTER 17 PREVIEW

On a Maryland Hillside

This chapter recounts a very personal story of a pivotal experience of God in my life. It begins with some additional reflections on Jesus, continued from the previous chapter.

WHO SHOULD READ THIS CHAPTER?

This chapter will be of interest to anyone pursuing a spiritual quest.

WHAT QUESTIONS DOES IT ADDRESS?

What experiences caused this author to pursue a spiritual search?

...when we came over the rise where the sea and land opened up to us, I stood in stunned silence and then slowly walked toward the waves. Words cannot capture the view that confronted me. I saw space and light and texture and color and power ... that seemed hardly of this earth. Gradually there crept into my mind the realization that God sees this all the time. He sees it, experiences it, knows it from every possible point of view, this and billions of other scenes like and unlike it, in this and billions of other worlds. Great tidal waves of joy must constantly wash through his being. It is perhaps strange to say, but suddenly I was extremely happy for God and thought I had some sense of what an infinitely joyous consciousness he is and of what it might have meant for him to look at his creation and find it 'very good.' ... he is simply one great inexhaustible and eternal experience of all that is good and true and beautiful and right. This is what we must think of when we hear theologians and philosophers speak of him as a perfect being. This is his life.

DALLAS WILLARD, *THE DIVINE CONSPIRACY*

CHAPTER 17

On a Maryland Hillside

The quote from Dallas Willard in the Chapter Preview rings true with me with a rare intensity. I remember sitting at my desk a few years ago, and a simple thought hit me "out of the blue" with similar intensity. It came in the form of a question: *Is it possible to have a thought of God that is too good to be true?* A God as wonderful as Willard described, a God of whom no thought can be too good, that is the God I have become convinced of and the God I have been seeking all my life.

That's why the teachings, story, and spirit of Jesus Christ have been so catalytic in my own spiritual journey. His life rings with this kind of vision of God. If I could somehow rescue Jesus from our miserable PR job (not that he really needs my help) and present him to people seeking faith, here are five things I would try to convey. (You'll notice that these observations have little to do with the doctrines of the Trinity, incarnation, atonement, or the like. That's not because these doctrines aren't important, but rather because this is a book on finding faith, not furnishing it or fine-tuning it.)

1. HE IS INTELLECTUALLY HONEST.

If there was one thing Jesus was clearly against, it was hypocrisy, pretense, cover-up, dishonesty. He wouldn't want you to recite a creed you weren't convinced of. He wouldn't want you to pretend. He'd rather have you say, "Lord, I believe, but yet I don't believe at the same time. I have my doubts, but I'd like to work them through. Help me."

One of the most fascinating phrases to come frequently from Jesus' lips was this: "Believe because." That's why those who attempt to be faithful to Jesus and to show their complete allegiance to Jesus by saying, "Jesus is the only way! Jesus is the only way!" can be wrong even if they're right. In other words, even if Jesus is the only way, exactly as they understand him to be, Jesus himself wouldn't go around claiming that for himself without providing evidence; he wouldn't demand people to believe that without giving them good reason. Can you imagine Jesus saying, "Believe that I am the only way. Why? Because I said so, that's why! And if you don't believe, then you're going straight to hell!" But isn't that how we present him through our slogans?

No, again and again we find Jesus saying, not "Believe because I said so!" but rather "Believe because of the quality of my teachings. Believe because you see the miracles I do. Believe because you see my disciples love one another. Believe because you see my followers displaying a mysterious but real unity. Believe because my words prove true in experience. Believe because you can see my profile in the writings of the ancient prophets. Believe because God somehow makes it clear to you. Believe because credible people tell you that they saw me alive after being killed. Believe because the fruit of my life was good."

In other words, the faith that Jesus calls for is an intellectually honest faith, not a phony, forced, or inflated faith. If you see things that seem unjust or that just don't make sense—like religious people giving all their money to the church, while neglecting their elderly parents, or like pastors working hard to make converts who then become more miserable and unfree than they were before, or like churches being fastidious about minor matters (like rigorously avoiding labor on the Sabbath) while overlooking major matters (like loving their wives, treating their children gently, or loving their neighbors of other races)—if you see these kinds of things, you don't have to pretend they're okay. You can be honest. You can call a spade a spade; dirt, dirt; and manure, manure. He won't chide you for telling the truth. If you read the accounts of his life, this complete, transparent honesty comes through.

For example, one of his chosen twelve, Thomas, was a doubter, and of him Jesus didn't say, "Boy, did I make a mistake choosing you. I want believers around here, not skeptics!" No, instead he said, "Blessed are you, Thomas, because you demanded evidence. And after you received sufficient evidence, you were truly open-minded, so you believed." In other words, "Thomas, you had your honest doubts, but then when the evidence came through, you were honest enough to believe. I applaud you for that."

If Jesus is right, then God doesn't want a faith that is false, forced, make-believe, faked; he wants a faith that is honest—full of doubt and hope, questioning and risking, tentative exploration, gentle persuasion, and hard-won conviction. In my search for a faith that is real, I find that tremendously exhilarating!

2. HE IS SCANDALOUSLY INCLUSIVE.

In the last chapter, when I seemed to knock those who say, "Jesus is the only way," some of you were thinking this: "But just a minute, Brian. Didn't Jesus' disciple John quote him as saying, 'I am the way and the truth and the life. No one comes to the Father except through me'" (John 14:6)? Isn't this "only way" language coming from Jesus' own mouth?

I would respond, "Yes. Absolutely. And I believe what Jesus said. But don't misconstrue that one statement; don't try to use it in a way Jesus himself never would use it." Because Jesus was not exclusive, at least not in the way the "Jesus is the only way" slogan makes him sound. Instead of Jesus *being* the way, the slogan makes it sound as if he's *in the way*—as if there are people trying to come to God and truth and life, but Jesus is blocking their path, keeping them out until they in some way acknowledge him. That's absurd. Rather, the reverse was true: Jesus was always the one helping *in* those whom others kept *out*! In the gospel narratives, we repeatedly see this theme of tension between exclusive followers (or disciples) and an inclusive Jesus.

For example, his disciples tried to exclude children, but Jesus said, "Let them come!" His disciples tried to exclude non-Jews, but Jesus said of one of them—a Roman centurion, no less!—"I have never seen such faith in all of Israel!" His disciples tried to exclude people who were doing spiritual works in his name, but didn't travel in their circle, but Jesus said, "Those who aren't against me are for me."

My friend Neil Livingstone says it something like this: In a world of religious in-groups and out-groups, Jesus created a "come on in" group. The kingdom of God is open to everyone who will come, he said. It's like a party to which everyone is invited, rich or poor, employed or unemployed, clean or dirty. So scandalously inclusive was Jesus' teaching that it took decades before his top disciple, Peter, could really accept it (see Acts 10), and even then, Peter waffled in his endorsement of Jesus' come-on-in policy (see Galatians 2). It was just too radical.

Driving Conflict

Even more dramatic than the tension between Jesus and his disciples was the tension between Jesus and the most highly religious leaders of his day, known as the "Pharisees," meaning the "Separated Ones." In many ways, this tension is the driving conflict in the drama of Jesus' plotline.

Though it meant he earned the derisive label "friend of sinners," Jesus scandalized the Separated Ones by refusing to separate himself from prostitutes, tax collectors, lepers, rabble. The Separated Ones feared being contaminated by the sin of the sinful; Jesus, in contrast, knew that the intense power of his love could decontaminate the sinners by bringing them to repentance. In fact, he said, many of the last shall be first, and the first last, for precisely this reason: The Pharisees and the other highly religious people thought they saw it all. They thought they had arrived first at the destination of holiness and were in no need of repentance. They were good and holy—and proud of it, too. For that very reason, according to Jesus, they risked exclusion. Ironically, it wasn't the whores and crooks that Jesus threatened with hell. Read the gospels and you will find it was the religious who heard the rhetoric of fire and brim-stone! The very opposite of our approach. Scandalous!

Here, then, the scandal worked in the opposite direction: The very people everyone considered most holy, most guaranteed of inclusion because of their immense knowledge of the Holy Scriptures and their rigor in obeying, were, according to Jesus, most in danger of exclusion. Perhaps you side with the Pharisees. That's certainly your choice. But I find Jesus' scandalous inclusion a powerful sign of his legitimacy. It rings true with me.

3. HE IS RELATIONALLY ELECTRIC.

As you read the gospel accounts, watch him interact with Peter—now encouraging him, now confronting him, now encouraging him again, bringing him along so patiently, yet so relentlessly. With Peter as with all the disciples, Jesus has the toughness and tenderness of the best of coaches, determined to turn paunchy couch potatoes into star athletes with lean muscles and strong backbones and a will to win. It's a little scary, but I find myself wanting to sign on the team.

Or watch him interact with a nameless young leader, successful and bright, a sincere spiritual seeker. Watch him feel along the edges of this fellow's character to the one fault line that must be confronted: his love for money. Watch him challenge the man, not rushing him or pressuring him to change immediately, giving him time, letting him leave, regarding him with love even as he walks away.

Watch him with a woman, a multiple divorcée, a member of a despised minority group, chatting naturally as a friend, beside a well in Samaria, gently kindling her curiosity, teasing out her spiritual thirst as he discusses physical thirst. Watch him bring up the sensitive issue of her sexual relationship with men, and watch him do so in a way that she runs back to town and invites these men, along with everyone else who had no doubt whispered about her affairs, to come meet Jesus too. Amazing!

You might say, "But how do you know these stories are true? How do you know that someone didn't make them up?" Of course,

I don't *know*. As we've seen in previous chapters, absolute certainty is not available on many, if any, things in this life for us. But I can say this: These stories are so improbable, so unexpected, so challenging to the status quo, so idiosyncratic, so earthy and rough and unedited and unrehearsed, that they simply seem to have the ring of truth to them, and so I *believe* them. And more, the truths that these stories yield are so inspiring that if they are fiction, whoever made them up would appear to deserve the honor we Christians give to Christ himself! But then again, if the stories are fraudulent, we are left with a paradox: It seems unlikely that a fraud—someone capable of perpetrating such a grand hoax—could ever come up with such spiritually inspiring fabrications. It seems unlikely that someone so sinister and dishonest could create stories of such simple genuineness and unpretentious grandeur.

Here's what strikes me after all these years of interacting with these stories: The electricity I sense as Jesus interacts with this amazing assortment of people, from prostitutes to Pharisees, from revolutionaries to military officers, resonates powerfully with the spiritual dynamic I sense in my own relationship with God. I sense this same electricity in my experience of life. Again, it rings true.

4. HE IS GRACIOUSLY DEMANDING.

Two kinds of religion are common in the world, it seems to me. First, there is no shortage of religion that is demanding—and graceless. Do this, don't eat that, travel here, say that, give this, accept that, observe this, forego that. And if you fail, you lose. Game over.

Second, and probably even more common these days, is gracious religion free of demand. You treat your wife like dirt? It's okay; after all, you weren't properly potty trained as a child. You broke your wedding vows? Nobody's perfect; it's okay. You make lots of money and keep it all to yourself? Not everybody's a Mother Teresa; it's okay. You drink too much, or listen too little, or complain excessively, or show gratitude infrequently or never? So do lots of other people, and we must maintain a good self-image, so it's okay.

Do you see the problem? Graceless demands leave us feeling guilty and defeated. Demandless grace leaves us apathetic and self-righteous. What we need is a demand that calls us to live a better life than we are currently living. But that call must come with compassion and grace, so that when we fail, we hear, "Father, forgive them, for they don't know what they are doing." This is exactly what I find in Jesus . . . and that strikes me as a livable path, a yoke I can bear, a yoke that is in fact easier and lighter than any other option I have tried or heard of. Another ring of truth.

5. HE IS POWERFULLY NONCOERCIVE.

Jesus was known for speaking in parables, in stories that would yield meaning on many levels. If you wanted to stop at the surface level, you could. If you wanted to go deeper, you could. The point was always on the deeper level, but Jesus never forced the crowds to dig for it, and never threw it in their face. Thus his approach with the general public was remarkably subtle and nonconfrontational; it was gentle, not harsh; magnetic, not pushy; inviting, not driving . . . an opportunity, not a threat. Take it or leave it. It's your choice. As he did with that successful young leader, he'll watch you walk away if you choose—no lectures, no getting in the last word.

A few lines from one of the ancient prophets (Isaiah) seemed to fit him perfectly: He wouldn't be heard yelling in the streets. He wouldn't snuff out a dimly burning candle. He wouldn't break a bruised reed. No, his approach would be gentle, like a shepherd carrying a lamb in his arms . . . not driving it, not whacking it, not threatening it . . . gently carrying it along.

And that approach makes perfect sense in the development of a faith that is real. It has to be free and unforced, a choice rather than a necessity.

A TRIPLE FORK

And that is how it has been for me. I didn't *have to* choose this path of faith. It came as a fork in the road—actually, a triple fork. One road represented following my typical adolescent urges. A second represented conforming to and complying with the calm and conservative rhythms of my religious heritage. Then there was a third path, a narrow, winding, uphill path leading off into the unknown, with Jesus' footprints in the dust. Here's how the choice happened for me.

As I have said, I grew up going to church, very conservative to be sure, but in many ways a good church nonetheless with sincere people who loved God and for the most part, each other too. At church and at home, I learned the Bible stories and learned to pray, and I cared about doing good and pleasing God.

But in my early teens, I did what a lot of kids my age do: I began to have my doubts. As I've explained, my religious heritage told me that evolution was a complete lie, that the earth had been created in six literal days some six thousand years ago. I had trouble with that in light of the growing evidence to the contrary. Furthermore, my church told me that we were among the very few who really worshiped God in his appointed way, but I found us to be not much if any better than other people I knew. So, although I had no one to talk with about these questions, in my heart I wondered. And I was afraid, because I thought I wasn't supposed to question or wonder or doubt.

About this time, I was invited to join a little rock and roll band . . . and everybody knew *that* was sinful. To my parents' chagrin, I joined, and we played at teen club dances and bar mitzvahs and parties, at which at least some of what went on was also . . . sinful. But all the same, to me, it was fun and exciting and free. I felt alive to be playing my saxophone, banging a tambourine, learning to dance. And I wondered, "If this stuff about God is true, then maybe I'm in danger of getting into trouble here. But if it's not true, then who cares? Why shouldn't I have a good time?" In that simple line of thinking, for the first time it mattered to me whether I believed "this stuff about God" to be true or not. I realized my decision would take me down two very different paths.

I grew my hair long (another no-no), grew a scruffy adolescent beard (a clear sign of rebellion), wore faded blue jeans at all times (an apostate fabric if ever there was one), and vehemently drew attention to every hypocrisy I could find in the church (with a degree of maturity that matched my scruffy beard). And I'm sure that many people who knew me at this time thought, "Oh, there he goes. Losing his faith."

COGNITIVE DISSONANCE

But the truth was, I was actually finding my faith. Yes, I was in a sense losing the faith that my parents and church had tried to give me. But this was necessary, because I had to find a faith with my own name on it, not just theirs. I guess psychologists would call this cognitive dissonance—that I had two conflicting value systems at work in my mind. But that cognitive dissonance created for me for the first time a fork in the road, one path being the attractive option that, if I wanted, I could drop faith altogether and "have a good time" like so many of my peers, without worrying about God and right and wrong and morality and all that.

Perhaps you see my dilemma. I was now presented with two unacceptable alternatives: Conform to my heritage and deny my doubts, or conform to my peers and deny my spiritual search.

A couple of things happened at this time, opening a third option for me. First, a fellow at my church invited me to join a Bible study group he had formed. Dave Miller was in college, a few years older than me, and at first, frankly, I didn't like him all that much. I was working hard on being a hippie, and he was a clean-cut, all-American athlete type. But he was persistent. He would drive forty-five minutes out of his way to pick me up for this Bible study group, and so I obliged him and went.

In that study group, the three or four other guys talked about their faith in a way I had never seen before. They related God and faith to their daily lives, to their struggles, to their fun, to their friendships, to their future plans, even to their sexuality. And it wasn't all about guilt and rules; it had more of the air of an adventure they were on with God ... an adventure with joy and reality and purpose.

Something else happened about this time. Largely because of this group, I started reading the Bible on my own. And I was fascinated. Sure, there were boatloads of things I didn't understand, and actually, quite a few I didn't agree with. But this Jesus, he fascinated me. He was magnetic to me.

MORE CONTACTS

About this time, I volunteered to be a counselor-in-training at a summer camp, and one of the other young counselors and I would stay up late at night talking after the kids in our cabins were asleep. We talked about life, girls, God, music, faith. This fellow, Tom, had been deeply into drugs—pot, mescaline, maybe some LSD too. Some months earlier, he had opened his heart to Jesus, he said, and his life had changed. He had little or no church background, but it was clear to me that the same spirit that I sensed in Jesus as I read the Bible was also in this guy, the same spirit I had sensed in Dave's Bible study group, something alive, genuine, purposeful, free, kind ... something I didn't quite have yet, but maybe was starting to wish I had.

At summer's end, back at school, I got to know another guy. This guy had been one of the main marijuana dealers at my school, but now he was telling everybody that he had changed. And he had. As in the others, I sensed in him that special spirit, that special vitality I could read between the lines in the Gospels. Through him I met more people who, for all their faults, seemed to have this same spirit too.

The question for me was, which way was I going to go? Several months passed with that tug-of-war going on inside me. At first I was eighty-percent no, and twenty-percent yes; then it was fifty/fifty for a while, and eventually, the yes part overshadowed the no part, and I found that the spirit I had sensed in these other guys was now growing in me.

ON A MARYLAND HILLSIDE

One decisive experience occurred about this time. I seldom talk about this, because talking about some things tends to cheapen them, but this seems like an appropriate time to mention it. I was invited by one of my best friends to attend his church's youth retreat. I don't think I had ever been on a retreat before, as our denomination didn't have retreats. We went to a ramshackle retreat center somewhere in the Maryland hills, and had the usual round of silly get-acquainted games, camp food, and talks by the pastor and his guest speakers. The first night, I was somewhat surprised to lie in the dark of the cabin and hear the other boys start telling dirty jokes. I wasn't above telling some myself, but I remember thinking that among church kids, this probably shouldn't be happening.

The second day, things went along alright until the afternoon. Midway through the afternoon, we were sent off for a time of silence and solitude. The idea was to get alone somewhere and talk to God. I found a tree along a path, and figured that climbing it and sitting among the branches would be a good place to get close to God. It wasn't much of a spiritual experience. First, I couldn't get comfortable. The bark was rough, and my butt hurt. Second, ants were crawling up and down the trunk, and I became a part of their roadway. Then the mosquitoes started biting. I would get out a sentence of prayer, and then would shift my weight, flick off an ant, and scratch my newest mosquito bite. I'd try to pray again, but would soon wonder, "When is that bell going to ring telling us this time is over?"

At some point though, I distinctly remember praying this prayer: "God, I want to stop fighting you. I want to be one hundred percent committed to you. I want to surrender to you. I want to say *yes* to you. I only ask one thing. Before I die, please allow me to see the most beautiful sights in the world, and hear the most beautiful sounds in the world, and feel the most beautiful experiences in the world." (Obviously, "beautiful" was an important word to this adolescent fledgling musician/hippie/spiritual seeker.)

ROUGH BARK, ANTS, MOSQUITOES, AND STARS

No lightning bolts or visions of angels ensued. Eventually, I surrendered to the bark, the ants, and the mosquitoes and left the tree and ambled back to the mess hall for supper. The evening brought more harmless if not inane camp games and songs, and we were about to go to bed for another round, I supposed, of dirty jokes. But a few friends and I decided to take a detour and look at the stars. It was a clear, dry, high-pressure-system night, and the stars were glorious. I went off by myself, a stone's throw away from my buddies on that grassy round hill, and I lay back in the grass and gazed. And a thought, or series of thoughts, came to me with a power that now brings tears to my eyes as I recall it. I felt loved. The thoughts went like this: "Those stars are glorious, but I am more precious to God than a star. God didn't send Jesus into the world for stars, but for me. The God who made stars and galaxies and space and time sees me lying here on this hump of dirt and grass, and he loves me. I am loved."

BEAUTIFUL THINGS

And with that realization, I started to laugh. It wasn't funny, exactly; it was joy. It was a pure joy that I have experienced on a few occasions in my life, but only a few, and it was so intense it almost hurt after a while. I remember almost asking God to stop it, because I was becoming afraid; I thought I was about to break or burst, unable to contain such joy and light in my soul. And then I began to cry.

My friends were talking intently to one another all during this, opening up in that wonderful way that young people do and older people should do. Apparently they didn't hear me quietly laughing and crying. When my intense feelings began to subside, I could again hear their voices through the silence, and I heard one of my friends say to another, and then to all the others, "I love you. I love all of you." And hearing that, I began to cry again.

More happened that night, but I don't need to go into it all. At some point in the early hours of the next morning, though, I remembered my prayer of the afternoon before, and I thought, *Yes, God has already answered it.* I had seen the most beautiful thing on earth—the glory of God shining through creation, making it ring like a struck bell, making it glow with wonder. And I had heard the most beautiful thing in life—human beings telling other human beings that they love one another. And I had felt the most beautiful feeling in life—to be loved, really loved, by a God who knows me—my secrets, my faults, my doubts, my wrongs, my shame, along with my strengths and dreams and hopes and gifts—simply to be known and loved.

The experience, of course, faded, and its memory fades a bit with each telling of the story, because gradually I seem to remember the telling, the story, more than the experience itself. But that's okay. Other experiences have come, like Willard's view of the sea, experiences that, in Wordsworth's words ("Tintern Abbey"), bring

> A presence that disturbs me with the joy
> of elevated thoughts; a sense sublime
> Of something far more deeply interfused,
> Whose dwelling is the light of setting suns,
> And the round ocean and the living air,
> And the blue sky, and in the mind of man:
> A motion and a spirit, that impels
> All thinking things, all objects of all thought,
> And rolls through all things.

The fact remains that it's twenty-five years later, and I'm still on that same path, learning to open my heart in new ways, savoring the same beauty, desiring that same spirit (or Spirit) of joy and love to fill me. I certainly have my ups and downs, and quite often that old "no" part of me stages a pretty strong counteroffensive. But the new spiritual "yes" seems to prove itself stronger than the old "no," and so I press on in this path, step by step, breath by breath.

And for this leg of the journey, I have felt that spirit prompting me to try to help you, across these pages, to find the path for yourself, so you can learn, in your own way and in your own time, how to say to God that one, life-changing word, *yes.*

YOUR RESPONSE

1. What one thing would you want to ask of God?

2. What yesses and nos are at work in your own life?

3. Is there any compelling reason for you not to say a whole-hearted yes to God right now?

4. The most important things I've learned from this book are:

5. The most important things I want to do next are:

6. The people I would most like to dialogue with regarding spiritual matters are:

RESOURCES

Consider getting away on a retreat of your own, either with a group or in solitude, to reflect on what you've learned so far in your spiritual search and to simply talk to God about it all. (*Note: If you would like to organize a spiritual retreat for spiritual seekers in your area, please contact the Finding Faith website for referrals to trained retreat leaders: www.crcc.org.*)

As a reader of *Finding Faith*, you are warmly invited to participate in the *Finding Faith* website on the internet, at www.crcc.org. Your comments and questions are welcome there too.

PRAYER

If a relationship with you could be compared to a home, and you were inviting me to come home to be part of your family, I would say yes. If it could be compared to a romance, and you were proposing a relationship of love and loyalty to me, again, I would say yes. If a relationship with you could be compared to a journey, and you were inviting me to follow you, I would say an enthusiastic yes. If a relationship with you could be compared to a school or a cause where you invite me to learn or work with you, I would say yes, yes, yes. I want my heart to be full of yes for you, God! I would like to express more of my feelings and desires and gratitude to you, God. . . . (Continue in your own words.)